POLICY MANAGEMENT IN THE HUMAN SERVICES

POLICY MANAGEMENT IN THE HUMAN SERVICES

John E. Tropman

Columbia University Press
New York   1984

Library of Congress Cataloging in Publication Data

Tropman, John E.
Policy management in the human services.

Bibliography: p.
Includes index.
1. Social work administration.   I. Title.
HV41.T74   1984   361.3′068   83-19029
ISBN 0-231-05614-1 (alk. paper)
ISBN 0-231-05615-X (pbk.: alk. paper)

Columbia University Press
New York   Guildford, Surrey
Copyright © 1984 Columbia University Press
All rights reserved

Printed in the United States of America

Clothbound editions of Columbia University Press Books are Smyth-
sewn and printed on permanent and durable acid-free paper

To my wife
Penelope S. Tropman
and my parents
Elmer J. and Elizabeth O. Tropman

CONTENTS

FOREWORD

Public and organizational policies that shape our human services often represent a curious mix of the objectives of special interest groups, the personal concerns of the policymakers, and prevailing political values. Social workers and other human service professionals are frequently active, if not always successful, in the multiple stages of policy formulation. The development phase of policymaking is addressed in this book in a manner that simplifies this task and should lead to increased effectiveness on the part of practitioners. Interestingly enough, however, once policies are enacted/adopted, many human service professionals seemingly become unconcerned about their effects as they move on to the next policy battle.

In this extremely useful book, Professor Tropman outlines a number of ways in which agency administrators and other practitioners can manage and massage policies to optimize the quality of services. In fact, there is so much useful information in this book that it may be possible for skilled professionals to manage policies in such a way as to win the war even if they lose the battle. Professor Tropman demonstrates that policy managers, like fiscal managers, personnel managers, and other senior employees in large organizations, have a crucial role to play in optimizing the quality of human service programs.

Although the purpose of the book is to assist professionals in the consideration, crafting, and implementation of policies, it goes well beyond these objectives. It is much more than a handbook or manual; the strategies and techniques proposed in the book are rooted in social science theory, and consequently the reader's understanding of theoretical issues related to policy formulation is greatly enhanced. But perhaps most important, the author fashions a framework that encourages professional and lay people to become much more systematic and analytical in their attitudes and behaviors regarding extant and needed policies. The thorough and enlightened treatment of the many factors involved in the implementation of policies is particularly interesting and useful to administrative personnel and policymakers.

For professional and lay people with policy-related responsibilities, this book transcends the more common publications that focus almost exclusively on policy analysis. In this sense it is a landmark publication and should prove to be a most valuable tool to shape a policy environment that will enhance the organization and delivery of human services.

Harold R. Johnson
Dean, School of Social Work
The University of Michigan

ACKNOWLEDGMENTS

Books are the crystallized products of diverse forces. The intellectual support of my wife Penelope and my parents has been acknowledged in the dedication. I would like to recognize as well the support of my children, Sarah, Jessica, and Matthew, who followed the whole process with encouragement and interest. Very special mention must be made of Ms. Sherry Massey, who labored long and hard to improve all aspects of the text. Robert Alexander shared his wisdom on specific portions. Barbara Aho and Dan Madaj typed numerous versions of this manuscript with clarity and accuracy. Many of my colleagues read and commented upon specific portions of the book and improved it greatly. Shirley Zimmerman of the University of Minnesota read and reacted to the entire manuscript. Anonymous readers at Columbia University Press made very helpful and important suggestions for revisions, which have been incorporated here. The editorial staff at Columbia was unfailingly interested and supportive. All shared with me the idea that ideas are important and need encouragement, support, and indeed, management. Without them, this book would not exist.

INTRODUCTION

Policy. The word crops up, it seems, everywhere. The problem, of course, is that it has many different meanings and connotations in several settings. Whatever else policy may be, it is an idea, and one which has been set down in writing and approved by legitimate authority. This book is for those interested in policy ideas, and discusses how to make the supply of them more abundant, their quality better, their language clearer, and their approval less trying and difficult. In short, it is about policy management or the guidance of policy through the process which runs from initiation, then approval, to programming.

Its first target is students of policy, whether they are in the many policy institutes, schools of social work, public health, business, natural resources and environmental conservation, education, or law, among others. I have stressed the professional student because s/he is interested in shaping and molding the environment, in changing it and making it better. Improved policy is certainly a way to achieve part of this end.

Different graduate programs have, of course, different foci. A proactive policy stance is not always espoused by the policy studies institutes. Often those centers have an analytic, if not contemplative, perspective on policy. Theirs is to analyze alternatives, often developed by someone else, or to assess policy which has already been developed, ratified, and implemented. My focus here does not exclude the role of policy analyst by any means, but it introduces a new role, that of policy manager, one who actively seeks to influence and shape the supplies of policy ideas within an organizational context much as the fiscal manager seeks to insure adequate supplies and developments of money and the personnel manager seeks to do the same for people.

And there is a movement in this direction. A new policy journal is called the *Journal of Policy Analysis and Management,* which is the journal of the Association for Public Policy and Management. Whether the intent of the phrases was to link policy and management or not is of little matter here; they are together and will doubtless grow more together in the future.

A second audience for this volume is those practitioners of the policy craft who are already in the field working as executives and deputies in governmental nonprofit or for-profit institutions, where part of their task is to assist in insuring the supply of new ideas and working on their refinement, presentation, and ratification.

Many of the women and men who do these jobs will not think of them in this way. American society, while founded by people of intellectual orientation, tends to value the pragmatic over the poetic. Ideas are assessed ambivalently within our culture, and the wo/man of ideas is thought, almost by necessity, not to be the wo/man of action. Hence, there is an inherent tendency for those who have the task of policy management to think of it in other, more current and acceptable, terms.

In the policy context ideas are action; policy is what makes organizations work or not. We can all identify those who seem to be good at crafting solutions, at getting new perspectives and data which permit things to go forward. We perhaps have not thought of them as policy managers. And most surely, they have not thought of themselves that way. The practitioners who read this book will find, I think, some of the "shock of recognition" that comes when someone recognizes what you have been doing, puts a name to it, and elaborates and systematizes it a bit.

These two audiences, however, have somewhat different needs for the presentation of material. For both, I have included a mixture of conceptual and practical material. Most chapters contain this mixture, with the emphasis tilting in one direction or the other. Some, like the chapter on having more effective meetings, are heavily oriented toward helpful steps; the same is true with the chapter on writing policy reports. However, each has important new conceptual elements as well. The chapter on value dilemmas, while heavily conceptual in orientation, contains suggestions for accommodating those conflicts as well. The chapter on social policy, most useful for the student rather than the practitioner, seeks to talk in some detail about one particular class of policies of interest to human service professionals.

Given the mix, however, I think that the practitioner might approach the chapters in a slightly different order than the student. For the student I would suggest the following order:

Chapter   1: Perspectives
Chapter   2: Problems
Chapter   3: Stages
Chapter   7: Roles
Chapter   5: Components
Chapter   6: Policy Machinery
Chapter 13: Social Policy

These chapters are largely conceptual and might be read as a group. Indeed, because of the practical pressures of the professional, they might be read second, and the next group of chapters might make a better beginning for the practitioner.

Chapter   4: Settings
Chapter   8: Policy Committees
Chapter   9: Policy Governance
Chapter 12: Value Dilemmas and Resolution
Chapter 10: Managing Effective Meetings
Chapter 11: Policy Writing

The second set of chapters helps executives do policy better; the first set helps them to think about what policy management is and about how they need to be more thoughtful and rigorous in approaching policy. Thus, the executives may define and distinguish policy problems and options and better understand the roles they can play throughout that process.

In a sense, the two approaches start with the focus of interest of the audience. The student audience begins with conceptual concerns and moves to practical problems; the practitioner's initial focus is on what helps get the job done and then s/he can move to think more about it.

One further point is worth mentioning. I have stressed ''human services'' in the title, meaning that to create special appeal to some groups while not excluding others. Both conceptual and practical elements will be helpful to students and practitioners in a wide range of agencies and instructional settings. My definition of "human services" is a broad one—agencies that are "people processing" and "people changing" in nature. Courts, schools, hospitals, the criminal justice system, the mental health system, and similar agencies are among those that would be included under this definition. There is debate about whether a given agency is people processing or people changing. Are graduate schools, for example, one, the other, or both? The point here is that organizations which have "patients" and "clients" have special problems of policy management, special because there is often a fundamental lack of clarity and understanding about what the goals of the agency or organization should be. There are often affect-laden conflicts about those goals. Interventions, like "professoring" or counseling, are often vague and unclear, hard to accomplish and hard to measure. The technology of intervention frequently involves the "software" of human interaction rather than the hardware of machines. And many of these human service organizations have multiple sources of funding, from clients/patients/students to people paying on their behalf (governments, parents) to grants and gifts (United Way contributions). Most are either public bodies themselves (departments of social services, colleges which are public) or "nonprofit" organizations. While the problems of public and nonprofit organizations are varied, they commonly lack a "bottom line" in the profit sense. Fees, if there are fees, may be assessed on a "cost" basis—but what should cost be? Human services can be elaborate and many, or simple and straight forward. Which is appropriate? And how do we know which is appropriate?

These problems of assessment and judgment certainly occur in materials handling operations, but to a somewhat different extent. Somehow, turning out widgits, however involving, has fewer of the ambiguities than turning out units of "mental health."[1]

All of these elements make "policy management" more difficult and more necessary. And there is yet a further problem. People processing and people changing organizations usually have an implicit theory or set of theories about the nature of man and her/his motivations and desires, along with what makes her/him change. Colleges have it, mental health clinics have it, correctional facilities have it. "It," of course, may vary a good bit from

1. However, it should not be thought that widgit production lacks passion. Tracy Kidder's book, *The Soul of a New Machine* (New York: Avon, 1981), points out dramatically how involving such activity (in this case, computer building) can be.

place to place, but "it" is always there, closely held, organizing deep commitments, serving as the basis for much of the intervention plans which the organization has. Because theories of human behavior are usually unverifiable, evidence from clients/patients/students now supports, now refutes, and is now mute on aspects of the theory and its postulates. Conflicts over what the evidence shows, and the theory itself, occupy a good bit of time within an organization. Staff tends not to think of it as theory, much less policy. It really is a hidden policy, of course, and one which tends to commit the organization to certain general courses of action and the avoidance of others. Given these problems, techniques of policy management are especially important. They will not solve the inherent problems, but the posture of proactivity proposed here can provide a stimulus which is now lacking for attention and examination. It is a tool for organizational self-analysis that human service organizations do not now have, as much as they need it.

The student and the practitioner, then, should find this volume helpful in organizing perspectives on the jobs of management within the human services system, as well as find practical suggestions for improvement of professional activity. This perspective is novel; people have not talked about "policy management" before, although, as I indicate in the text, there are some who come very close, and the new Association for Public Policy Analysis and Management is but a step away. Ideas are a vital organizational resource. And perhaps they are an unrecognized one. This volume is a step toward making them more plentiful and of higher quality.

POLICY MANAGEMENT IN THE HUMAN SERVICES

1

PERSPECTIVES ON POLICY MANAGEMENT

In recent years the idea of "policy" has become an important topic of study within the whole management realm. In many institutions there are Institutes of Public Policy Analysis. Many departments within schools and colleges are developing policy sections or components. There is a Policy Studies Association which has grown from just a few members to several hundred. Yet the focus of these efforts has been largely upon policy analysis. The idea of policy as something that needs to be managed or something that even could be managed has not really been part of the approach. This book seeks to introduce that concept and to provide some beginning perspectives and skills that will assist the student, the executive, and the manager in thinking of policy as a target of action and change.

The Elements of Policy

What is policy? It is an idea that has been elaborated and set down in writing, ratified by existing authorities, and designed to guide action.[1] Each of these components of the definition is important.

Policy Is an Idea

First, policy is an idea. It is a concept of the way things should go, the way things should be. It is, one might say, analogous to "theory" within the practice realm. It represents a set of assumptions and expectations that have been somehow brought to the surface, at least in part. Thus, one thing we need to know about policy is precisely that it *is* an idea or a set of interrelated ideas, and we need to think about how to create a personal and organizational climate which fosters the development of ideas.

Policy Is Written

A second component of our definition is that policy is written. A will, for example, is policy. Intentions about what to do with one's estate are not policy. Policy is thus open to scrutiny precisely because it is written. One can look fairly carefully at the language of policy (or of a policy). One can explicate the implications of a policy. One can assess whether or not the assumptions and expectations in the policy document are legitimate in the light of current knowledge and experience or whether they seem unreasonable, unrealistic, or unenforceable. Implicit, of course, in the whole idea of policy analysis is the very fact that policy is indeed written. Yet, from a practical point of view much of what people popularly think about policy is not written, but is rather conventional understanding about "the way we do things around here."

Policy Is Ratified

The third component of the definition is ratification by legitimate authority. Consider the case of the will. Acceptance by legitimate authority in that

---

1. Harrison defines it as ". . . a course of action or an intended course of action conceived as deliberately adopted, after a review of possible alternatives, and pursued, or intended to be pursued" (Harrison 1964:509).

case means that the person or persons making the will must, after it is written and reviewed, sign it in the presence of witnesses. That act of signature makes the will legitimate. Additional modifications to the will, or codicils, can be made, again in writing, if they are signed by the individual in question. At the level of a social agency or small organization, the board of directors or the stockholders usually have to approve major policy initiatives, and until that approval occurs, the policy simply is a proposed policy, not an actual policy. At the city government level, the city council or board of supervisors in the county, typically, has to ratify a particular proposal from the county government or city government staff or from any other source. The same is true at the state and national levels. Ratification by decision-making groups is a crucial component of policy.

There is some legitimate authority which is executive rather than legislative in nature. That is, it tends to be more related to a very small group of individuals or a particular individual rather than an elected group of approvers. Where an executive can issue an exectuive order, that also constitutes legitimate authority. The signing of the will can be done by the individual (or individuals) in question. It does not require approval of any legislative group. But even within the realm of executive action, there are often decision groups which act as important ratifying components. Sometimes, for example, even though a decision may be made by an executive, it must be approved by some other group, an advisory committee or advisory council. Sometimes there are staff groups which need to approve particular policies. So both legislative and judicial approval is sometimes required; in other instances, legislative approval only; in still other instances, executive approval only. The crucial element in each of these is the formal legal requirement. Policy is not policy unless it has met the formal legal approval requirements.

Legitimate approval is more than a formality however. It is stressed because that approval implies not only affirmation but choice, not only the approval of one particular direction of action but a rejection of other possible directions. As such, the choice juncture, or the point of ratification, typically involves selection among a range of possible alternatives. When that does not happen, when choice is made from only one alternative, we consider the ratifying body a rubber stamp. That does not make its approval any less crucial however, though it may make it less informed. It simply means that ratification and choice have occurred at two different points in the policy system. Whether that was wise or not is something to be considered. However, ratification is the formalization of choice and, thus, of crucial importance.

Policy Is a Guide to Action

The last component of the definition follows logically. Policy is designed to be a guide to action. It is designed to be a benchmark and reference point to help provide the basis for deciding a series of actions or events in the future to guide people's activities as well as adjudicate them. It is strategic in that very guiding sense. It shapes and focuses people's expectations. In that sense, policy represents, or should represent, one of the most fundamental aspects of life, whether it is personal life, agency life, community or societal life itself. It represents official choices among competing claims and alternatives as implied by the notion of ratification. Considering the background of policy just outlined, one can see the importance of "managing it," not in a Machiavellian sense of secretly or covertly directing it, though that of course is always possible. Rather, we seek to improve the quality of policy that guides our club or organization, our social agency, our city and state, and our nation. We seek to have the most sensible, most well-informed policies. All too often, in fact most usually, the policy process is a haphazard one with intelligence applied to it only later by analysts. Little attention is given to insuring a supply of alternate problem definitions which the policy system can think about and develop into policy proposals. Little attention is given to insuring a supply of policy proposals with an adequate range of options available. Little attention is given to the choice point within the ratification process. Because of its more immediate nature, greater attention is sometimes given to the planning process, that part of it that occurs after policy has been enacted and involves the definition of operational guidelines for putting a policy into effect. And only relatively recently has attention been given to evaluation and assessment of policy, which is both the last step and in a sense the first one, since evaluation is the policy trigger for the feedback loop that returns us to problem definition. Presumably, sensitive and informed policy evaluations provide the basis for problem redefinition.

The Policy Process

Policies *are* decisions, but they are not *only* decisions. They represent a total policy process which extends from ideas about problem definition through the generation of idea-solutions (options) to the point of selection and ratification, into planning and evaluation and then loops back again to problem definition. In order to insure that an organization functions well and is taking appropriate account of its environment, anticipating the difficulties that it will face and providing guidelines and directions for the organization to follow, there must be management of the policy process. The ideas which guide our lives and our organizations are too important to be left to chance. The point of importance here is to make the argument that management of the policy process is crucial to the successful operation of any system.

Policy is:

- An idea, which is embodied in
- A written document, which is
- Ratified by legitimate authority, and serves as
- A guide to action, and is
- The result of the policy process.

The Idea of Policy Management

Good Ideas

The argument here is a simple one. Things are likely to go better if one thinks about them, plans for them, secures the relevant information, and tries to integrate that information into what is already known and being done. It is possible to spontaneously come up with good ideas or the right ideas, but it is unlikely that one can rely, as an operating procedure, on such a system, especially because organizational structure and organizational environments are becoming increasingly complex. Thus, since policy is an idea, we need to ensure that a continual new and adequate supply of ideas about organizational activities flow into the organization for consideration just as we need to assure adequate supplies of money and staff.

Orchestration and Interlinking of a Policy Over Time

Management, however, implies both the generation of resources and the application of those resources to organizational goals. When one is thinking of money, for example, one thinks of the generation of income as one part of the management process, and the assessment and tracking down of that income as it is applied to the achievement of organizational goals as another part of the management process. Managers need to conduct themselves and their organizations so that there is an adequate supply of income on the one hand, and the most intelligent application of that income to organizational subgoals and mission and role on the other. Policy management thus involves not only the assurance of an adequate supply of ideas and options—a crucial portion of a policy management process, to be sure—but also involves the orchestration and interlinking of that process itself in its several components. Good ideas are not much good if they get lost long before they get considered for ratification. Innovative problem definitions are not helpful if they never get translated into policy proposals. Quality ideas, once ratified, are not very helpful if the planning process that succeeds ratification does not implement them in a useful way or establishes operational definitions that change the nature and intent of the policy itself. Hence, managing the longitudinal or "flow" aspects of policy is an important aspect of policy management.

Orchestration and Interlinking among Policies

The third aspect of policy management has to do with the horizontal integrity of the policy process. Policy is a collective noun. When we mean one policy, we tend to say a policy. Thus, speaking of policy management implies a plurality of policies—many policies—that might well guide an organiztion, a person, or a community. Since the policy process is such a loose one, there is nothing to assure that these policies are consistent each with the other, that they are mutually reinforcing and extending, that a new policy in area X takes account of what has happened before, and so on. Hence, there needs to be some scrutiny of what has gone before and what else is going on in the policy system so that the array of policies as a system accomplishes organizational purpose.

Mitigation and Utilization of Conflict

So far, the idea of policy management has had three core components. One is to assure the supply of good policy ideas. Second is to attend to the interrelationship of those ideas and their transformation over time. Third, it is important to attend to policy synchrony so that at any given moment policies complement each other. There is a fourth aspect that needs to be mentioned—the management of policy conflict. The different political and intellectual interests characteristic of the kinds of environments we are talking about mean, invariably, many different points of view about what should be done, how problems should be handled, what is the appropriate way to proceed. To complicate matters further, it is not only competing interests between groups and individuals that we need to take into consideration, but competing interests within individuals and groups. Many of the values we hold are themselves contradictory. We want, of course, adequate income for our staff, but we also want equitable income for our staff. On some occasions, those two principles provide us with conflicting courses of action. There is no magic solution by which conflict can be "managed." When people differ in their views on how a situation is to be handled, especially if they may gain by one solution and lose by another, there is no clear-cut way that all contenders can be satisfied with, at least in terms that they would find totally acceptable. However, crucial to the idea of policy management, the management of ideas, is the fact that we are too often prisoners of particular perspectives and faulty frameworks, which, unfortunately and inadvertently, commit us to conflicting, or more conflicting than necessary, approaches to the situation at hand. A good policy management process not only assists in conflict management by explicating the bases on which conflicts may exist, but provides alternative solutions that might be considered.

Policy management cannot *resolve* conflicts any more than fiscal management or personnel management can *resolve* fiscal or personnel conflicts. These are resolved, if they are resolved, in the decision process: to allocate money to a project or not, to hire or dismiss a person or not, to follow a particular strategic course or not. However, it should be clear that in all of these cases policy management, fiscal management, and personnel management conflicts are exacerbated by a paucity of alternatives and by a haphazard, helter-skelter approach to the decision process. In addition, conflicts are inflamed as crisis looms. Management styles in policy, fiscal, and personnel areas can be bad for many reasons, not the least of which comes from the tendency to delay decisions. Unfortunately, as decision time approaches, options become fewer and narrower. Timing is crucial. They cannot be too far away from the problem or they appear unreal; if options are too close in time to the problem they are not too useful.

The Leverage Principle

This proposition, which I call the leverage principle, suggests that if one is a moderate distance from a required decision point, the greater the range and desirability of options there are. This means that the ability to choose is enhanced, the ability to combine and sequence options is strengthened, and the ability to orchestrate both choice and sequence is enhanced. Conflict frequently results because options are limited due to the press of time. Had more time been devoted to anticipating the elements that would be required for a decision, a greater range of acceptable options could have been generated.

In a sense then, policy management *is* crisis *management*. It is not crisis resolution, personnel rectification, or fiscal amalgamation. Rather, it is the process by which problems are identified, options selected and sequenced, constructed and crafted, decisions made, and implementive strategies designed and put into place.

Policy management:

- Has good ideas
- Orchestrates and interlinks a single policy over time
- Orchestrates and interlinks different policies at given moments in time
- Mitigates and utilizes conflict
- Employs the leverage principle

Policy Management, Fiscal Management, and Personnel Management

I have mentioned fiscal management and personnel management as two analogous kinds of concerns that human service and other executives have as part of their daily routine. Indeed, they tend to loom much larger than policy management and tend to be the idioms through which policy management actually occurs. Much of the discussion around how we should spend money, or whom we should hire or reassign, deals with larger policy management questions than are implicit in the fiscal or personnel questions themselves. There is, of course, a fiscal policy and a personnel policy, but these seem to be narrowly constructed policies aimed at the fair and equitable handling of people and money within the framework of agency goals and objectives. No one would seriously argue that the discussions of money should be *in fact* a discussion of agency goals, although it often is such a discussion. No one would seriously argue that one should hire first and decide what to do second, although discussion of agency direction are often implicit in hiring decisions. (This is especially true when one is hiring the executive, and much of the search committee's activity, in almost every instance, focuses upon "where do we want to go" and "what do we want to do," which inform the choice of "whom do we wish to have to go where we want to go and do what we want to do?")

Fiscal management and personnel management are, of course, crucial components of any organization's range of responsibilities and area of activity. Insuring adequate supplies of fiscal resources and their appropriate allocation has already been mentioned. One might also note the need to guide against misappropriation of funds, theft of funds, and other problems that fiscal managers must concern themselves with. Personnel management, too, needs to pay special attention to securing an adequate supply of people who have the abilities and talents appropriate to and requisite for the enterprise at hand. However, neither of these two concerns deals, necessarily or directly, with the supply of ideas. To survive in an increasingly complex environment, an organization needs, along with a supply of money and skilled personnel, a supply of concepts, views, and perspectives, which can become bases for policies that assist the organization in dealing with its environment.

For a variety of reasons, discussed in chapter 2, organizations are as likely to suffer a conceptual deficit as a fiscal one. Organizations tend to spend a lot of time on fiscal and personnel management and deal indirectly with matters of policy management via fiscal and personnel matters. This tendency makes the consideration of fiscal and personnel matters less adequate, more confused, and subject to a range of perspectives and concerns that is probably too great, while at the same time not dealing directly with issues of policy management. There is no question, of course, that these three elements interrelate. But, at least in the perfect world, fiscal and personnel matters should be subservient to policy matters of a goal and mission sort. For example, *how* one spends money and *whom* one hires depend upon *what* goals and missions are to be accomplished.

It should become clear by now that policy management has two important senses, both of which overlap with fiscal and personnel management. In one sense policy management refers to the entire range of organizational policy, which includes goal and mission policy, fiscal policy, and personnel policy. Hence, when I speak of policy management here, in one sense at least, I am referring to the need for ideas in all three areas, the need for attention to and focus upon policy in the goal and mission area, in the fiscal area, and in the personnel area. Some people like to think of policy as referring, really, to only the first area, that is, goal and mission ideas. And certainly a primary focus of policy management is to ensure the flow of goal and mission ideas. However, policy management seen as the supply of ideas must also take into account, as I have just noted, the need to have a supply of ideas about fiscal policy and about personnel policy.

Thus, the policy manager really has two major missions. One is focused on the nature of goal, fiscal and personnel activity; the second seeks to improve their operation. One is change; the second is improvement. Just as money serves to be important in putting ideas into effect through people and people serve to put ideas into effect through money, ideas serve to direct money and people. There is an interaction, therefore, among the three elements—ideas, money, and people. Ideas tend to cluster for the most part around organizational goal and mission and secondarily around money and people as well. These are the two areas where policy management is best used.

A Perspective on Policy: Sectors and Levels

Thinking about "policy" in the "human service system" tends to bring a variety of images to mind, not all of them involved (if, in fact, any of them are involved) with running the agency. While that is an important focus here, it is also necessary to consider the broader types of policies, all of which are, or can be, the subject of policy management.

Public Policy

When one is thinking about human service policy, somehow there is a tendency to focus on things governments do. Certainly that is an important type of policy, and often the phrase public policy is used when referring to policy made by governments. Typically, such policy is aimed at a broad group of citizens—citizens of a nation, citizens of a state, citizens of a country or local municipality. The target of the policy is the behavior of those citizens rather than the government operation itself.

Private Policy

Public policy, however broadly one ordinarily construes it, is only a portion of the types of policy one could consider. The competing aspect is private policy, that is, policy made by private organizations. It may be comparable in scope to governmental policy and operate at the federal, state, or local level. Consider a large national corporation (or even a multinational corporation). Its activities may well be as important as those of the national government, at least for certain purposes and in certain areas. Private policy has been typically thought of as subject to only the most minimal constraints and the limitations on the activities of boards of directors (as a chief policy-making instrumentality) have been minimal.

The nonprofit organization stands, in some sense, like a public utility—halfway between a public policy and a private policy orientation. Among other differences is the overall level of self-aggrandizement which may differentially characterize public and private policy. Public policy is supposed to be aimed at the common weal and have fairly traceable benefits, even if the primary beneficiaries are individuals or special groups. Nonprofit institutions may well aim at a narrower scope than this, with their targets being both their own operation and, to some degree, specification of client groups' behavior and desired outcomes. The basis of judgment, however, is supposed to be the organization.

The distinction between public policy and private policy is one that is perhaps less clear than one might have thought. Public policy obviously affects, often in profound ways, private individuals. Private policy affects, often in profound ways, the public weal. Thus, the distinction is probably most useful only as a descriptor of the source of ratification.

Policy Levels

Another way to think about this situation is to consider "levels" of social organization, ranging from the person through the family and group to the organization and community to the society or state itself.

What does a look at levels of social organization in terms of the types of policy they engender reveal? At the level of personal policy, we would find various agreements entered into and signed by the individual to borrow money, to go into the army, to do this and that. All individuals are surrounded by a range of signed documents that obligate us to do this or avoid that. In retrospect, the wisdom of these documents is frequently questioned. Often, pressures at the time make it seem as if they were a good idea, or lack of information about alternatives makes a particular course of action seem wise, and so on. While it is not possible in all cases, we can in some discern a pattern—the borrower, the lender, and so on and so forth.

Family policy is, primarily, the will and any intrafamily gifts that involve the exchange of property or obligations from one portion of the family to another. Sometimes there is a social policy that affects family policy. For example, state laws sometimes specify the ways in which property must be divided in the event of a marital rift, or states may set minimum standards for the care of children.

Agency policy derives from official actions of boards of directors. Those actions are binding on the whole organization, whether the organization likes it or not. And most boards do not expect their policy simply to be offered up as a window dressing. They expect the executive and the executive core to enforce it. But executives also make policy—often within delegated areas where general policy has been set by the board or by statutes and of a clarifying and implementing sort.

Community policy is one of the least clear policy arenas that we have to deal with, perhaps because the idea of community is itself ambiguous. One can, of course, talk about municipal policy, city policy, or county policy, but these are public policies made by governmental bodies. There is an entire private sector which is not involved and which frequently seeks to become involved as time goes on. Even within subsectors of interest there are public and private organizations responsible for their own policy, and hence without the necessary ability or willingness to "pull together" and set aside petty grievances (or sometimes not so petty, but questions of power nonetheless). With community policy we begin to see that as the level of social organization becomes more complex, the number of policy actors become exponentially more numerous. Simply being aware of the range of actors is sufficiently difficult to comprehend, but when one contemplates their interaction as well, the system begins to look very complicated indeed. It is this complexity that lends a certain perverse credibility to the "inside dopester" who "really knows what is going on" or to the conspiracy theorist who can offer a plausible interpretation of what is happening. In reality, of course, these explanations are more satisfying than accurate.

The state level, of course, and the federal level represent still more superordinate policy-making collectivities. In most cases we are talking about the state government or the federal government. However, in other instances we are referring to organizations with a state-wide focus or a national focus.

Each of these kinds of policy is subject to policy management considerations. The fact that some may be social policy and some may not is of less concern than the fact that some kind of weakly ratified document states principles by which our life is guided. The fact that it is ratified means that it cannot be changed at a whim and that penalties are attached for noncompliance. Hence, these policies are important, identifiable, and workable targets of change.

Policy Boundaries

Policy has become such an omnibus term, so often used for so many things, that it is often hard to know where policy ends and some other types of activity begin. Some consideration of the relationship of policy to other important organizational processes can help provide a richer sense of what policy is and what it is not. These distinctions are not hard and fast, but rather they help to develop a sense of place for policy, planning, practice, and administration.

Policy vs. Practice

Much of what is discussed as policy, in my view, is better termed practice. Policy is what is written and legally approved; practice is what is done. There may be a practice in an organization to do a particular thing for birthdays. When one speaks of family planning practices, one is asking what do people actually do about family planning; it is not implied that "practice" is at the level of policy. "What we do around here" is a legitimate and important organizational form. I think accepted practice is a good phrase, which for our field carries exactly that meaning. While it is often confused with policy, it is not policy. The relatively recent development of client contracting, that is, developing specific written agreements with clients, is an effort to convert practice into policy and to clarify the set of expectations between worker and client, to set goals, and target progress.

Policy vs. Planning

Frequently, discussions of policy will also mention, as a synonymous term, planning. Planning is sometimes referred to as that which comes before policy and involves the anticipation of policy. In my view however, planning is that which takes place after ratification has occurred. As will be discussed in a later chapter, it is most useful to consider planning within the context of approval and ratification. All too often, within the human service sector at least, planning occurs without appropriate policy in place. Operational activities proceed with no authorization, with little sense of where these activities are to go and what purpose they are to serve, other than being good or doing good for people. Since planning is inherently more specific than policy and assumes the legitimation and approval that a policy brings, it seems that we should not think about plans as containing the level of generality that a policy would. Nor should we think about a policy as normally containing the level of specificity and detail that a plan would. All too frequently we run into situations in which people develop policies in the form of plans, that is, more detailed, more specific sets of procedures, and then find themselves in a very difficult position when those who have to approve the policy object to certain aspects of the plan, format. Or they are critical of plans developed without some sense of approval and legitimation. We have even incorporated these words into organizational titles, such as Community Planning councils and Social Planning agencies. To me, it is very useful to keep the planning/policy distinction alive and well and to think about community policy organizations, for example. Such an organization would assess demographic, economic, and social trends and develop proposals for the community as a whole, or subsectors within the community, to handle those types of changes. Once they have been approved, such an organization might well develop the more specific plans required for actual implementation.

In sum, policy is general, goal defining, and formally ratified. Planning is more specific, goal accomplishing, and works to implement formally ratified policy. When policy approval bodies get plans in lieu of policies, several types of problems can occur. The specific nature of plan language often diverts consideration from the policy issues into detail, much to the detriment of systematic policy assessment; objections to specifics become at times objections to the general, even though not intended; discussions of goal definitions become enmeshed in discussion of specific means to accomplish a particular goal; discontent about proceeding so specifically prior to overall policy approval is generated.

Policy and Administration

Most typically the idea of management is associated with administration rather than policy. Wilfried Harrison suggests that administration is:

co-operative activity within an organization, conceived as serving certain ends which are not necessarily those of the cooperating participants and which is also conceived as being organized for this purpose in a hierarchial manner. (Harrison 1964:10)

There has been the idea that "policy" makes decisions and sets directions while "administration" is involved in carrying out policy. Within the political realm, this distinction sometimes was called the "politics versus administration" dichotomy, because policy and politics became fused in that the ratifying body, the policy body, was also (though, of course, not uniquely) a political body—a legislature, a city council, or some other governmental form. Increasingly however, administration is recognized as having policy influence if not policy authority. Why is this so?

First, administrative activity through the development of organizational practices "sets" policy through the authority of convention. While one might consider such *de facto* policy as lacking formal legitimacy, which it does, it may also have the power of normative consent. And though policy and practice need to be sharply distinguished, administration is still involved in policy in this way.

Second, administration has the power of interpretation, of assigning an event or problem to the "policy" realm or to its own. As items for decision are allocated to administration and administration decides them, the policy activity, if not the authority of the administrators, is enhanced.

Third, administration, as comprised of women and men who are "on deck" most of the time, has the ability, if not the authority, to "commit" the organization to courses of action (or to avoiding courses of action) which later can be ratified by the policymaking group. In such cases the policymaking group may have little choice other than to follow the lead of the administrative action, because the action may have preempted, in terms of the flow of events, other options of significance.

Each of these tendencies or possibilities is, perhaps, more common in human service organizations because of the separation of realms of policy-makers and administrators. In a human service organization, where there is a "volunteer" board of directors of people from other occupational arenas, the power of the executive staff may be enhanced. The board may not meet often enough (even once a month can be too infrequent in fast-breaking cases), so there is temporal distance between the executive and the policy ratification body. The volunteer and professional split between board and staff may also serve to permit the executive to commit the organization in areas of her or his "expertise," and if it is claimed as a commitment that is professionally "correct" it becomes difficult for a lay board to countermand it.

While distance from the day-to-day activities, both temporally and so-cially, is a factor which involves administration in policy, closeness is too. Haft (1981) points out for corporate boards, at least, that the practice of having "inside" directors, that is, directors who are employees of the or-ganization, may lead to lack of independence and judgment in policy review functions. In this case, policy and administration are merged because the people are, for the most part, the same.

Rather than seek to continue to find two completely independent spheres for policy and administration, I suggest that we use here an interdependent spheres conception, as outlined below in figure 1.1 (after Tropman 1981:25). Policy functions are those which are decisions of 1) broad scope and impli-cation; 2) commit the organization's people and resources in a substantial way and in a substantial direction; 3) are hard to reverse; 4) are precedent setting, and 5) have force over time.

Joint policy/administrative functions involve the intersect of policy and administration—policy oversight from the board's perspective and issue gen-eration from the administration's point of view. The executive lies at the center of the policy/administration interface and attends to that interface as a primary responsibility. Policy management involves especially the policy and policy/administration spheres. It not only attends to the supply of ideas and concepts, alternatives and options (policy quality and quantity), but also seeks to assist in the recognition of items appropriate for policy considera-tion (policy vitality) and to promote a balance among the functions, pre-venting policy atrophy. For reasons of temporal and social distance, many human service organizations look more like figure 1.2. Policy, in this more common illustration, becomes a tail wagged by the dog of administration, arriving too late with too little.

Figure 1.1
Interrelationship of Policy and Administration

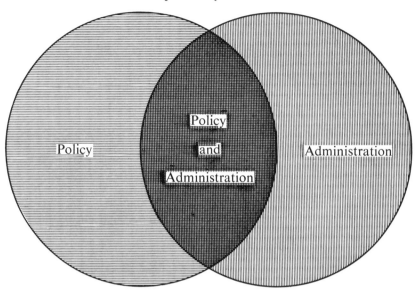

Figure 1.2
Asymmetrical Relationship Between Policy and Administration

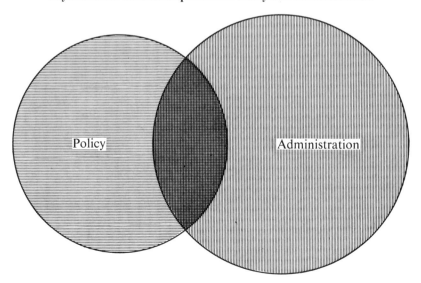

Almost anything improves if one cares about it and spends time and attention on it. Policy is no exception. It cannot be an afterthought. Policy direction for human service organizations is especially difficult because of the inherent ambiguity in our business, lack of clarity about which of many ways to go could be the right way, and the fact that our income sources come less from customers and more from appropriations bodies, which have, or may have, quite different ideas about what customers want or need (see examples in Drucker 1973:49). Finally, because clienthood itself, as a definition of someone's position, implies and even demands that we disregard the client's wishes and views because "client" in some important sense is a synonym for incompetence, creates difficulties.

These difficulties, however discouraging they may be, demand policy management, not policy abdication. Salvation will not come through administration only; rather, effective and efficient performance will come from high quality decisions, well implemented. Without high quality decisions however, the human service organization will suffer from policy atrophy, a precursor to organization atrophy.

Policy management requires:
- Sensitivity to the difference between policy and planning
- Awareness of distinction between policy and practice
- A balance between policy and administration

Policy Roles

The very idea of policy management implies that there are individuals who have certain tasks and assignments with respect to the entire task of problem analysis, proposal development, policy shepherding and ratification, assurance, planning, programming, and evaluation. And, indeed, there are such roles. They vary, both in terms of the place in the policy development process where they occur as well as in the nature of their target.

The first distinction has to do with the difference in roles between those whose primary task is the mobilization of people and those whose task is the mobilization of ideas. The former, one might call the community organizer. This is in no way to say that ideas are not important to the community organizer, but rather that the focus of the community organizer's effort is primarily on individuals, groups, coalitions, and various combinations of individuals, groups, and coalitions to build support for particular policies (or to develop suggestions for policies). The policy specialist, on the other hand, is one whose primary task is aimed at the development, presentation, and movement of ideas within the social system. People are, of course, crucial at all these points, but occupy the same general position for the policy specialist that ideas occupy for the community organization specialist. Each has a dual focus, but one is dominant and one subdominant.

Within the policy specialist role are some sub-roles. The policy analyst is one whose main assignment is the dissecting of problems, assessing their relative causes, and providing scenarios and solutions to be considered. Imagination and analytic ability are the primary skills of the policy analyst, and the policy analyst is not necessarily the individual who is most capable of getting a suggestion accepted and implemented. Often such persons are known as "idea men" or "idea women," a phrase that points to special talent in generating new and innovative solutions to problems and indeed identifying previously unknown problems.

The policy manager, on the other hand, is one who has as a primary focus the movement of ideas through the policy process. Such a person may also be an analyst and may have as a special skill that sense of interconnection between one stage and another. After all, these stages are largely defined on an ongoing basis. No trumpets blare heralding a phase of ratification versus a phase of problem analysis versus a phase of proposal development. As we will discuss later, those phases represent crystallized points (often meetings) during which influence can be brought to bear. It is also true that during the interstitial periods between phases and meetings influence can be brought to bear. The policy manager sees to it that enough time, but not too much, is spent on problem identification; that enough options, but not too many, are developed; that links with the community organizer are established; sees to it that a reasonable set of proposals moves into the arena for ratification; tries to link the formal and informal systems of approval; and so on and so forth. The manager also performs these tasks within an appropriate time frame.

Once approval has occurred, the policy manager shifts to a planning role. Such a role involves the more detailed specification, as I have already mentioned, of the more specific instrumentalities that would be involved in carrying out a policy. Finally, of course, we move to the programming or actual running of an operating program and at this point the administrator becomes more centrally involved. The administrator has, of course, been developing an involvement as time has been going along, but this represents the turning over of the program from the policy specialist to the administrative specialist.

Often the executive is seen as the "policy specialist" within the organization. And to an important extent this perception is correct. The executive position is most certainly a blend of policy and administrative functions. For many executives however, the administrative portion of the job tends to drive out the policy portion. Administrative tasks are numerous and demanding. They can easily fill up a day, and leave one with the feeling that one has put in a full day of work (and one has!) The problem is more one of the issues on which time has been spent, rather than whether time has been spent. Thus perception creates, but does not reflect, reality. The executive, who is seen as a policy manager, often needs assistance and perspective in getting to that point. This problem may be true generally, but it is certainly more true in the human services, perhaps because we have more recently than most come to understand the importance of administration and because many of the executives come from a different, and clinical, orientation.[2]

Perhaps not strangely, policy literature does not mention anything like the policy manager. However, Daft and Bradshaw touch on this in their study of why new university departments are created (academic and administrative) within a university. They point out that the departments (one could read here programs and services) arise as a product of two decisions. "The second decision, which is visible and often studied, is the formal choice among alternatives" (Daft and Bradshaw 1980:455). Formal choices among alternatives, however, imply that someone, somehow, has come up with alternatives that can be considered as options. The generations of these alternatives, the provision of ideas within the "policy mill," is the first decision.

The first decision, however, occurs before the formal organization choice. Someone senses a problem and decides to propose and champion an idea as a solution. This "idea champion" interacts with the environment in his area of expertise and responds with action. . . . We know almost nothing about this choice activity, such as who idea champions are, why they act, and how they differ from colleagues. . . . The idea champion provides energy to move the system, energy to gain acceptance for a change. (Daft and Bradshaw 1980:455)

2. Talcott Parsons posited three levels of organization—technical, managerial, and institutional. Each represented different types of skills, and success in one was not automatically predictive of success in the other (Parsons 1960).

The idea champion is the role close to that of policy manager, and it appears to have arisen spontaneously within the university setting at least. I suspect that it is present in other settings as well, and that "new programs" and new departments are not the only ideas that such idea champions have. The idea champion role, structured, systematized, more normalized and more regularly played, institutionalized as a part of the organization's role array, is, I think, that of the policy manager.

Policy Management Difficulties in the Human Services

The idea of administration has received some attention in the human service field, but even so it has only recently been accepted as a legitimate area of work and inquiry within schools of social work and major agency sectors. All too often those persons elevated to administrative posts were people who had had most of their experience in direct practice and, because of the competence they displayed, were offered other positions in agency management which did not at all use the things they did well. Indeed, there is a broad consensus that many human service organizations are poorly, if not badly, managed. Such conclusions must be in part drawn from observing the problems of those who, with little background in administration, seek to administer.[3] For a profession to systematically use those untrained in administration for administration is perhaps trusting more to luck than is appropriate.

Administrative Training Programs Are Few

These problems have been sufficiently recognized now to have generated a number of administrative training programs around the country for human service professionals—some in schools of social work, some in schools of business, and some as combination programs between schools of social work and schools of business. Large organizational systems have begun to develop intramural training programs along this line as well. The United Way of America, for example, has an extensive training program for its execu-

3. This pattern continues today. At the University of Michigan School of Social Work we get many calls from people who have just experienced this kind of promotion and who seek a "quickie" course in the essentials of administration because of the pressures of the job as they are experiencing it. For this reason, we instituted a certificate program in human service management.

tives around the country and has developed a range of courses and materials for them.

Bias against Administration

In general, the human service profession has been slower to recognize the levels of social organization beyond individual ones and slower still to develop training and educational curricula for their management. In the strong days of casework, group work was suspect. After group work had been accepted, community organization remained a small program. As community organization increased, administration began to develop. And now that administration has been legitimized as a social work method, an important one remains—policy. This book is about the realm of policy and the importance of developing skills in policy guidance and management, as well as in other areas for the human service profession. Indeed, I would argue that the deficiency here, in the ideas and concepts, could undo all or much of what has gone before.

Why is there this hesitancy on the part of human service professionals? There are many reasons, but surely one lies in the fact that as one moves from the level of the individual to "higher" levels of social organization, there is a different focus, a different orientation, different theoretical bases, and conventionally different points of reference. Administration, for example, is often thought to be the province of "business," and somehow it appeared unseemly to think that human service organizations should be administered or "managed."[4] The very words carry a connotation of lack of "freedom," and somehow it is or has been thought that such organizations would run themselves. Organizations, of course, run themselves as well as data speak for themselves, but a negative evaluation made progress difficult.

Then too, there is the idea, expressed by my inclusion of "higher" levels of social organization in apologetic quotes, that somehow work at these levels demeaned the individual, made the individual less important, less prominent. It is, indeed, a curious paradox that within the social work/human service profession, which explains poverty and disadvantage so heavily in terms of the "system," there is such a strong emphasis on treating the individual. One would have thought that the general orientation of the human service field would have led to a set of strategies more consistent with its ideology. The reverse seems to be the case. It is almost as if the ideology—

---

4. The very phrase "management" goes against the grain of "client self-determination" in the field.

the culture of the profession—and the actual structure of activity in the profession work in opposite ways. One could say at "cross purposes" or, alternatively, argue that they serve as a complementary balance. While I am inclined to the latter view, it is of small moment here. What is significant is the understanding that such cross purposes exist, and that they have implications for the development of policy guidance comprehension, training, and action.

Assessment Difficulties in Human Service Organizations

The focus upon the policy management idea evolves naturally from the development of the field of policy itself. Increasingly, as the complexity of society makes decisions ever more difficult and at the same time ever more fateful, the policy management process will be at the center of consideration. Our focus here is human service organizations, those enterprises which have the helping of people (people assisting), The moving of people (people processing), and the changing of people (people changing) as their primary goals. Such agencies range from prisons and detention facilities (people processing) to organizations that provide adoptive children, chore service, transportation (people assisting) to those that seek through various means to change people (people changing). One agency can have a function that meets (or seeks to meet) two or all three of these goals or it can have subparts that work in each of these areas. The key problem that these "nonprofits" have is that without the push of "profit" as a margin for measure of performance there is less likely to be the push for new ideas as well. Hence the potential for stagnation is greater. But that is only part of the problem nonprofit people agencies face. Their environments are more turbulent, the values which support them are less secure than is the case with other organizations. They can be subject to rapid swirls and eddies of support, something that again stresses the need for a savings account of ideas and approaches that can be called upon in time of need.

Problems of Public Sector Management

Human service organizations are not all within the "nonprofit" sector however. Many are in the public governmental sector, ranging from the large megabureaucratic public welfare department in a state government to the vast Social Security Administration within the federal establishment. All of these public agencies have needs for policy management as well, as Curtis (1980) points out. They face the same kinds of pressures as the "non-profit" organization (lack of profit pressure, turbulent environment) and the additional difficulty of high value conflict within the public sector. Curtis identifies such special problems as separation of powers, services not bought by users, the spoils system, and managing in the public eye as among those public managers have.

Multiple Publics

Both the public and the private agencies have multiple consumers—because the client is not, in many instances, the one who pays for the service. Hence, the client's view is doubly removed from the organization—first because the client (like "student" or "child") is automatically, by definition, suspected of having poor judgment, and second because the client's financial connection to the operation of the agency/bureau itself is a tenuous one. Not only is the client "once removed," but other funders, community representatives, and legislators have things to say about how people can be best helped.

The Pressure of Human Problems

Human service organizations have two other pressures on them. By and large, they are overworked and pressed by day-to-day problems. Daily routine drives out policy and planning to some degree. The variety and complexity of human problems is endless. Because of the definitional difficulties mentioned before, it is hard to find limiting rules (how many times? how much service? how often?). The pressure of problems does not serve, like the pressures of profitability, to define a cost benefit line.

The Pressure of Staff

That problem is compounded by another. Human service workers *want* to help. That is why we got into the business in the first place. The push of problems combines with the selectivity of staff to make overload even more troubling. Both tendencies mitigate against policy management.[5]

5. One variation of this point comes from the nature of the professions themselves. Professions, because they involve doing, tend to be action oriented. Policy management is heavily conceptually oriented, focusing upon the development and managing of good ideas. Hence professions may be less attuned to policy management.

Yet the more pressures there are that mitigate against policy management, the more it is needed. Hence, whatever improvements can be made in the quality of ideas and concepts that inform the agency and in turn become the policies that guide it, the more satisfying and helpful the organization is going to be, and the higher the quality of service will in turn be.

And that, finally, is the goal of policy management, to provide high quality decisions that guide and direct the agency. Part of the reason it needs to be emphasized within human service settings is because of the high need for it there, and the many organizational forces that make it even more difficult.

Among the special problems faced by the human service systems are:

- Few administrative training programs
- A bias against administration
- Outcomes are hard to assess
- Public sector management is difficult;
- Multiple publics
- The pressure of human problems
- The pressure of staff

Conclusion

Policy management, then, is an idea about ideas—it focuses upon the generation of policy ideas and their refinement, processing, storage, and ratification. It refers to their generation and improvement as well as to their review and refurbishment. Some policy ideas will become ratified and become policy for the organization. The need to insure an orderly process of development, assignment, and assessment is as important for policy ideas as it is for dollars and people, and it is indeed important that ideas are, after a fashion, discussed. But one should not let dollars and people drive the organization. Rather, the organization's mission and role should be the driving force, and dollars should be distributed and people organized to serve those ends. Systematic attention to mission and role ideas is one major component of policy management. Fiscal and personnel ideas, which help serve the mission and role ideas, are another. And constant working with those ideas so that they can be current and appropriate, and of the highest quality is a third. It is to the accomplishment of these goals that this book is aimed.

CASE ILLUSTRATIONS

THE CHILD WELFARE AGENCY

Children's Helpers, one of the oldest child welfare organizations in the city, was yet one of the newest. It had begun its work well before the turn of the century and had had its share of friendly visitors and psychoanalytically oriented psychiatric social workers. But it also had added some new staff and programs in recent years. Grafted onto and only partially integrated with the older part was a runaway house, a drug treatment center, and an information and referral center for lost children. The board was in a state of irritation at the moment because the adoption division had just passed up to it a recommendation that it found astounding. The division had proposed that this child welfare agency seek to move into the area of surrogate motherhood, arguing that there were a number of young women at the college nearby who would be willing to be surrogate mothers for the price of tuition and that with the dwindling supply of adoptable babies such a plan was gaining ground all over the country. Wouldn't it be better, the adoption division argued, for a reputable and legitimate child welfare agency to start a program that could benifit everyone concerned—the mother and the adoptive families—in the context of social work concern and service. The child protective division had sent a strongly worded memo opposing this unalterably. There were plenty of adoptable children, if people could get over the notion that every child had to be a perfect child. This division knew how many unwanted children existed and was trying to promote the adoption of children who had suffered the trauma of child abuse.

People in the community were uncertain about the role of the agency at this point. The proposal to move toward surrogate motherhood, questionable in itself to many in the community, seemed to symbolize the pattern of the organization: to seek and do whatever was currently popular, with little thought or perspective. Indeed, some of the workers themselves shared this view. Others in the social work community sensed that there was an erosion of mission and role, that the agency was trying too hard to be all things to all people. Wherever there were a few dollars to be gained, this agency came up with a proposal. While everyone supported the idea of securing funds, they also thought that there needed to be some limits. The clinical styles which had come to characterize the agency seemed more to reflect the staff at the moment, rather than to represent any overall approach. There was a sense that the agency could certainly vary, but such wide variation made it very difficult for other agencies in the community to relate. When the board got this proposal, it was shocked into an attention that it had not paid in recent years. Some said that the acting executive, who had replaced the previous executive who had had thirty-years tenure while a new director was being sought, had deliberately permitted this proposal to come to board attention to, in fact, get the board's attention. This contention, of course, could never be proved.

Discussion Questions

1. What has happened to this agency?
2. Are the new proposals good? Why or why not?
3. How can policy management help here?
4. Does the agency have problems "typical" of human service organizations? Why or why not?

THE WELFARE PLANNING COUNCIL

The Welfare Planning Council had a good reputation for planning within the human service sector. However, in recent years it had seemed more wobbly and uncertain than had been true in the past. A number of new planning organizations had emerged in the community, including some in health and hospital planning, a coordinating council which sought specifically to pull together the public agencies, an area agency on aging which sought to pull together a number of the agencies involved in providing senior services, and a center for human service research and statistics at the local university. The effect of all of these organizations had not yet fully crystalized, and the welfare council was beginning to wonder, in private of course, whether its days might not be numbered. After all, it had over the years pulled together many of the human service agencies. In fact, it had been a premier organization, and when it spoke it spoke for the whole human service community. That was certainly no longer true. It had also collected data. Its annual meeting, during which the service and social problems statistics were presented, had been a highlight of the community, for the press and human service providers alike. Now, almost no one came. The executive and staff were aware of some of the problems, but as yet the community had not sensed the peril in which this organization seemed to find itself. An additional problem had cropped up with United Way. Increasingly, the United Way organization represented only a part, rather than all, of the organizations in town. It was interested in planning for its sector of organizations and was pressing the planning council to focus special effort on the United Way agencies. Historically, of course, the Welfare Planning Council had had a very close relationship with United Way and its views were a powerful consideration. On the other hand, there was the community as a whole to think about. What might be good for it? What might the total range of agencies and citizens want and how could one find this out? Was there room for a total citizens' body or should the focus be on the special interests? The executive knew that there would be no one point of decision, but rather a span of decisions. Once that span had been traversed and decisions made, the community would wake up one morning to find a strengthened and vigorous welfare council with a specific role being carried out energetically, or it would find the shell of a once powerful organization, devoid of staff and essential support services, seeking, perhaps pitifully, to maintain itself, but recognized by all as on its death bed.

It was with these concerns in mind that the executive confronted two problems that had come across her desk recently. One was from the public library. It was worried about vandalism at the branch libraries and had had to divert funds from a number of accounts to increase security and, it seemed to her, fortifications at the local branch libraries. How puzzling, she thought. Some of these libraries are centers of learning, surrounded by people who can't read. Isn't there a way we could bridge that gap? But then, is this an appropriate task for a welfare planning council to undertake?

The other problem seemed more traditional. The director of a local settlement house had written. Most of its previous clientele had moved to the suburbs and it was considering moving. Could the Welfare Council suggest a way to dispose of its building and provide it with enough capital to make the move to the suburbs to follow the ethnic populations with which it had worked so well in the past? How can we solve this problem? thought the executive. That settlement house is currently a round peg in a square hole. We could move it to a round hole out in the suburbs, but then there would be just an empty, unfulfilled need in the place where it was. On the other hand, it's not filling a need now and we could convert it into a square peg. But then it would be something different. With these thoughts in mind, the executive went home for the day, not sure whether to respond to either request and with no good ideas about what to do in either case.

Discussion Questions

1. Should the council accept the two assignments? One? Which one? Why or why not?

2. What are theories of community planning bodies today? What is an ideal role for them?

3. How could the council begin to become more policy related?

4. What kinds of ''new ideas'' would help here?

2

THE PROBLEMS OF POLICY MANAGEMENT

The idea of policy management—that is that ideas are a crucial resource for an organization and require management and shepherding—has a number of problems associated with it. These problems are of different types. One set has to do with issues of why we do not now have something like policy management. Another has to do with its more specific application within the human services area and some of the unique problems that the human service organization presents. A third problem has to do with the difficulties in actually performing policy management functions.

This group of problems is complicated by two features inherent in American society. American society is pragmatically oriented. The very notion that ideas should be a topic of attention and development is a subdominant theme within our culture. While it is true that we have contributed, through documents like the Constitution and the Declaration of Independence, ideas of historically global importance, we nonetheless take as much, if not more, pride in our practical "hands-on" day-to-day kinds of skills and competencies. Ideas are general, abstract, speculative. They do not have the concrete feeling of money and people. Thus, the very cultural context of our society makes the policy management task seem impractical, something that does not contribute a lot to the organization's development. I would argue, of course, that good timely ideas are among the most practical of organizational resources. And yet, since they are not perceived in this way, they are not pursued and cultivated as appropriate.

The second general problem, which may stem in part from the first, is the crisis orientation of American decision-making styles. Time after time, as one talks to executives in human service and other organizations about planning ahead, about thinking about alternative paths, one gets the reply, "I don't have the time. There's this crisis and there's that crisis." The current crisis as the arbiter of time allocation within the social agency or human service organization is not unique, and while the concept of crisis is used as an explanation for the inability to plan, few see that the lack of plan may be the root cause of the crisis itself. There is little question that unsystematic and casual attention to mission and role, to the allocation of other resources, to organizational tasks is likely to be itself the generator of crisis—not only because potential difficulties are not foreseen, but the simple interlinking of complex arcs of activity within the organization are likely to cross and spark. Fire fighting has always been more dramatic, more exciting than fire prevention. The dramatic surgical repair of a face smashed in an automobile accident has always seemed more worthy of attention than programs to wear seatbelts. As Mazzolini says: "triggering search for a new course of action in non-crisis times when the organization's health is good requires a strong initiating force" (1981:92).

Mazzolini's point, of course, is that crisis tends to motivate us while good times tend not to. And that is a great shame, because it is in the periods when the organization is doing well that it has its greatest energy and resources and its scope of decision alternatives is the widest. That, of course, is the leverage principle.

A third set of general problems that inhibit policy management functions is the nature of the problem itself. Policy management tends to deal with the more difficult, the more complex, the more troublesome areas of organizational life. These are likely to be avoided in any case. Rittel and Webber (1973) call them "wicked problems" and point to a set of difficulties that are especially unique to wicked problems:

1. There is no definitive formulation of a wicked problem;
2. Wicked problems have no stopping rule;

3. Solutions to wicked problems are not true or false, but good or bad;

4. There is no immediate and no ultimate test of a solution to a wicked problem;

5. Every solution to a wicked problem is a "one-shot operation"; because there is no opportunity to learn by trial and error, every attempt counts significantly;

6. Wicked problems do not have an innumerable (or exhaustible describable) set of potential solutions, nor is there a well-described set of permissible operations that may be incorporated into the plan;

7. Every wicked problem is essentially unique;

8. Every wicked problem can be considered a symptom of another problem;

9. The existence of a discrepency representing a wicked problem can be explained in numerous ways. The choice of explanation determines the nature of the problem's resolution; and

10. The planner (I would say policy manager) has no right to be wrong.

(See Exercise 2.1)

This set of ten reasons provides ample enough justification for avoiding the wicked problems that policy management tends to deal with. However, here as in other difficult areas, the intractability of the problem promotes avoidance, which in turn only makes the problem worse. There are, to be sure, some problems, like some illnesses, which will go away if one does nothing and it is likely that this "avoidance" solution occurs with sufficient frequency to make it strategically appealing. However, there may be an appropriate generalization here from regular or ordinary problems to wicked problems. And one might add an eleventh category to those offered already by Rittle and Webber, viz., that wicked problems will not go away of their own accord. Hence, the most difficult problems we face and the ones that press us most to avoid them are the ones that will, through the generation of crises, at some point demand our attention. These three elements then— lack of interest in focusing upon ideas, tendencies toward crisis management, and the nature of wicked problems—all tend to contribute to an anti-policy management climate in which it is hard for the idea of idea management to surface. But there are a number of confusions about policy itself that add to the set of problems policy management faces.

The Problems of Policy

What are some of the problems of policy? And in what ways do they confound the process of policy management? Two principal confusions stand out as important. The first of these is a lack of clarity about the concept of policy itself and the second has to do with some confusion about policy elements.

Conceptual Confusion

If policy is an idea that has been elaborated and set down in writing, ratified by existing authorities, and designed to guide action, then it must be a decision and, in fact, is a series or cluster of decisions that are involved in policy. Most policies involve both series and cluster decisions. The *series* decisions are those made over time and involve necessary precursor and post-cursor decisions on policy substance as well as meta-policy decisions involving such questions as the amount of time and resources to be spent on a particular policy area. *Cluster* decisions represent that group of items to be considered which are decided at the same time. Frequently a personnel policy, for example, will involve a whole range of decisions, but it is called *a* policy because it is decided all at once and written on a single sheet of paper or within a single booklet. The word policy can thus focus on a specific decision or specific decision cluster or a loose aggregate of similar decisions, which seem, upon review, to characterize a particular posture. The larger the system, the more complex the system, the more one speaks about posture rather than policy. And while it is true that policy requires a decision, a collectivity of unrelated decisions cannot be considered as policy because that collectivity has not been ratified as such.

It is this middle ground, the policy sequence and the policy cluster, which is the first line of responsibility for policy management. To make a sequence of policy decisions intelligible, coherent, and interrelated, and to facilitate the process of policy review and policy decision making and the subsequent planning and implementation are substantial tasks. However, the very fact of the size of this responsibility means that people tend not to understand it, feel that it is unmanageable, cannot be attended to, and thus tend to overlook it. We tend to operate at either end of the continuum, picking out some specific decision which has to be made and focusing upon it in a sort of policy individualism approach. Or alternatively, we talk about policy as if it represented the sum total of an agency's posture with respect to a particular sector of its environment. This confusion over policy itself and the different levels and meanings of the very word, the different references and points of view that surround it, makes it very difficult to develop a policy management focus.

Confusions in Descriptions of Policy

To this confusion we must add another set of confusions which have to do with lack of clarity in thinking about policy models. Zimmerman, in her excellent 1979 piece on ''Policy, Social Policy, and Family Policy: Concepts, Concerns, and Academic Tools,'' identifies a number of models, including the rational model, the organizational process model, and the bureaucratic process model. These tend to be confusions between models of policy itself and models of policymaking, both of which are important. But one deals with characterizing the nature of the particular decisional cluster according to its own characteristics (comprehensive or limited, liberal or conservative, proactive or reactive—the list could go on), while the other focuses upon what influences the policy process.

How might one characterize policy itself and why is it important? It is important, considering the second question first, because of the likelihood of misattribution. Consider a policy developed and put into effect which fails. Was the policy deficient? Only if one tautologically assumes that any policy which fails is by definition deficient. And in some sense that is perhaps true. However, it may well be that exogenous factors which could not have been anticipated caused the policy to fail. So an assessment of the decision in its own terms, as well as an assessment of the process by which that decision was achieved, is important. If one looks at the other side of that point it becomes even more important. Suppose that a policy intrinsically in error somehow succeeded. The Type A error, in which an appropriate policy failed because of exogenous factors, is bad enough. A Type B error, in which an inappropriate policy succeeded because of exogenous factors, may be even worse on the grounds that false confidence is perhaps more dangerous than false doubt. These two examples give a partial answer to the first question and suggest at least two dimensions of assessment. Success is one dimension, although one must be sensitive to the fact that success may not be related to the policy, but may be due more to luck. Another, of course, is the quality of the decision itself assessed in its own terms. And throughout this volume we will suggest some other criteria, such as simplicity of implementation, clarity, lack of complexity, and ability to communicate and to be understood with relative ease. The point here is not to provide a set of categories for assessing policy, but rather to stress the point that the distinction between assessing policy itself and assessing certain features that influence policy is an important one to make.

Elements Affecting Policy

What are some of the elements that affect policy? Three seem of primary interest here: assumptions about the decision process, the organizational structure for decision making, and structural and cultural conditions in which the organization and the decision are meshed.

Assumptions about the decision process are usually offered in model terms—the rational model, the satisfactory model, a zero-based model, an incremental model, a crisis model. Each of these "models" is a way of describing and characterizing the way people think about how decisions are made—that is, how they make decisions or how they think others make them. It provides main starting points for decision-makers and policymakers to take as points of departure.

One can also look at the decision process and ask questions about how the organization is structured to make decisions of a policy nature. Many human service organizations have no particular identifiable system for making policy decisions. Those I have talked with usually identify a loose coalition of those involved, plus members of the board, with a proposal or policy ultimately going to the board for final ratification. This might be characterized as an "interests" system, with those whose interests are most affected by a particular situation being involved in resolving it. However, a different structuring might involve organizational elites as the typical decision-making people. Alternatively, under either the interests system or the elite system, there may exist a veto system, in which groups are given the opportunity to reject a particular course of action by vetoing it. The extent to which decision systems tend toward consensus, incidentally, approximates the extent to which they have a veto system.

There are also structural and cultural conditions that influence policymaking and these can range all the way from the distribution of social problems in one's community, the demographic structure of community, staff, or clients, to shifts in social norms and laws, which make, for example, abortion possible when it had not been, or drinking illegal when it had been legal. Each of these is important and useful as a point of understanding for the policy manager. However, clarity between analysis of the decision itself and analysis of factors that affect that decision is important, since the policy manager may wish to manipulate both.

These confusions, then, over what policy is and a lack of clarity between a policy fragment (or individual policy) and a policy cluster and sequence and posture make it very difficult to know where to target one's work. Additional confusion between aspects of the policy itself and aspects of the system that influence policy further confounds the policy management process. Each of these concepts is one that in time will be elaborated, discussed, researched, and taught about. But for the moment we can simply point to them as problems that have held back the development of the focus on policy management.

Three crucial elements affect policy:
- Assumptions about the decision process
- The organizational structure of decision making
- The conditions under which decisions are made

Problems of the Human Service Organization

The human service organization is a unique organization, one aimed at providing "social services" of a hard or soft variety to a contested and often threatened group of clients. Human service organizations run the entire gamut of types from the United Way organizations to the Sectarian Counseling Agency to Planned Parenthood to public welfare and other large-scale public organizations. Policy management in these organizations is hard, in part because of a number of differences between human service organizations and other types of organizations. I do not mean to imply that all human service organizations, or all not-for-profit organizations for that matter, have the problems that I will detail. Nor do I mean to imply either that only not-for-profit organizations have these kinds of problems. But rather, it seems upon reflection that on balance the problems I am going to mention—"misdirection by budget," values subdominance, turbulent environment, suspicion of quantitative data, lack of generalized organizational information, clinical focus, little stress on the external environment, and little attention to tactical follow-through—combine to make the problems of policy management in the human service organization even more difficult.

Misdirection by Budget

This phrase is Peter Drucker's, and he uses it to refer to what in his view is a crucial point of division between the human service organization and other organizations. He comments:

The one basic difference between a service institution and a business is the way the service institution is paid. Businesses (other than monoplies) are paid for satisfying the customer. They are only paid when they produce what the customer wants and what he is willing to exchange his purchasing power for. Satisfaction of the customer is, therefore, the basis for performance and results in a business.

Service institutions, by contrast, are typically paid out of a budget allocation. Their revenues are allocated from a general revenue stream that is not tied to what they are doing, but is obtained by tax, levy or tribute. Furthermore, the typical service institution is endowed with monopoly powers; the intended beneficiary usually has no choice.

Being paid out of a budget allocation changes what is meant by "performance" or "results." "Results" in the budget based institution means a larger budget. "Performance" is the ability to maintain or increase one's budget. The first test of a budget based institution and the first requirement for its survival is to obtain the budget. And the budget is, by definition, related not to the achievement of any goals, but to the *intention* of achieving those goals. . . . It is obviously not compatible with *efficiency* that the acid test of performance should be to obtain the budget. But *effectiveness* is even more endangered by reliance on the budget allocation. [Italics in original.] (Drucker 1973:49–50)

Drucker's point, and one I think a very useful one to keep in mind, is part of the reason for fiscal prominence in the organization of human service delivery. There are always more services which can be given, more needs which can be met. As far as one knows, the meeting of needs is, relatively speaking, a bottomless pit. Hence there is never any situation in which more money cannot be used, more programs cannot be offered, more services cannot be structured. And because of this problem of misdirection by budget, more is thought to be better. The press for quantity of resources replaces (or can replace) decisions about quality of services, and balance among services.

Misdirection by budget also has another limitation which Drucker implies. Actual results with clients tend not to be the criteria used. Rather, various substitutes for results, such as number of client visits, number of worker home visits, number of interviews scheduled, can be used as measures of service delivery effectiveness. What the budget processors must justify is the intention of doing good, not proof of whether good was done or not.

Subdominant Values

Human service organizations operate generally within the realm of what might be called subdominant values (see chapter 12). Subdominant values are ones to which we are all strongly committed, but we are perhaps not as committed to them as to some more dominant value orientations. For example, we wish to provide counseling, but we do not wish to provide counseling interminably; we wish to provide food and other housing services, but again, for a limited period of time. The American perspective is one which suggests that the business organization is really the bastion of accepted values and the social work organization seeks, perhaps too often, to "emulate" business. And even though some aspects of business, as Haft suggests and we shall note a bit later, seek to emulate human service organization structures in the board area, there is still a feeling that the making of money and profits is the first order of priority and the providing of counseling and charitable help is a second priority. As Boulding points out, "Perhaps therefore we can identify the "grant" or unilateral transfer—whether money, time, satisfaction, energy or even life itself—as the distinguishing mark of the social just as exchange or bilateral transfer is the mark of the economic" (1967:7).

In a society such as ours where reciprocity is so important the fact that many clients of human service organizations are in positions of reciprocal asymmetry—receiving, but not giving—puts them at a disadvantage, and, as Boulding suggests, may even alienate the giver.

Turbulent Environment: The Clash of Values

The various perspectives, both positive and negative, in which many of the clients and services that human service organizations offer are seen, create a turbulent environment. Hence a considerable, and perhaps an inappropriately considerable, amount of time of the human service organization is taken up defending itself for the very job that it is doing. It is the subject of repeated attacks in the press and by public figures. The human service organizations are never praised for the good they do, they are blamed for the wrongs they cannot prevent. The public's unrealistic hopes for human service intervention as well as the public's ambivalence about what to provide, how much, for whom, and under what conditions, turns the job of the human service employee into a series of jarring jousts with the civic culture at large. Strains and wishes to improve human service activities, to make them both more effective and efficient, and to increase them are not greeted with the praises for which they would be met in other sectors. Rather, they are greeted with suspicion and hostility—simply spending more public money, whether it is tax money, United Way money, gift money, or whatever. The job of policy management is difficult enough and the turbulent environment and its perils is perhaps one reason why it is even more discouraging.

Suspicion of Quantitative Data

The human service field dealing, as it does, with "the whole person" and sometimes the whole family, is not a field that has been characterized by its support of quantitative data. Research and statistics courses in schools of social work have not been among the more popular. We prefer to paint a qualitative and affective picture of the needs of clients rather than use a quantitative and empirical approach. Sprafkin (1978:615) supported the computer as suggesting what I have in mind here. "If we want to avoid our becoming obsolete in a few years time, we have to begin with accepting the newest techniques that help in planning and preparing, and look to the computer as a means to overcome our individual limitations. Whether we like these *mechanical monsters* [emphasis added] or not they're here to stay and can be helpful." As an agency executive, Sprafkin's support is helpful and suggests the general problem involved in getting quantitative data on which to base our conclusions, a point Shapira (1971) also stresses heavily.

Lack of Information

The lack of quantitative information is part of a generalized lack of overall information available to human service organizations for policy management purposes. An information and retrieval system, which involves only numbers of clients, frequencies of visits, numbers of meals provided, and so on, is only the basis for the more analytic type of information which is really proportional in nature. We not only want to know how many meals were provided, but we also want to have some idea of cost per meal and of how much time the really difficult cases actually take, the ones that everyone claims take so much time. We might even begin to develop a scale of case difficulty which could be used to assess both assignments and expected results. The suspicion of quantitative data deprives us of an important base. But quantitative data, important as it is, does not really constitute information, since information tends to be more analytically focused and organized around sets of questions. There is a vicious cycle here. Without information, some of it of course quantitatively based, it is very difficult to do policy management tasks, especially in the earlier phases of problem specification and option generation. On the other hand, without some kind of policy management, even informal and unacknowledged, it is very difficult to generate pressure for the collection of useful information. Into this information vacuum flow conventionalized understandings about "what is going on." These conventionalized understandings pervade agency life and extend to stereotypical references to the community, the profession, the agency itself, to general and specific clients, and to other workers. Both lack of information and conventional wisdom tend to extend to measurement of outcome, to what works and what doesn't, what's good and what isn't. Without these kinds of analytic perspectives, policy management is made more difficult.

Clinical Focus

Human service organizations tend to be run by people who have had clinical backgrounds. Scurfied comments in his study of social work administrators:

It is suggested, however, that the majority of administrators continue to place a high value on the relevance of clinical perspectives and orientations to administrative role performance. Such a posture strongly suggests that the expected transition to an outlook on orientation appropriate to administration had not occurred unless one considers that clinical knowledge and skills may be useful or central to many aspects of administrative role performance. . . . These findings raise serious questions as to how adequately prepared, educationally and motivationally, many administrators are for administrative roles. The fact that post-MSW education in administration is generally a voluntary pursuit has apparently produced a generation of social work administrators who have little formal or theoretical preparation for the job. (1980:53)

He picks up this theme in another article entitled "Clinician to Administrator: Difficult Role Transition?" (1981), and Shapira (1971) also stresses it. Perhaps because of some of these problems Austin and Lauderdale feel that "the future public welfare administrator is less likely than in the past to be an established professional in the human service field" (1976:14). Not only are more educational programs within universities needed, but a more vigorous focus on in-service and post-university training as well. One can see the problems that this kind of recruitment pattern portends for policy management. Since policy management requires some understanding of sophisticated management techniques and approaches, to the extent that this understanding is not present within the executive core of the human service agency, it is not likely that a policy management approach would be supported, the need for it recognized, and the resources for it provided.

Little Stress on the External Environment

Perhaps because of the problems discussed, or some version of them, the human service profession has been a bit slower to adapt to and adopt the strategic planning focus which is becoming an important, if not pivotal, point of departure in business. Strategic planning is "getting top management to go through the process of taking the time to think about their business, where they are with the business, where and what they want to be as an organization, writing all those thoughts and ideas down on paper; and then developing, evaluating, and implementing action programs and plans to get from where they are to where they want to be at the end of a reasonable, foreseeable horizon" (Donnelly 1981:3). This process is essentially what Sprafkin calls long-range planning. He almost defines the policy manager role when he says:

an integral part of the leadership role of the executive director is to *think* [emphasis added]. He or she needs to think about what should happen three or five years from now. This calls for *ideas, new ideas* [emphasis added]. To produce new ideas . . . is not easy. . . . It requires an ability to envision an everchanging future. (1978:619)

This thinking, involving what he calls long-range planning but I would call policy management, helps to fill what he sees as "the managerial gap" (p. 614).

Morris (1980) talks about identifying emerging social, economic, and political trends, further and securely, identifying key publics who are or will be important to the company (from our point of view, the human service organization) and third, the need to improve and understand credibility. Perhaps the very turbulence of the environment itself makes it difficult for organizational managers to undertake strategic planning or even long-range planning. Doubtless, that is part of the explanation. The lack of organizational intelligence, facts, figures, data, and information that could serve as a basis for such assessment is also a factor. And we must not overlook the lack of training that many of the managers report in certain technical areas (Scurfield 1980).

Then there is the ideological notion that a technique must be somehow "appropriate" to social work practice. Scotch and Haskett (1978) make this point when they suggest that social work managers learn the skills of budgeting, cost accounting, cost effectiveness analysis, and cost benefit analysis. Even within their summary they argue that "the discussion of each will include its appropriateness for social work practice." Hence, at least for some human service practitioners, there is a reluctance to use "business-oriented" techniques at the same time that there is envy of their efficiency and effectiveness. While some of this reluctance may stem from lack of knowledge and training, a substantial portion may well stem from a feeling, however correct or incorrect, that the techniques lack humanity and compassion. For whatever reasons, and there are doubtless others than the ones mentioned here, human service organizations tend not to take a strategic view of their environment, its strengths and problems. Hence, they are more often than necessary caught unaware and find themselves in a reactive rather than a proactive position. And yet, like Sprafkin's, there are some calls for a policy management approach that would systematically look at the context within which the organization works and seek to take advantage of that context to prepare for its challenges and to thwart its dangers.

Little Attention to Tactical Follow-Through

Decisions made within the organization must be based, of course, on accurate information about the external environment, at least to some extent. Yet here again human service organizations tend to be less than eager to undertake the kind of assessment that would be required. Naylor (1981), for example, mentions the planning audit, or an assessment of the kinds of decisions needed and the way in which they can relate to the strategic plan. The strategic plan, which is the larger scale set of policy directions, needs to be implemented through daily decision-making and Naylor speaks of the planning diplomat (someone who comes fairly close, it seems to me, to the policy manager). "The role of the planning diplomat is to help motivate senior management not only to participate in the design of a planning system but to use strategic plans as the basis for decisions'' (Naylor, p. 60). In the human service organization, for example, if certain service criteria are set up, it would be important for the policy manager to motivate case supervisors and others to seek to meet those service criteria. Otherwise the strategic plan does not have any implementation. This is what Reeser (1981) calls tactical planning and it focuses more upon the day-to-day activities. Without some day-to-day attention to some of these problems, which could be one of the roles a policy manager could undertake, they will undermine the best policy efforts.

Human service organizations have eight crucial problems:
- Misdirection by budget
- Subdominant values
- Turbulent environment
- Suspicion of quantitative data
- Lack of information
- Clinical focus
- Little stress on external environment
- Little attention to tactical follow-through

(See Exercise 2.4)

The Problems of Policy Management

The problems of policy management, therefore, are several-fold and once the idea of policy management itself has been introduced there follows the problem of acceptance. But even after that, there are a number of practical difficulties involving organizational and professional orientation and structure which serve to inhibit the organization from considering a policy management role and function. Yet withal we seem very close to conceptualizing this policy management role. I have already mentioned the concept of the idea champion (Daft and Bradshaw 1980). Naylor (1981) has the planning diplomat; Frankfather (1981) mentions the entreprenurial administrator; Michael (1980), in discussing the concept of feedback, introduces the concept of feedforward, which provides lead time to solve problems before they affect operations. While he does not designate a particular person as a feedforward manager, one can certainly take that next step based on his work, and it links perfectly with the leverage principle. Klein and Newman (1980), in introducing their acronym for strategic planning—SPIRE (*S*ystematic *P*robe and *I*dentification of the *R*elevant *E*nvironment)—speak of the SPIRE manager, a concept very similar to that of feedforward.

In sum, people concerned about the whole matter of improving the way organizations relate to their environment seem to be very close to the point of identifying an important role very much like that of policy manager. There are enough concepts close to that of policy manager to make the policy manager idea credible. Admittedly, the business management literature seems a bit more closely linked to it than the human service literature, although Sprafkin's concept of the managerial gap and Frankfather's concept of the entreprenurial manager come close.

Let me emphasize that policy management and some of the skills which will be suggested later in this volume are not meant to substitute for the technical skills of personnel and fiscal management. Those skills are needed and important. But at the moment, as I argued in chapter 1, they have tended to become the means through which policy management is carried out. Despite some of the problems, policy management will merge and grow as an area in human service activity.

CASE ILLUSTRATIONS

THE CHILD WELFARE AGENCY

At this point the surrogate motherhood idea was put on hold, as were many other recommendations to the board, for the Child Welfare Agency was in crisis. The coffee room buzzed with dismay and apprehension. The executive had been closeted with his key staff all morning. "Was it true?" people asked. "Could it have happened?" "What about our jobs?" others asked. The cause of this dismay was the announcement of a double blow affecting the agency, people thought. It had been reported late the night before that United Way had responded to community pressure and sharply cut the funds that would be given to the organization. At the same time the local public welfare agency had made it clear that the reimbursement rates for the group homes run by the agency were going to be revised sharply downward and might be cut out entirely. Staffers had known that there was dissatisfaction in both areas, but the previous executive had indicated that there really would be no problem. It was simply a matter of budgetary "machismo," to use his phrase, and once all the dust settled the agency would continue to be funded much as before. It looked very much as though this was no longer going to be the case. The dismay was aggravated by the fact that nobody seemed to know what was happening or why, or how the agency was responding. Sam Jacobson, a casework supervisor, thought that he needed to know what was going on. He felt a little sorry for the new director, even though he was only acting director. It had been one crisis after another during the two weeks that he had been in office and the old executive had taken off for Florida. One of the most disturbing things that had come to light since the old executive left was the fact that the endowments, on which everyone had relied and which everyone thought were the ultimate source of the agency's stability, had been spent down to a devastatingly low extent. No one seemed to know how this spend-down had been achieved, or where the authority for it came from. Sam personally knew the current treasurer of the board, a man who had himself been in office for only a short time. He said that the records were so ambiguous and vague that they were hard to follow. One thing was clear, however. The funds were drastically lower than anyone had thought. And other problems had come to light. In these days of high market interest rates, the agency funds had for some reason been left in very low interest passbook accounts, incredible as that may seem. Furthermore, in the past six or seven years the agency had received almost no gifts and no additional bequests. The historical source of the money for innovation and improvement was simply not there. Sam mused sadly to himself that an awful lot of money must have been going to those assistant directors and associate directors. "We're top heavy," thought Sam. "That's where all that money is going. We don't need more people, we need a good idea or two."

Discussion Questions

1. What are some of the problems that (might have) brought CWA to its current state?

2. What are the key environmental forces impinging on this organization? How can (should) they be dealt with?

THE WELFARE PLANNING COUNCIL

Madeline Deaker, the director of the Welfare Planning Council, had resolved to sit down with the executive committee and begin to discuss some of her concerns about the agency. As a start, she thought, I'll raise some of the issues with the staff. That was a problem, though, and she needed to think about just how to do that. She did not want to panic the staff or make them think they were in serious trouble, even though she herself thought they were in some difficulty. She wanted to create a situation in which the current reliance on the historical prestige of the agency could be converted into a kind of investment capital that could be used to risk new ventures and try new things, rather than serve as a source of standpatism. She recalled somebody's definition of the status quo as "the mess we're in," and grimly thought it aptly appropriate. The problem was that even on her staff she had a couple of nay-sayers who had been with the organization for a long period of time. They represented a sort of arteriosclerotic element, or what she had heard businessmen refer to as an example of hardening of the organization's, arteries, a stiffening, a resistance. They didn't want to even think about anything new. They're the kind of people, thought Madeline, who would drive a car until it absolutely wouldn't go another inch and then express surprise and shock that anything had happened to it. One of them, Jim Ashcraft, had a favorite phrase he used all the time and that Madeline hated, "If it's not broke, don't fix it." He was hardly the one to talk, she thought. His workday consisted of a leisurely reading through of the daily *New York Times,* a project that didn't end until about ten or ten-thirty each morning. She had spoken with him about this and he had been incensed. "It's my job to be informed about what is going on," he said. In a way, she agreed, but his productivity was very low, his resistance to new ideas very high, and all in all he was a very large pain in the neck. For the past two years he had received no increments. He had been angry, and she had tried to explain to him that his productivity really left a lot to be desired. He took an absolutely opposite view and argued that it was his role as one of the longer term employees of the council to preserve tradition, to be a mentor to younger planners, etc., etc. "All of which meant he didn't do any work," thought Madeline. Despite the problems that raising some of these issues in the staff group would cause she was resolved to try. I really don't have any choice, she thought. But before she did that she called Jim in and told him the kinds of things she had in mind to discuss. He began intoning his usual status quo litany, which burst forth with the regularity of a Gregorian chant. She looked him straight in the eye and said to him very cooly, "Jim, you're the oldest employee the agency has and you're going to be the first to be fired since I've become director if you keep this up. I'm not going to tolerate any more. You are negative and show lack of support for anything new. You are a nay-sayer and a well-poisoner. I'd like to hear some positive words from you at the staff meeting, and if you don't feel that you can contribute anything positive, if you don't feel you can join with us in exploring new alternatives, then I suggest you take a sick day." Jim was absolutely stunned. It had never occurred to him that at age fifty-five he might be fired. His face white, he left the office. It would have been difficult for Madeline to know how desperately he had wanted her job and how much he resented her in it, and now she might fire him. His plan to make her look bad and force her to resign so that the board would come finally, and with apologies, to him looked as though it might fail. He would have to reconsider.

Discussion Questions

1. Much of the council's difficulty seems centered on one employee? Do you agree? Why or why not? What else is important here?

2. What kinds of new ideas might be useful?

3. Is there an "idea champion" here? Why not? What prevents one from arising?

3

STAGES IN POLICY
MANAGEMENT

Policy management involves a structure, or it might be more accurate to say, a series of structures. One set of structures has to do with the locations in which the policy management task might be performed and that is the subject of the discussion in chapter 4. Another aspect of structure has to do with the roles that a policy manager might play as opposed to the locations where one might play those roles. Roles are the subject of chapter 7. Ideas need to meet certain tests and the structure of those tests is discussed in chapter 8. In this chapter, however, we focus upon the structure of the process itself. Because, as Hillsman (1964) says, policy is politics, it is a confusing and confounding process. As when waves hit a beach in a storm, one is hard put to discern any coherent structure. Problems surface, proposals float around, people come and go, and somehow work, withal, is done. In a sense it is a garbage can model of decision making (Cohen, March, and Olsen 1972), and if we were to take that garbage can and begin tossing it around, we might have some approximate idea of how the policy process might look to those who are in it.

Nonetheless, stepping back reveals the shape of a structure and it is important for the policy manager to have some rough map of the policy terrain, because, while it is true that things are confusing, contradictory, and full of tensions, and that is especially true the closer one gets, it is also true that there is a rough order to the way things happen. And this rough order needs to be perceived and worked with because it involves plateaus of crystallization and valleys of transition. While often in any specific situation it is difficult to know whether one is on a plateau or in a valley, it is helpful to know overall that there are a series of steps that one follows in moving from plateau to valley to plateau. Apart from the overall perspective on the policy process such a model gives, it suggests some of the areas of potential vulnerability and difficulty that one needs to be alert to.

There is, for example, the notion of sequence itself. What happens when things get out of sequence, when a problem is "solved" before it is identified, when planning is begun before ratification occurs? These difficulties of sequence present a number of problems.

A second type of difficulty occurs because the cast of characters shifts in the play of policy. This change in the cast means that while many of the same people are involved, some new people are also involved. The problem here, of course, is to provide continuity for those who remain while providing adequate "input influence" to those who are new.

A third problem might be called policy wandering and travail. Because the policy system is what one might call "loosely knit," it requires a policy manager to guide the policy process itself and the specific policy in question. Often, because of the lack of policy management, policy is simply permitted to drift from one stage to the next, in the frequently forlorn hope that in the end something workable will emerge. The fact that so often something does emerge, albeit after a long period of time and with unnecessary conflict, is a tribute to the system's functioning. It is also a tribute to the fact that there are people who are assigned or who perform the roles of policy manager in a very informal and *ad hoc* manner. Neither the assigners nor the assignees often recognize that that is the case. However, a boss may say "Harry, why don't you take some responsibility for the new personnel policy? Find out what other people are doing, sit down and talk with the personnel committee and with other people in town and let's see if we can't update our policy." To the extent Harry does that job, carries out that assignment, he functions as a policy manager. How well Harry does depends, in part at least, not only upon his own personal skills but also upon the cycle of policy.

The purpose of this chapter is to outline five phases of the policy process that I call the five P's: the problem phase, the proposal phase, the policy ratification phase, the planning phase, and the program phase. As each of the phases is discussed, there is emphasis upon the people who are important in that particular phase, the ideas that tend to characterize that phase, and the requirements for blending the ideas and people during the phase.

People, Process, and Policy

While the task of idea generation and analysis is central to the policy manager role, so is the blending of people and ideas for successful outcomes. As I mentioned, the policy system is a process of decision sequences, or perhaps fragments of decisions, developed over time and in evolving contexts. People need to be involved at all phases of policy process, not only because of our political heritage (no taxation without representation) and because people have good ideas and are sources of good ideas, but because people also have to carry out the policy. Policy managers rarely are involved in the actual implementation of day-to-day administration of policy. For these reasons, and others too, involvement is a hallmark of the human service organization. This principle is one which is applied not only at the community and group level, but also at the client level. As clinicians, we eschew making decisions for clients. Rather, we will work with the client to come to a decision, but the decision is made by the client. The same, of course, is true at the group level. The principles of community organization have long stressed the need for involvement. Lest we think that this process is unique, let me quote from the eminent Harvard sociologist Ezra Vogel, who describes a version of the Japanese process of decision making in his book *Japan as Number One,* in which he seeks to account for the high quality of Japanese decision making:

If one factor stands out . . . it is the involvement of all relevant parties in the decision making process, and their thorough commitment to the resulting decisions. In English, this process is sometimes referred to as "decision making by consensus" but this does not adequately describe the Japanese decision making process. In Japanese, the term used is *nemawashi:* root binding. The term originally comes from gardening, where it designates the careful untangling and binding of each of the roots of a tree before it is moved. The Japanese bureaucracy provides vigorous direction on many major issues, continuing over a long period of time, and during this process they are in close touch with all relevant groups to make sure they understand the evolving decisions, that their roots are bound. . . . Not all a tree's roots can always be smoothly bound, but a majority is not enough and a serious effort is made to include as many roots as possible.

An important part of root binding is to give each group ample time to adjust to the emerging decision, to explain the goals of the decision and let them understand the information that leads to this conclusion. . . . The public may complain about imperfect plans from arrogant bureaucrats but in the end it is not "their plan" but "our plan" and the roots stick with the tree. (1979:93–96)

This kind of process seems to be a good summary of the role of the policy manager and the people in the making of policy decisions. The manager is involved in doing the intellectual work, culling and synthesizing ideas, and presenting them in written form, and is also responsible for being in touch with the range of "roots," subcommunities' interests in individuals who have a say in the process, of involving them in the decision-making process, of explaining to them what is being proposed and why, and of adjusting the proposals based on their feedback. This process is not an automatic one. It is a creative one in which the final result is a superior blend of ideas and people that result in an exceptionally strong decision fabric.

How then might we think of the policy process? I have suggested that there are five stages. I would like to say a bit about the stages overall and then discuss each one in particular.

The policy manager needs to attend to:
- Ideas
- People
- The mix of people and ideas

The Five Ps

The policy process, or the policy cycle, is one that involves a series of different phases which blend together in ways that sometimes make them indistinguishable. Nonetheless, each phase has a center and a periphery (to use Edward Shils' apt phrasing) and the periphery or boundary of one phase is likely to blend indistinguishably into the periphery or boundary of the next phase. It is important for the policy manager in the human services to have an extrinsic sense of what these phases are because there will be no trumpets, no letter in the mail saying Phase 1 is ended, Phase 2 has begun, except in the most unusual case. One needs to recognize when one is in the center of a process and when one has reached the periphery.

The importance of these phases comes from the fact that differing perspectives develop and impinge on the policy during each one. That is, different sets of ideas become germane at each phase of the policy process and different sets of actors become involved. Thus, policy management is not an uninterrupted smooth flow of water, but rather a series of jerky shifts with important interstices between the major centers. Often, policy managers, having involved one group at one phase, forget that a different group at a different phase is also likely to wish involvement. These new actors are ignored, and problems are created because of it.

Five Phases

The five phases of the policy process that I have identified are the (1) *Problem Phase,* in which a group of actors determine what in fact the problem is. This is followed by the (2) *Proposal Phase,* in which some solutions to the perceived problem are generated. From a range of potential solutions a few are selected as recommendations and go to the (3) *Policy Ratification Phase.* In the policy ratification phase, one solution, or an amalgam of several recommended solutions, is crafted into a policy. At that point there is formal legal approval for a policy to be carried forward and the fourth phase begins, the (4) *Planning Phase.* In my view at least, planning does not begin until policy has been ratified. Planning implies and requires, indeed needs, the kind of legitimate assurance that policy ratification gives it. Planning without policy creates a terrible dilemma for the planner because there is no authority available to plan. In our case then, once the overarching policy has been crafted, legitimized, and is in place, the policy manager becomes a planner involved in more detailed description of exactly how the proposed policy would work and begins to set up the machinery for implementation. As that machinery is hoisted into place we are in the (5) *Program Phase,* which is the actual operation of a policy. It is at this point that the policy manager leaves to the administrator the carrying out of the policy, although administrators have surely been involved a good bit prior to the actual program start up. Policy managers and staffers continue to be involved during the operation of the policy because they will be looking for fresh problems which will begin the cycle again.

This system is similar to one developed by Mazzolini (1981:88–90) which begins with (1) "decision need identification"; goes to (2) "search for alternatives for action"; followed by (3) "investigation of courses of action;" followed by (4) "reviews and approval;" concluded with (5) "implementation." Mazzolini's scheme is notable because it does contain an approval phase—one that I call ratification. However, he lumps all of implementation into a single phase whereas I am inclined to think that once approval has been given, once ratification has occurred, there is a "sort of operational definitions phase" which I have called planning—or the translation of the more generalized policy document into a set of operational guidelines that can be used by the people who have to administer them. In a sense, his deficiency is remedied by Anne Westhues (1980:333–342), who talks about the planning stage specifically and gives it three subparts—program design, program implementation, and program operation.

The key element here is to introduce a dynamic sense into the policy process. All too often it is viewed or talked about as if it were a static process, that problems were somehow specified, alternatives identified, information sought about those alternatives, review occurred, planning and implementation developed, all within a single moment in time. The fact that this process occurs over time means that there are a number of ongoing changes in the system as the very remediation of that system is being attempted. Sometimes, for example, the initiation of policy activity in one sector signals the initiation of policy activity in another sector. Within the human service field, by way of example, it is not uncommon to hear as justification given for a particular activity, "if we don't do it the federal government will do it." The temporal changes within the policy process and the effect of time itself on the policy process have not really been studied in any detail. We can, however, lay out in a sequence of steps some reasonable phases that can be used to guide the policy practitioner until such time as more empirically based information is available.

The five phases of the policy cycle are:
- Problem
- Proposal
- Policy Ratification
- Planning
- Program

The Problem Phase

The problem phase is one in which the initial discomfort emerges as a problem to be solved. This phase has the greatest leverage for the policy manager because, defining the problem here, causes all else to follow in the way that it does. If, for example, the problem is defined at the level of the individual, it is most likely that individual strategies will be the ones thought about, proposed, passed, and implemented. If, on the other hand, it is decided that the problem is a systemic one, it is likely to be systemic strategies which are discussed, proposed, ratified, and so on. Depending, too, upon the definition of the problem, differing groups of individuals and interests come to be involved.

The policy manager should pay particular attention to pulling together a broad range of ideas about the nature of the problem during this *initial phase*. If this is not done, there is likely to be premature closure because we all have pat answers for pat problems—"everybody knows" that delinquency is caused by this or that. Without a fuller exploration of possible causes, an entire policy process can be truncated inappropriately, because not enough groundwork has been done in generating alternative ideas. This phase is one of the most intellectually exciting and the staffer should seek to exploit it to its fullest, bringing to the attention of superiors and people involved in the community a possible definition of the problem and listening to a wide range of individuals who have suggested definitions. Particularly in the human service field, we should take great care to be sure to present options which focus on the *individual,* on the *system as a whole,* and on the *interaction between individual and system.* If we can touch base with at least these three possible orientations, we will have protected ourselves from premature closure with respect to problem definition in most instances.

The people involved in the initial problem definition also represent a wide spectrum. Included here would be relevant professionals, people from the academic community, people from the news media and other sources of public opinion, as well as people from the community and others directly involved in one way or another in the problem. Always look to at least a small report from those most directly involved as clients or recipients. It is much better to conclude later that their comments missed the mark than to assume that they will do so and never ask.

The intensive review of possible causes from a conceptual point of view and the intensive discussion from a "people" point of view should provide a rich set of possible problem identifications to compare. However, it may be that the conceptual and theoretical investigation already done by the staffer provides a common denominator with which apparently different points of view can be harmonized. Should this be the case, the staffer will have already been doing the essence of the staffer job, which is the synthesis and blending of a series of people and ideas with an eye toward crafting a solution to the problem. Once the initial problem investigation process has gone on, the staffer can prepare a fairly comprehensive list of alternative problem definitions which, after some reconsideration, should filter down to a fairly small number of alternative definitions. At this point one begins to move into the second phase, the proposal phase.

The Proposal Phase

Given the alternative definitions of the problem, the staffer then begins to check back with individuals about the problem definitions, doing so with an eye toward getting their proposed solutions to the various problems as they are defined. This involves the individuals, encouraging their reactions and feedback to the problem and asking them to indicate what they think would be a solution to the problem if it were defined in the way of "a", in the way of "b", in the way of "c", and so on. Frequently, each problem definition will have multiple solutions, so that in effect we have a set of two lists. On the left hand side of the list is a set of problem definitions, on the right hand side a set of solutions commonly proposed, even though offered for different definitions of the problem. During this phase the staffer begins to condense and integrate the proposed solutions in a process similar to that gone through with respect to the problem.

A key element in the proposal phase is the idea of malleability. One does not like to define problems in such a way that there can be no solution. Therefore, the manager should seek to reshape problem definitions in such a way that something can be done about them. This is particularly true within an American context, as Americans are action oriented and such strategies as waiting, doing nothing, biding your time, do not appeal to Americans even though such a strategy may be the wisest course. Similarly, theoretical definitions of a problem that seem to yield little chance of solution should be set on the back burner in favor of problem definitions that contain a greater possibility for intervention. Similarly, proposals, once the problems are defined, should be looked at in terms of reasonableness, administrative efficiency, and the ability to proceed quickly. This list of proposals is a preliminary one, and thus the staffer should include all possibilities because they will be culled fairly ruthlessly at the policy ratification phase.

During the policy proposal development phase, staffers talk to individuals on two somewhat separate occasions. Initially they talk to secure proposed solutions. Then there is a period of staff work in which these solutions are compared, contrasted, crafted together, and a set of proposed solutions developed. At this point people are talked to again, to see what they think about the proposed solutions and what suggestions or modifications they might have. This is particularly important for those whose interests might be negatively affected. Another way might be found that would confer benefits on those adversely affected and this solution might well be pointed out in advance of the ratification phase. At this point we talk about the clearing processes, during which relevant individuals participate, entering into the discussion, and changes are then made in the set of solutions offered.

During the proposal phase the manager makes the first of a series of reports or proposals that will ultimately become policy. The problem is described and defined in a report, the set of solutions-options proposed, and a set of recommendations developed blending ideas and political preference. Often this and subsequent drafts of the reports are shared with the relevant individuals, first by sending out the draft, then by a series of meetings. In the proposal phase, several drafts are likely to be developed, changed, redeveloped, changed again, and, when one feels that there is a fairly reasonable set of recommendations, one moves into the third phase, policy ratification.

The Policy Ratification Phase

The policy ratification phase is the one during which the actual policy is approved by a policy legitimating authority or policy committee. Following the suggestions outlined in the chapter on report writing, a proposal is submitted to the appropriate body. It need not be that one, and only one, problem definition and one, and only one, problem solution be presented at this stage, because it is within the process of the stage itself that the final determination will be made. If it is possible, and the intellectual and political current seems to indicate a single or uniform definition and solution, fine. If, however, the situation is more typical, and such that there several solutions are possible, then these should be outlined as previously suggested, along with a separate section on staff recommendations.

It is in the recommendation section that the staffer or policy manager has the opportunity to propose what seems to be the ideal blend. The policy ratification committee, however, may disagree or may seek to craft its own blend. In any case, special attention should be given to the ratification phase because much work can be undone there. It is often wise to check informally with the ratifiers in advance of the official meeting to see whether they favor a particular type of alternative or not. This approach falls under the "know your audience" prescription in the chapter on writing. It is here, too, that failure to touch base with involved individuals is likely to bear bitter fruit. Such individuals, if ignored, can come to the ratification session and raise a host of problems which may lead the policy ratifying group to postpone a decision. Such individuals may, of course, raise objections anyway. As Vogel indicated, not all roots can be bound. There should be a predominance of affected interests, whose views and opinions are reflected in the final document and, if possible, in the final proposed recommendation. This assures the policy ratifying group that they can proceed to act. A positive vote moves the document from the policy proposal phase to the planning phase.

The Planning Phase

Once a document has been passed, in whatever form, it then moves to a phase in which a set of plans is developed for implementation. At the federal level these are often called "the regs." They, in effect, represent a series of ancillary and supportive subpolicy decisions made by the administrative staff, which serve to further define and put into operation within the intent and spirit of the law, or policy, the proposed solution. It is frequently at this point that administrators become heavily involved, though as indicated, they would have been involved throughout as one of the key groups normally checked with. However, at this point policy managers and administrative managers begin to work together to develop the actual operation of the policy, which may vary greatly in extent depending upon the nature of the policy. In a number of instances the policy is relatively self-sufficient and needs only an announcement that it has been passed to bring it into the purview of people. On the other hand, a fairly extensive program of community information may be required, involving meetings throughout the community to indicate what has been done and why and how it will affect those involved. Usually there is a need, as well, to develop plans for informing agency staff of what has gone on.

There are really two aspects, or two sets of plans, developed. One is a set of regulations that enlarge the policy proposal itself and provide more specific interpretations and definitions. A second is the plan for implementation of the policy. The first I call policy planning, and I would like to distinguish it sharply from other uses of that phrase, or from a phrase that might be called the planning of policy, which is awkward, but one that could be used for what I have called the proposal phase. Policy planning deals with the set of regulations, definitions, and other administrative interpretations that have the force of law and serve to enhance the policy itself. Policies, as passed by policy ratification groups, are seldom completely sufficient. Often, terms are left undefined or specific actions are left up to the discretion of the administrator. It is therefore imperative that an additional set of definitions be developed.

Policy planning, then, is the carrying out of the process of policy elaboration. Program planning, on the other hand, deals with taking a policy and developing the programmatic aspects of it. These, in turn, include two phases. Within the planning phase, program planning begins with the process of informing relevant communities of what has been done and thus comes somewhat after the policy planning phase. Program planning also takes into account the actual development of a set of instrumentalities and mechanisms, if required, for the policy to take effect. If a policy, for example, says that there shall be a grievance committee, then there needs to be a mechanism to select such a committee. Such a committee must, indeed, be selected and must, indeed, have files, offices, and so forth. The planning of this operation is what I call program planning. It is in the transition from policy planning to program planning that we move into programming itself. Not all policies require a program and so in many cases the policy stops right here. The policy has been passed, a policy plan has been developed, and a program plan has been developed, but there is no actual program because there is no particular action that needs to be carried out beyond this point. The grievance committee has been set up, but until there is a grievance nothing needs to happen. Let us assume for a moment that the policy involved setting up an office at a remote site. The board passed a policy that said such an office would be set up within reasonable cost limits. The policy planning process went on and definitions of reasonable costs were established, which then informed the program planning phase, a phase which, in turn, laid out the required square footage, located an office, located furniture, identified staff, and so on. Once that actual programming has occurred we move into the program phase, the last phase of the policy process.

The Program Phase

Picking up the example just given, we have an office established at a remote site and on a given day the office opens, the phones begin to ring, clients begin to come, and the general functions of an office occur. What begins to happen at this particular point is that the policy manager, or staffer, shifts from a more active role to one of oversight, working with the administrative staff to spot problems and develop a list of potential difficulties that might call for policy revision as time goes on. Usually, it is a good idea to specify some period of time as a target date for a fresh look. During the policy ratification phase, for example, the board may indicate that in a year or two it would like an evaluation and during this period information is collected for any systematic evaluation that might be done. During the policy planning and program planning phase, aspects of the required evaluation would be developed along with other aspects of the plan. During the program operation phase, those evaluation elements would be carried out and would blend into a fresh problem phase at the end of the evaluation period.

The Policy Loop

Implicit in the discussion at the end of the programming phase is the notion that the policy manager begins to study, rather than operate, the implementation from the perspective of "looping" back to a new set of problems that may need to be handled. It is in this sense that we have a cyclical, rather than a linear, notion of policy process. The whole idea of using program assessment as a first step toward policy definition is an important concept to keep in mind. All too often, once program implementation has been achieved, the policy manager moves on to other types of activities and the program managers and administrators are left to struggle as best they can with what they have. There are some roles for the policy manager here, although not quite as intensive as they have been in the past, and I have specifically located them in a separate section, "The Policy Loop," in order to indicate their special nature.

One of these tasks is the designing of assessment instruments. Sometimes outside researchers and consultants are used for this process, but there is no reason why the policy manager cannot be involved (indeed she or he should be involved) in the creation of instruments designed to measure the program activity. Part of the reason is simply to see what is going on. All too often, within the human services, we rely on ideological and impressionistic assessments of even such basic questions as: do we have more clients or fewer? are the problems different or similar? do we have an increasing number of single parents? Sometimes these basic pieces of program information are simply not available because they are not collected. This relates to the impressionistic portion of the point. There are also ideological elements, for example, people who are committed to taking more or fewer minorities, who are committed to the idea that men have greater problems than women or women's problems are greater. And it is not unlikely that these impressions become parent to the deed with respect to reporting requirements. Hence, some kind of ongoing empirical assessment of basic program data and basic ratio data—how many clients per worker, how many this per that—becomes an important policy manager activity.

A second task, related to the first, is designing benchmark assessment periods when the policy and planning goals can be compared with the program activity. Often, during the first year of a new activity, quarterly benchmark conferences are useful. If one seeks assessment in a period shorter than three months, it sometimes is difficult to get a feel for what is happening. On the other hand, if one goes much beyond three months, at least initially, it is possible to get quite far off target before one realizes it (one problem) and the opportunity to take corrective action becomes more limited (a second problem). Therefore, the design of benchmark conferences, in which the operational goals developed in the planning period and the policy requisites (to the extent they differ from the operational goals and were contained in the earlier document which was ratified) can be looked at with respect to current activity. I mention the benchmark conference as second to the assessment instrument construction because it is very difficult to have such conferences without some data. One can sit down and inquire how things are going, but there are a number of problems that occur without data, detailed by Argyris (1982), including a certain amount of distancing in which individuals seek not to recognize particular problems and a systematic misperception of the responsibility of self and others. Data provide a way to look at some of these issues neutrally, without directly and personally attacking the credibility of people. It is important to stress the policy loop in particular, because, without some attention, it is unlikely that sufficient attention will be given to the development of measurements and to the benchmark meetings. Often, establishing a new service within the larger human service framework involves a number of additional problems and difficulties. Frequently, the press of these difficulties, which are really the responsibility of the program administration, do not permit systematic and focused attention on the larger question of whether programmatic goals are being met and, more importantly, whether the assumptions on which the policy was based are reasonable.

This point is also important for the policy manager as well as the agency administrator and program manager. Policies are based on a number of assumptions. Frequently, in the proposal development stage these are checked insofar as possible with empirical data. Nonetheless, the flow of time, as Cohen et al. (1972) point out in their garbage can model of decision making, is always a factor. It is never possible to fully check, to fully verify all of the assumptions. Is a new service needed? The evidence points in that direction, but the evidence is never complete. Will people use a new service? Preliminary estimates indicate they will, but preliminary estimates are only, after all, preliminary. Does it duplicate another service offered by another agency? Initial inquiries seem to indicate that it does not, but the other agency's program has not as yet been fully developed and will have to wait and see. The list can go on and on. Policy decisions are best guesses made with the evidence available.

The policy management function seeks to insure that the very highest quality ideas, the very best evidence, are in fact available and taken into consideration when the decision is made. Following this process will insure a higher quality policy than typically is the case. However, one should not forget, and readers of this book least of all, that we are still dealing with estimates, probabilities, incomplete evidence, evidence whose validity and reliability can only partially be checked. Therefore, in the programming phase one may wish to carry out something I call an assumptions audit. It is hoped that during the process of policy development, structuring, ratification, and planning, the policy manager has kept a note—physical or mental—of the key assumptions on which the particular policy, plan, and program are based. These need to be specifically checked and, in the development of assessment instruments, special attention might be paid to an assumption audit inquiry. Some of the information will, of course, come from other sources too, because the problems, difficulties, or holes in the information on which assumptions were based previously may, on completely separate grounds, now be able to be identified.

Hence, there are really three specific areas of focus within the policy loop—that period which transforms programming into new sets of problems to be solved within the policy cycle. The design of assessment instruments is certainly one. The scheduling of benchmark conferences is a second, and the assumption audit is a third.

Policy Loop areas are:
- Design assessment instruments
- Schedule benchmark conferences
- Plan assumptions audit

Conclusion

In this all too brief discussion of the policy process, I have tried to identify the key points or junctures at which policy crystalization, of one sort or another, occurs. Crystalization begins during the problem phase and further crystalization occurs during the proposal phase. A formal crystalization occurs when the policy is ratified and one then moves into the phases of policy planning and program planning, and finally into program operation. The main role of the staffer during the program operation phase is policy evaluation and assessment leading to a fresh problem phase. These phases are loose phases, as I mentioned initially. There is no particular point that one can identify, with the exception of the actual moment of ratification, when one moves from one phase to another. However, if the staffer can keep these general progressions in mind and keep in mind as well that ideas and people need to be freshly checked and freshly combined at each phase, it can be of great assistance in achieving an integrity of the policy process that is not present in many policy scenarios within the human service field.

CASE ILLUSTRATIONS

THE CHILD WELFARE AGENCY

The new acting executive, James Whitelaw III, was not easily rattled. He came from a patrician family and had gone into social work as a job he liked and a way of expiating in part for his family's sins, or at least what he perceived to be their sins. But he had to admit that the first days and weeks on this job had been enough to try the patience of Job. One thing he had firmly resolved for himself: he would never stay in any job as long as his predecessor had. Over time, what had seemed to happen was that the board has receded into an almost honorary role, routinely approving, even on an *ex post facto* basis, actions of the executive. Long ago, so long ago that he couldn't even find it in the minutes of the board, it had stopped being a decision-making body. It was not even a rubber stamp at this point. It looks a lot more like a box of wet Kleenex, he thought, and even that might be giving it too much credit. The problem of the depleted endowment funds was only the first of a series of rude shocks he discovered upon taking over as acting director. He couldn't get over how much his predecessor had deceived him. Perhaps he was deceiving himself as well, thought Jim. The man had retired and left town. He hadn't been asked to retire and there was no sense that anybody had known how bad things were. Poeple simply had come to rely on him and more and more had done so. When he had reached age seventy, he left. Jim wasn't sure that the agency could be saved. Its structure at the moment looked like something created by Rube Goldberg. Programs that had never been approved by the board in any way he could find existed all over the county. Leases had been signed to rent decentralized sites. The agency owned a number of Winnebagos used to deliver mobile services, but many were rusting here and there in parking lots around the county. The central building was old and hadn't really been refurbished in many years. With the exception of the director's suite, which had been recently redone, and sites for other executives, the place had a desperately second-hand look. There was no coherent definition of the problems the agency was addressing or of alternatives they might propose to attack those problems. The executive who had left seemed to approve whatever program the person in his office pushed hard for. The entire agency structure looked like a backyard that had been let go for many years. Everything was overgrown and it was hard to know, from an outside perspective, what should be retained, where the central structure actually lay, what were weeds that should be cut down and removed as quickly as possible. The agency had no coherent personnel policies. Everyone did everything.

Discussion Questions

1. This organization had money and people, yet it had begun to decline. Why?

2. How could the decline be reversed? What could be done?

THE WELFARE PLANNING COUNCIL

The discussion of agency directions had actually gone better than Madeline had had any right to hope. Even her nemesis had for once put down his *New York Times* and come up with an idea or two. She wondered whether she could ever get that tough again and felt a little bad that she hadn't done so earlier. Out of the discussion a glimmer of a possibility had emerged. One of the things that seemed wrong with the agency, very much so to her but to others as well, was that for quite a while now the agency had been developing "social plans" at the suggestion of this or that group or aggregation of interests. Once a plan for action had been developed the agency began a process it called implementation, in which it sought to get the plan accepted by people and put into action. The way in which the agency sought acceptance was twofold. First, those involved were often called to serve on a "study committee" or a "review committee" to look into the problem and formulate solutions. It was hoped that their participation would insure the success of the second step, when the agencies or institutions that had to take action were asked to do so. But there was a flaw here, which seemed to be that the plans were developed outside the context of any policy framework. This well accepted process was perhaps all right when all the agencies concerned were somehow affiliated with the planning council. However, now that they were not, there was no longer the informal package of influence that was needed nor, perhaps as important, the informal package of agreements that informed the planning process itself. We need to move back in the process, she thought, and become an organization that defines and articulates problems and lays out possible courses of action. Once those courses have been selected, perhaps by the relevant agencies, we can make ourselves available within the context of approval to design the programs necessary to carry them out. These can then be fed back to the agency which can run the programs. Or perhaps the agency itself will want to design the program. But we need to take a broader view of the process and locate ourselves somewhat differently in it. For the first time in a long while she felt good, not because everyone would agree with this definition, or because the process of moving the agency toward this goal would be easy, but because she herself had a concept of where to go. I'm like the captain of a ship, she thought, who's been sailing under cloud cover and now the clouds have blown away and I can see the stars. I know how to navigate. Whether I'll make it or not is another question, but at least I know the course to take.

Discussion Questions

1. The operation of the Planning Council seems to be "out of phase" with the 5 P's Cycle. Do you agree? In what way could that be so?

2. How could the organization reorganize itself to be more "in phase"?

4

SETTINGS FOR POLICY MANAGEMENT

Given the policy cycle then, where does policy management occur? Where might one find a policy manager or, more likely, someone who is performing policy management functions? A corollary to that question is one that asks where policy management might be needed, where is there a situation that could benefit from a more structured, focused, systematic approach to the generation and processing of ideas, and that at the moment, at least, is functioning in a haphazard and unattended way.

The answer is simple, if surprising. The major setting for policy management activities is in a committee. Policy management goes on through committees. It is committees that stimulate, review, and ultimately ratify policy documents. I shall have occasion to pay more specific attention to the policy committee as an object of analysis in later chapters. The important point here is to begin the process of recognizing that the committee is a policy instrument and therefore a crucial setting—indeed the crucial setting—where policy occurs.

This point of view immediately brings to mind the myriad committees with which we are typically associated in the human service system. They are agency planning committees, board planning committees, office-party planning committees, search committees for staff and directors, standards review committees of various sorts, coordinating committees, advisory committees—the list could go on and on—and, indeed, each represents a policy center or policy locus where some type of policy which affects the agency could occur, or more often does not occur, or sometimes occurs by happenstance.

All kinds of human service organizations are involved in policy activity. The range extends from the smallest family and children's service in a relatively small community that may have two or three staff members and an executive to the megabureaucratic departments of human services or social services that may spend millions of dollars each month and have annual budgets that run at times well over a billion dollars a year. They extend from the counseling agency to the community organization agency to the agency whose primary concern, one might say, is policy—the social policy organization. The purpose of this chapter is to provide some sense of the various kinds of committees that deal with policy and to suggest some of the elements that may affect their structure and functioning.

Settings for Policy Management

A number of elements in the social structure affect the policy committee. Two dimensions, however, seem most useful for preliminary discussion. One has to do with the focus of policy and a second has to do with the base of the committee itself.

Committee Base

Social agencies and human service organizations deal essentially with two types of policy committees—those generated by the organization and based within it, and those generated outside the organization and with which the organization must deal. In both cases membership may vary a bit. Consider, for example, the organization-based committee. Typically, it is made up of members of the organization who have been assigned to pursue some area of organizational interest. Once that assignment has been completed the committee members tend to return to the appointing authority with some kind of report or set of recommendations. Often, they will seek involvement from non-organizational members. Sometimes this involvement is on an *ad hoc* or visiting basis. Thus, a committee appointed to consider personnel policy may invite testimony or opinions from members of other organizations. This informational interchange simply brings the committee looking at these matters up to date on what other organizations are thinking. Sometimes however, by design or requirement, such a committee may have a member from outside the organization. There may be external standards which must be met and it is most useful to have ongoing participation from a representative of a standard-setting organization. This could be another human service organization, for example, such as the United Way or the Child Welfare League of America, depending upon the particular focus of the group. Sometimes, human service organizations generate policy committees which seek to interact with the environment. Thus, an organization may stimulate an inter-agency committee of some sort to develop, let us say, a standard intake form or some other commonly useful document. Organizationally based committees may consist of organization members only or they may, for a variety of reasons and in a variety of ways, reach out to others in the community whose activities are relevant to theirs.

The inverse is true with respect to environmental- based committees. Consider, for example, a community committee set up to review and assess a particular human service organization. Traditional practice in the human service field, plus good sense, suggests that one not undertake such a review without the cooperation and involvement of those affected. Hence, review committees, for the most part, will seek membership links with those to be reviewed. There are a number of other community and national groups on which organizational members serve, whose purpose is to suggest or initiate policy that would affect the organization in question. These settings are important for the organization, because they represent strategic foci within the environment that the organization needs to be aware of and may influence. Hence, there is the desire on the part of the human service organization to provide time for at least some of its employees to participate. From the other point of view, that is of the environmentally-based organization which seeks members, the involvement of those concerned is of primary importance because they can provide at least the parameters of possible pieces of crucial information the external organization needs if its policy is to be successful.

Focus of Policy

A second important element in settings has to do with the focus of policy. That is, what is the target or intent of the policy being considered here? It is impossible, of course, to partition policy into completely distinct targets. There are a number of reasons for this difficulty, including the fact that policy aimed at one target also implicates another target and the sum of the considerations relating to that second target are often involved in thinking about the primary target. Hence, we will talk about the primary policy focus and, in thinking about that primary focus, understand that other policy foci come into consideration.

Basically, four divisions, or four foci, of policy seem to be appropriate for our purposes here. The first might be called *intra-organizational policy*. This has to do with policy for the human service organization concerned with the internal aspects of the organization, its structure and operation— personnel policies of various sorts, policies relating to treatment of clients, number of clients, workload, and so on, all of which fall within the intra-organizational policy system. Sometimes these policies need to be approved at the agency board level, but often they can be approved at sub-board levels, perhaps with some board involvement. For example, a finance committee may be appointed by a board to work with certain elements of the staff of the human service organization to approve particular kinds of expenditures within the acceptable range of agency policy already set up and approved by the board.

Agency policy is the second type of policy focus. By agency policy I mean to suggest that set of policies which set the mission and role of the organization, specify its goals and objectives, and give it a strategic location within the human service notwork. Policies which set the main type of client to be served and the focus of that service are another example. An organization may, for example, in its bylaws specify that it wishes to focus especially on those who are needy within the community and primarily provide a family counseling type of service. Occasionally there are major changes in agency policy and Goldberg's discussion of the Community Service Society of New York's shift in attendent problems is one example (Goldberg 1980). Agency policy may also focus upon the strategy of funding. For example, an agency may choose to seek or not seek federal and state support. An agency may seek to have a certain fee structure for clients. An agency may seek to generate a certain proportion of its income through fees. An agency may seek to pursue a number of bequests. All of these are examples of a fiscally strategic posture appropriate to the board of directors of a human service organization and not to subunits of the organization. The agency may also seek to specify its posture vis-à-vis professional staff. It may seek to have some mix of MSWs, BSWs, and paraprofessionals, for example. Agency policy locates the agency strategically within the network of human service organizations in the community, taking into account relevant laws, regulations, and legally required missions and seeking to put them into operation in a reasonable way, taking into account local conditions, emergent stresses, and difficulties.

The third type of policy is *inter-agency policy*. Here the organization seeks to specify its posture and its relationship to elements of its environment with respect to those elements rather than with respect to itself. *Agency policy*, of course, is always an environmental statement and, in that sense, always takes account of the environment. However, there are a number of pressures upon human service organizations to join in specific and focused relationships within the environment. An *inter-agency policy* may be required to specify the nature and limits of that participation.

The fourth area of policy with which human service organizations may be involved is *social policy*. The idea of social policy is a complex one and the subject of my final chapter. Nonetheless, it becomes important to mention here the point that organizations sometimes feel the pressures of social policy. Some agencies, of course, have the job of making social policy. Governmental organizations, or megabureaucratic organizations, may be specifically policy deciding organizations with respect to some realms of social policy, or their own agency policy or their inter-organizational policy may have the effect of social policy. Consider, by way of example, a large state department of social services which sets reimbursement for group homes or sets AFDC budgets. While the organization may simply view these activities as agency policy, others may view them as having the effect of social policy.

Most human service organizations feel the imperatives of social policy (or at least their understanding of social policy) as they make agency and inter-agency policy for themselves and their community. Let me give one example. A part of social policy seems to involve focus on the disadvantaged. Thus, a typical human service organization seeks to retain or feels the imperative to retain some of that focus. This might be accomplished through sliding fee structures or through a limitation on the number of fee-paying clients. The agency may see itself as a model for the community or, as Goldberg (1981) points out for the Community Service Society of New York City, for the nation. Sometimes the agency feels called upon to make policy statements or express policy sentiments giving its perspective on a particular policy arena. Nuclear war, an incumbent President, gay rights are among the types of social issues on which the agency may wish to comment. Whether this is wise or appropriate in specific or general instances is not the point here. It simply is to indicate that there is a general sense of obligation from the social policy perspective that suffuses and informs, rightly or wrongly, agency policy.

A Policy Settings Grid

These two dimensions, the base of the policy committee (organizational vs. environmental) and the focus of policy (intra-organizational agency, inter-agency, and social) form a grid which helps us locate eight types of policy committees that provide settings for policy work (see table 4.1).

Table 4.1
Focus of Policy

Locus of Policy Committee	Intra-Agency	Agency	Inter-Agency	Social
Organizations	1	2	3	4
Environment	5	6	7	8

Organization-Based Committees

1. Organization-Based Intra-Agency Policy Committees

In the first row, we see such committees as the agency planning committee, the personnel committee, the finance committee, the executive core committee, the administrative team, listed as organizationally-based committees that focus on intra-agency policy. The policy manager may be a member of or a staffer to these committees. They and other intra-agency committees become the central vehicles for defining agency operations policy.

2. Organization-Based Agency Policy Committees

The second cell identifies such agency-level committees as the board of directors itself, policy analysis units that might exist within a very large organization, search committees, or bargaining committees. These are committees whose actions tend to be organizationally fateful with respect to the mission and role of the organization. The board, of course, in all of its deliberations can be organizationally fateful. Once it becomes separated from a sense of what is happening in the organization, as Goldberg (1981) points out, it can take steps to activate its potential power and change agency operations to those more to its liking. For large megabureaucratic organizations, such as human service departments in states, the board is really a combination of the state legislature and the governor. At certain key confluences, such as the appropriations juncture or appointment of the executive, links with those governing groups need to be made, and it may be at that point that latent hostilities and displeasures will surface in ways costly to the organization. Sometimes those larger organizations, because of the great space between the governing group and the organizational operations, require special policy analysis units. I shall speak more about such units in the chapter on roles, but it is important here to note that the larger megabureaucratic organization may have such a facility available to it.

Search committees for new executives are typically fateful for the organization, though they are relatively atypical and we do not have a great deal of experience with them. It is obvious to the committee when it begins to work that the selection of the executive depends, in part at least, on some formulation of the mission and role of the organization. Is it to be the same or different? Is it to emphasize this or that? These kinds of questions tend to plague search committees, and frequently they will spend some time trying to develop a sense of the direction of the organization in order to recruit and select the new executive. Similarly, of course, the new candidate wishes to query the search committee on these exact points. Hence, decisions are often made by search committees that have a far-reaching policy effect contained within the search process. Bargaining committees, of course, are also policy committees of high importance because they deal with the basic posture of the organization vis-à-vis staff. This involves the allocation of personnel and money and it involves, as well, the kind of picture they wish to present to the community.

3. Organization-Based Inter-Agency Policy Committees

The third cell stresses inter-agency policy committees, and among those committees are inter-organizational coordinating committees and joint planning committees. It is important to recognize that these committees are often initiated by the organization and represent an attempt on the part of the organization to influence, if not control, the external environment. It is sometimes difficult to know with respect to the inter-organizational committee where the initiation began. Often there are different perspectives on who really got the inter-organizational planning committee "going." Too, as time goes on, the deference which is usually given to those who have initiated an enterprise may fade. And while a family and children's service of a particular community may have played a key role in initiating the joint family agency planning committee in the beginning phase, after several years that may no longer matter. Involved here as well are those community and state agencies whose job it is to set up inter-organizational systems and to monitor and nurture those systems. Community Welfare Councils, United Ways, Area Agencies on Aging, and the like are among those who have inter-organizational responsibility and use inter-organizational committees as a main operational vehicle which defines and serves the larger good of the community. Hence, policy and planning organizations may be among the main initiators of activity here, seeking to involve direct service agencies in participation.

4. Organization-Based Social Policy Committees

The last category in the organization-based maze has to do with social policy formulation itself and here we are dealing mainly with national organizations which are policy-setting or policy-recommending organizations for the whole human service sector. Consider, for example, the code of ethics set up by the National Association of Social Workers. Since, in effect, "charges" can be brought for violations of the code, it becomes an important standard for human service organizations to attend to. Similarly, there are standards for child welfare agencies, for family service agencies, for hospitals, and for clinics. There are also standards for colleges and for schools of social work. While none of these may be all that we would like or hope for and while they may generate disagreement in one area or another, they represent important sets of rules with which most organizations must comply.

Standard setting, in its technical and legal sense, may be the province of state and national human service organizations which have that responsibility as part of their mission. However, it should not be thought that the regular community-based human service agency does not engage in at least standard recommending activity. Many social agencies have public policy committees or join with other organizations in taking public social policy positions on such matters as national social policy standards, AFDC grant levels, and environmental issues, as well as on state and community issues. In fact, it is often a matter of some controversy as to whether the organization should take these positions and, if so, on which issues and how frequently? For these kinds of policy recommendations one must conceive of an abridged policy cycle that goes only as far as policy ratification. Typically, under these kinds of situations, a public policy committee will initiate policy activity with respect to a public issue. Studies will go on, recommendations will be made, and a policy statement may be approved by the board of directors. At that point it may be sent to the media or to other interested organizations. The fact that the social agency does not itself make the policy does not keep it from seeking to be a policy influential within the policy context.

Environment-Based Policy Committees

The policy process is, as stressed here, a multiple and interactive one and the distinction between organization-based and environment-based policy committees is an example in hand. Human service organizations initiate policy activity and respond to it, and while this distinction is useful as a way to partition the policy environment, many exceptions and interactions may require tempering the distinction in actual practice. Nonetheless, organizations do respond to pressures from the environment and that is the particular area, as I mentioned, which is the focus for strategic planning.

5. Environment-Based Intra-Organizational Policy Committees

In the fifth cell, under intra-organizational environment-based committees, one might think of such groups as client and alumni groups, which the organization may sponsor and which may relate to former members of the organization's client community. Client committees can either be of current or past clients, and they may be used to comment upon organization operations and make suggestions. Members can even be future clients. For example, some agencies with long adoption lists seek to involve potential adoptive parents in an advisory and educational role, so that the agency can better inform the parents as to what is the likely course of events. They can also be responsive to the parents' needs and concerns on an ongoing basis before adoption takes place. Group work and recreation agencies have for many years maintained alumni groups, and frequently these groups, like college alumni groups, span the years with people getting together who went to Camp XYZ in 1950. While they are not employees of the organization, they may be at least involved with the organization and may seek to become informed about it and provide support for it. Sometimes support is not in a form that the organization wishes. It may involve criticism or complaint, and the fact that there is "a dissident" committee within the organization seeking to implement certain changes is one of the problems with which the organization has to deal. All too often, the organization views these groups as potentially hostile rather than potentially helpful. Sometimes the help is perceived as exclusively financial. It is quite possible to use these groups as a source of ideas for the organization, especially in the early phases of the policy cycle—problem formulation and options generation. They are also an important aspect of the "policy loop," because these are individuals who have passed through the system and who have a perspective, albeit not a complete perspective, on their experience and the way it affected them.

It is especially important to view these groups as policy committees, at least in part, because of the point Drucker (1973) made concerning the separation of human service organizations from their client or customer stream. The focus on budget generation which characterizes many social work agencies tends to place client feedback at a fairly low point within the organization's hierarchy of interest. This may mean that ideas and perspectives of great utility to the organization are present but cannot move through it to other centers of policy generation and decision. For this reason the organization should pay even more attention than it currently does to client committees and alumni committees.

6. Environment-Based Agency Policy Committees

One of the kinds of committees the agency at the board level often needs to deal with is the policy advisory committee. This committee is often appointed by external bodies or is required by federal legislation or some other legal requirement or is appointed by the agency but under pressure from outside groups. The committee may consist of clients, professionals in the same field, professionals in different fields, or, in general, may be comprised of a wide range of fairly disparate types of individuals with different types of interests and different types of hopes and expectations for the functioning of the policy advisory committee. It is often unclear to the advisory committee whom they should advise and it is not infrequently the case that advisory committee sessions deteriorate into a sort of "bull session" with the agency executive. When this happens, there is likely to be disappointment on both sides. The executive feels that there is a lack of coherent and thoughtful advice on important problems. The advisory committee members feel that they do not have the opportunity to give such advice since issues always (or often at least) come up too late for a systematic study to be done. Here again, an opportunity, in my view, is missed. While it is true that there are hostile advisory committees and that many advisory committees do not fulfill a useful function, much of this, in my experience, is due to poor planning and preparation, lack of role clarity from the committee member's point of view, and a lack of understanding of their purposes and potentials from the executive's point of view. When that kind of package gets put together, it is almost certain to be one which all of the participants find disappointing.

In addition to advisory committees, there are other kinds of committees created by environmental forces that impinge very directly on the organization. Among the more important ones are accreditation and evaluation committees. Few human service organizations escape some kind of systematic evaluation at various points in their organizational life course. Small or "mini" evaluations frequently occur around budget time and with respect to particular programs and particular funders. However, what I am referring to here is the larger scale, or in-depth, evaluation that may be initiated on a scheduled basis by a major local funder like a United Way or may be initiated when problems occur or are perceived to have occurred. The accreditation visit is threatening, but less so, because it does occur on a scheduled basis and because people have time to prepare for it. Accreditation may involve a committee visiting the human service organization and making various kinds of compliance assessments with respect to previously established national standards for its type of operation.

Nonetheless, even though one prepares for the organized visit of the accreditation team and feels that there has been time to work through a number of issues with staff and members of the community, there is the possibility of a negative judgment and that brings some feeling of anxiety. The interesting role for the policy manager here lies in the possibility of proactivity. While this does not always occur, looking ahead a year or two before the accreditation visit can give an organization with the proper structure and motivation a very useful opportunity to look at itself first and to chart some new directions. Sometimes this occurs, but often, as one may guess, it does not. And as with other deadlines, the accreditation visits often sneak up on agencies and seem in too many instances to take them by surprise.

The evaluation visit is somewhat different from the accreditation visit because it often begins with some sense of problem or peril in the environment. While it should not be the case, evaluation is all too often a step in a discontinuation process initated by a funder who has for good or ill already made a preliminary judgment that this specific agency needs to be looked at very closely. Sometimes the initiation comes from outside concerns and is pressed upon external funders by dissident groups. Other times the funding agency itself, using its own internal assessments, has questions. There are still other occasions in which dissident elements within the organization feel that an outside review is imperative. Whatever the reason, agency evaluations are threatening and are very hard to turn into productive, policy proactive situations. Nonetheless, they are episodes which do have high policy impact for the organization and with which the organization must deal.

7. Environment-Based Inter-Agency Policy Committees

Environment-based inter-agency committees are those set up by environmental forces which cannot help but affect the human service organization. Thus, agencies involved are virtually forced to provide participation because the penalties for nonparticipation are likely to be greater than any losses that might occur with participation. What might some examples be here? One, of course, could be a standards review committee. Such a group flows out of the accrediation standards just mentioned. Those standards themselves are often challenged by individual agencies and over time most standards develop a legacy of complaint around them. Such a legacy need not reflect the poor quality of the standard. It may have been excellent when it was originally formed (or it may well not have been excellent). For the excellent standards, time and social change may make them inappropriate. Caseload size, cost per client, square feet per staff person, and so on are all professional standards that may well come under scrutiny for either increase or decrease as time goes on. Most organizations have a high degree of vested interest in assuring that the standards are ones they can live with and thus seek, if possible, to participate in standard setting, review, and refurbishment activity.

Coordinating committees also exist here and these are ones not stimulated by the human service organization in question. Rather, they are proposed again by elements in the organization's environment; funders concerned about duplication of services and seeking a greater degree of horizontal integration, and standard-setting organizations concerned with a problem of vertical integration—that is, the integration at the local organization with state activities in the same area and thence national activities as well.

8. Environment-Based Social Policy Committees

These are committees in which the social agency may not participate directly. They may be national groups or state-wide groups which are engaging in social policy review and development within a particular area. The organization in question may seek a limited involvement via testimony, the preparation of background material, or the loaning of a staffer with policy management experience who can help in the requisite activities of the social policy group. At other times the organization may be asked to provide a range of assistance. Sometimes the organization even brings clients for public testimony or seek to use examples from its caseload about how bad things are or how much things need to be improved and so on. With this as a background, organizations can participate in and influence social policy at state and national levels. Sometimes "elite" groups of executives and "leaders" in the field get together to influence the course of social policy in the state and nation.

Other Factors Influencing Policy Settings

Each of the arenas or areas just discussed is a setting in which policy management can occur. It is a setting available for the development of ideas, their codification, their assessment, and their shaping into options for ratification by various groups. In some, the agency itself will be the ultimate ratifier and will then move programmatically to implementation. Generally speaking, organization-based activities of an intra-agency or agency sort are most typical here. To some extent, inter-agency activity, which the human service organization initiated and in relation to which it will modify some of its own activities, also qualifies. The same is true in a sense for the first two environment-based categories. Client committees and alumni committees, as well as other advisory committees, usually require the organization to take some action. Whether the organization does or not is subject to a number of uncertainties, but the potential is there. Social policy and the environment-based inter-agency activity tend to be policy relevant areas in which the organization participates where it does not make final decisions. Rather, ratification of various social policy proposals or standards comes elsewhere. The organization is influential, but does not determine what goes on there.

Given the potential for policy activity, why are some organizations more active and influential than others? Obviously there are a number of unique factors, but some general ones worth noting are often important.

System/Agency Differentiation

One important variable is the degree to which relative systems—the agency system and the environment system—are differentiated (see Hasenfeld and Tropman 1979). The organization can be relatively simple or relatively complex. To the extent that a human service organization is relatively simple, it will not need a great deal of policy management, though it will continue to need some. Matters concerning its purpose, mission, and role remain difficult ones to solve whether the agency is small or not. In fact, in one respect the smaller, less differentiated organization is the more vulnerable among human service organizations because it has less "cushion" in terms of staff, clients, funds, or alternative missions to turn to as the environment shifts and turns. A small organization, for example, can be put out of business by a single negative decision of a large public bureaucracy. A large human service organization, however, probably has the resiliency and the resources to withstand one or two or even several, such shocks before being fatally injured. Not only are environmental shocks more perilous to the smaller human service organizations, but they are less likely to be aware of them, partly because they do not assign people the task of environmental monitoring and strategic assessment. Those tasks are very close to aspects of the policy management task. Staff, including the executive, are too busy "getting the job done" to assign people to the tasks of strategic scrutiny and assessment that are required to be involved. If the environment is relatively simple itself with only a few relevant variables, a more basic pattern of policy management may well be successful. The problem for the small organization comes as it develops and moves into a more complex environment. Consider, for example, the small block club organization in a major city. There the agency is relatively simple in structure, yet the environment with which it must contest, in which it must compete, and with which it must cope is very complex and diversified. One of the reasons such organizations tend to have relatively short lives is because they simply are unable to deal with the complexities of the environment while at the same time carrying out their tasks.

The highly differentiated human service organization faces another set of problems. There, policy management activities, especially intra-agency ones are absolutely necessary for the agency to function. This agency has two sets of problems facing it (among others). One set deals with organizational coordination and articulation within its own operation. It can be coordinating different functions each with the other or similar functions at different sites, or it can be concerned with problems of policy that occur at different levels—local, regional, and state. Each of these difficulties is very serious and policy management is a necessary function within the organization, to say nothing of the need to scrutinize the perils of the environment. That really represents the second set of problems, and one that is similar for the smaller organization. Both face environmental challenges and competitions. Policy management, in this setting, aims at providing an articulation between the problems faced by the organization and its ability to respond. If a complex organization exists within a relatively simple environment the problems are not too severe with respect to the organization, but they are perhaps severe with respect to the environment. That condition is a setting in which the human service organization is likely to dominate the environment inadvertently. Consider, for example, the highly differentiated field office of a large state human service bureaucracy in a relatively rural and unpopulated county. The resources available to the organization, since it can draw not only on its own field office staff but the larger state staff as well, are greater than those available to the county itself. Hence, the regional office is likely to become a dominant force there, whereas in other counties it may not be anywhere near so dominant.

Generally speaking however, complex organizations exist in complex environments and, to press that proposition a bit further, the internal differentiation of complex organizations tends to be, relatively speaking, parallel to or isomorphic with the crucial environmental structures with which it must deal. These include client structures, financing structures, and administrative structures. What keeps the complex human service organization on track is that the relevant substructures are, or should be, alert to changes within the components in the environment for which it is responsible. These changes are noted by an organizational subunit, and the executive core (administrative team) of the human service organization is alerted to what may be on the horizon. What makes these settings crucial for policy management is that changes can occur rapidly and without a great deal of warning in the strategic environment of the human service organization and they may be overlooked by the appropriate personnel within the organization. Hence, environmental changes in this way "creep up on" the organization via substructural malfunction.

Input-Output Concerns

Human service organizations also face another type of problem. The pressures at input are sometimes very different from the evaluations at output. This seriously complicates the tasks of policy management. Most human service organizations are, in one way or another, people processing settings. Their goal is to handle or keep the people whom they are assigned to process. Sometimes they are asked to do people changing as well. And indeed, almost all human service organizations prefer to think of themselves as people changing rather than simply people processing. However, society's wishes, despite society's rhetoric, are often for people processing—we may insist that more people go to prison, that all children be in school, that all mental patients be institutionalized. And this may well increase the input into human service organizations. However, society, because of its ambivalent posture on some of these points, does not always like to provide (or ever like to provide) the resources for people changing. Rather, it likes to speak of people changing while providing resources for people processing. This gap means that those who control crucial inputs into the organization in terms of people may have somewhat different views of what the organization or other professionals would have. They may also have unrealistic output expectations and may seek simplistic formulas that tie outputs to inputs.

Policy management has several tasks in this kind of situation. One is to provide the articulation between the external systems, which may control the flow of input, the (different) external systems, which control the flow of resources, and the organizational structure itself. Second, the policy manager helps to interpret the nature of the organizational outputs to the service system as a whole. Both of these boundary-spanning activities typically involve agreements of various sorts—who is seen by the agency, for how long, and under what conditions; who gets discharged, and when, and to where. In specific cases these human service functions are the stuff of social work activity; what is often needed, however, is a set of policies and guidelines which can aid the worker on the line in approaching these problems and can at the same time forge links with other inputting and outputting units.

The Policy Cycle

The policy cycle itself influences the setting for policy management. As implied in the previous input/output problem, a single problem may occupy two settings. In that instance, the policy manager may seek to interpret output problems to input controllers on the one hand, while interpreting input problems to output controllers on the other hand. Both may take a dim view of the policy manager's role, and indeed one might fairly say, imitating Gilbert and Sullivan, that "the policy manager's lot is not a happy one." Implicit there are dual settings and the policy cycle concept suggests multiple settings. When I discussed the policy cycle I discussed it as if those elements within the cycle occurred within a single setting. And indeed that is sometimes the case. It is best when it is, but it is not as often the case as we would like. Not infrequently policy definition occurs in one type of setting; policy option generation occurs in another; ratification in yet a third; planning and programming in yet a fourth and fifth. This situation is likely to be especially true when the human service organization is a large one and when there is plenty of opportunity for intra-organizational differentiation. Even the small organization, however, may suffer from multiplicity of policy settings because, being small, it may have to be satisfied with policy definitions generated by policy elites in other organizations, with options suggested by policy influentials in still other organizations, and what comes to its board may be less a product of its own work than that of others. Such a situation is even more likely to be true if the relatively simple social agency exists in a complex environment.

Factors that influence policy settings are:
- System agency differentiation
- Input/output concerns
- The policy cycle

Conclusion

In this chapter I have tried to provide some sense of the settings in which policy management may occur. These settings are likely to be committees and, for that reason, knowledge about committees, their activity, their problems, their stresses and strains are of crucial importance to the policy management process and will occupy two later chapters. The purpose here is to introduce the idea that the policy process is, in large part, the committee process. And it is in committee settings that a great opportunity for policy management occurs. It is certainly true that there is individual work in securing information and generating alternatives and the whole raft of personalized opportunities which the policy manager has. Still, properly handled committees are a great source of ideas, the group processes is a strengthening and enlarging one with respect to the options available, and at various stages of the policy process usually a "sign-off" kind of activity is required. That sign-off tends to mean that a committee will consider a number of problem definitions and settle on a few. While that is not ratification in the formal policy sense, it does suggest that effectiveness in the ability to deal with committee activities is central. The chapter on policy roles will suggest a number of more specific activities that the policy manager might undertake and a number of more specific job assignments that can be combined with policy management activities. Suffice it to say for now that the starting point, at least, for consideration of policy management settings is the policy committee.

CASE ILLUSTRATIONS

THE CHILD WELFARE AGENCY

During the first few weeks of the hectic crisis at his agency, Jim had been able to hold things together and forestall a series of devastating cuts in the agency's budget. He and the president of the board had met with the major funders, listened to their complaints about the agency, and promised to make the requisite adjustments. What he needed was time during which he would try, with the help of staff and community support, to turn the place around. He and the president pointed out that there were not that many organizations that could fill the kind of need that their organization could. He stressed its historical importance to the community and the bad reputation that would affect all human service agencies if the oldest were allowed to go under. He had previously talked with the president, who, with the concurrence of the board, had agreed to delay looking for a new executive for a year. Then the board, the funders, and the community would assess where they stood. Jim sent a memo to the staff, informing them that things would pretty much remain stable, as far as funding was concerned, for a year. After that, he indicated, it was uncertain what would happen. In the note, he shared some of the thinking that he had done so far. He outlined the problems that beset the agency and some of its historical difficulties. He soft-pedalled the problems he thought exclusively due to the former director's inordinate tenure and his habit of making decisions solely by looking in a mirror, getting no other counsel or feedback. He indicated that there were a number of ways the agency could go and he would look forward to hearing from people in writing and in discussion about what ways they thought would be appropriate. He further indicated that whatever way was chosen there would have to be some rapid reorganization and job reassignments. He was confident, he said in the note, that he could rely on the staff to cooperate in this difficult time. "By pulling together," he concluded, "we should be able to come out of a difficult period even stronger than before."

Jim's first problem was how to deal with the four associate directors. Each was making about $25,000 a year plus liberal benefits. He met with each one and indicated that henceforth the job would be only a one-half-time associate directorship for reasons of finance. The other half of the time would be spent in direct service. Privately, he felt that he wanted to reduce all of them and bring in somebody new, but he needed some of their expertise at this point and didn't want to make too many radical changes at all points in the organization. They had been appointed by the previous director and, while not necessarily responsible for the current situation, had not done anything to prevent it either. They were committed to the old way of doing things and, he thought, did not have enough freshness of focus to be helpful. So he reached down into the ranks for Sam and asked him to become his assistant. Sam's job was to talk with a number of people about what needed to be done in the organization and assemble a list of suggestions so that at least one suggestion or observation from every staff member at the professional and secretarial level was available. Then he was to collate these to see whether any themes emerged. At the same time Jim asked the associate director for finance to prepare an outline of where the strengths and weaknesses were so that he could begin the process of pruning. He himself got on the phone and began to talk to a number of executives in the community and, during the next couple of weeks, began to amass a series of ideas from them about what ought to happen. He had to do this in a way that did not generate a perception of weakness among the other executives, although he was pretty certain that everyone knew his agency was in bad shape. But at least he wanted to have a full set of available ideas to play with. He had also asked Sam to make a short list of individuals who seemed most vigorous and who had made the most interesting contributions. He was going to form a small task force to pull together some ideas and chart new directions. At the same time he had the cooperation of the president and some of the board members. His presentation to them suggested that he would have to cut and prune fairly quickly and he asked for rather extraordinary authority for a short period of time, with the understanding that whatever reorganization was done would be reviewed at three-, six-, and nine-month periods. He was candid with them and indicated that he would like to work closely with the president because it was not going to be possible, given the emergency situation the agency faced, to follow the usual process. He agreed (it was really his suggestion) to send them almost weekly bulletins of what was happening. If they had any serious questions, they were to give him a ring and they would talk about it right there and then. It was an odd procedure, but one everyone felt was appropriate in the circumstances.

Discussion Questions

1. The director is seeking to change the course of the agency. What is good about what he is doing? Why?
2. What is bad about what he is doing? Why?
3. How do you assess the agency/environment balance here?

THE WELFARE PLANNING COUNCIL

The director didn't have a lot of money, but one of the things she wanted to do was to begin to get some new ideas pumped into the organization. She asked one of her staff to initiate and coordinate a half-baked idea seminar in which the new thinking of individuals could be shared. She indicated that a premium would be placed on the imaginative and the creative over the practical, at least during the first four or five months of the seminar. In this seminar no one could criticize any idea brought up. That would help stimulate the flow of new thoughts. On alternate weeks she would invite university people, other professional people, a visiting author, or somebody from the census department to come in and make presentations to the staff.

The agency, she thought, needed a shot in the intellectual arm. There was no sense of creativity and vitality. She got a small grant of $3,000 from a local foundation. She asked her old nemesis, the "stick-in-the-mud," to plan a one-month trip that would take him around the country to different welfare planning organizations. She wanted to know what other organizations were up to, what their thinking was, how they were coping with the problems they faced. He was astounded, and then overjoyed. The very thought of it he found somewhat stimulating. Despite the fact that he had wanted her job and wanted to force her to fail, he began to think that she might not be all bad. She asked another staff person to review the history of the organization as represented in its minutes and its annual reports and anything else that could be found and to assemble a relatively comprehensive list of the different roles and functions that it had performed over the years. Special attention was to be paid to those which might have applicability to today, although they had been discontinued years ago. She took some initiative and called a meeting of the other planning and policy council executives in town, something that had never been done before, and put to them the question of the possibility of a sharing group that might meet every so often, perhaps once a quarter, to let others know what they were up to. Several of the executives didn't know the other executives, but the idea seemed good to everyone, at least for a while.

Discussion Questions

1. Consider a range of ways the executive could improve agency/environment relations. Is she moving in the right direction? Why or why not? What should she be doing?

2. Agencies in town concerned with planning and policy seem not to have got together until recently. Why might that have been?

3. What are some examples of committees which could have been set up to smooth and facilitate environmental relations?

5

POLICY COMPONENTS

If a major task of policy management is to supply a fresh set of ideas as solution candidates for the problems of the agency, the community, and the society, there needs to be some way to assess the ideas offered. How can someone filling a policy manager's role know when or if an idea is good? The answer is, of course, that one can not. But there are some touchstones, some criteria, which can be of assistance.

Scientific Correctness

Ideas which guide action can be of varying accuracy, and it is important that the ideas be "right" insofar as knowledge permits.[1] As obvious as this criterion is, it is likely to be overlooked or set aside, sometimes because

---

1. By right here I do not mean moral rightness. Rather, especially in the human services, there is a need to link policy to what research has said on the subject, to the current state of knowledge. For example, if an agency is going to have a policy on short-term counseling visits, what is the best number of visits to pick for the cut-off point as a "scientific" basis for beginning the discussion?

people have pet theories they do not wish to examine, and other times because they do not have the latest information.

Policy as Theory. Policy is to practice what theory is to research. Policy, in fact, represents an implicit (and sometimes explicit) set of assertions about cause and effect, along with the appropriate remedies based upon this set of ideas. If one believes, for example, that the body is helped by the letting out of "bad blood," then one might well embark on a task of bleeding someone who is ill. If one believes that juvenile delinquency is caused by lack of work among teenage boys, one is inclined to develop a jobs program. If one notices that much of the delinquency appears to end once age twenty or so is reached, one might conclude that delinquency is a transient adolescent state, and do nothing.[2] It is crucial to understand that these incipient theories are, in fact, contained in policy ideas, because they could be wrong for several reasons, including myth, stereotype, and lack of accurate scientific information.[3] Ideas of the most atrocious sort can permeate policy thinking—for example, those of racial inferiority or male superiority. Such ideas are often held with remarkable tenacity and are, at times, resistant to scientific information. "Everyone knows" what causes what, and to suggest something different is to threaten conventional wisdom, conventional practice based upon that wisdom, and thus, by implication, the integrity of the service provider. Such a situation may be more common in the human services, where there is, after all, not a great deal of evidence anyway. While there is research available on various techniques of psychotherapy, various approaches to different problems, and ranges of group techniques, much of this evidence is less than conclusive. But even when scientific information is available, in some areas of the National Science Foundation's work, as Bozeman and Blackenship point out: "formal scientific and technical information (recorded data) play a secondary role in planning and decision making. As such, it is filtered into planning and decision making or 'trickles up' from the specified program director" (1979:55).

The Latest Ideas. It is a crucial task of policy management to be aware

---

2. A humorous reflection of this point comes in the song "Officer Krupke" in the musical *West Side Story*. In this song a group of delinquents sings through a series of theories about what makes them bad, including one which says, ". . . deep down inside me I'm no good!" For each theory they also sing a solution. One line offers the idea that juvenile delinquency is purely a social disease, and they respond, "So take me to a social worker!"

3. Consider, for example, that if a social agency is going to take a position on salary increments for staff it would want as much current data as possible on current practice.

of the latest thinking on the realms of policy under consideration and to bring those ideas into the policy process. Such activity may involve simply education (where little or nothing was known before) or reeducation (disabusing some system of a set of ideas and presenting substitute ones).

It is only through a process such as this that policy making can be thoughtful in the fullest sense of that word. All too often, policy is blind, guided by ambition or by incorrect beliefs about the world. The pressure of day-to-day activity is a contributing factor here. It is important in the process of policy management that "the available evidence" be carefully considered in the development of a policy proposal.[4]

For policy to be scientifically correct, it must:
- Make relevant assumptions about the solutions and causes of the problem it addresses
- Touch base with the latest writing, both scientific and quasi-scientific, relevant to those assumptions
- Take any conflicts in the field under consideration

(See Exercise 5.1)

Ideas of Quality

This criterion is somewhat more difficult to define, but it tries to pinpoint the importance of *good* ideas, rather than trivial ones.[5] It is difficult to make high quality policy from third-rate ideas, and one task of policy management is to bring fresh alternatives into the picture at a time appropriate to their consideration and to seek to synthesize the available ideas into a new one. The Ford Motor Company made this orientation one of the hallmarks of their advertising campaign during the late 1970s. There were various versions of the layout but essentially a picture showed a shining light bulb (often used to depict a good idea) with the words "FORD Has a Better Idea." There they emphasized the idea or concept aspect of their work. Whoever had *that* idea surely had a good idea.

What is a Good Idea Anyway. How does one recognize a good idea? It is not easy, but simplicity is usually a good indication. Simplicity does not mean simple-minded or simplistic, both of which are characterized by ig-

4. A more subtle factor is the lack of intellectual interest characteristic of most professions. A profession is charged with doing something, and the day-to-day activity of most professionals leaves little time for the kind of thing I am describing, unless it is explicitly planned for and organized.

5. Or, as in the previous criterion, *wrong* (insofar as we know it) ones.

norance of the relevant facts and by an inappropriate reduction of the complexities of the situation. Rather, simplicity refers to the process of reducing a problem to its most essential features and proceeding from there to craft a solution that deals with these features. Any time policy ideas become too complex, look again. The ideas may well be in need of improvement.

Several years ago Herbert Simon and his colleagues (1950) gave some criteria which can be used as a test of ideas. A couple are worth mentioning here.

Simon says:
- Good ideas make compliance easy.
  (Does the idea propose something that is easy to do or is it very complex? Can people "do" it without trouble?)
- Good ideas make noncompliance difficult.
  (Is the idea something that people have to go out of their way to avoid, or will, under criterion 1 above, compliance occur in the routine course of events?)

(See Exercise 5.2)

Political Sensitivity and Involvement

Knowing. In any political environment certain interests need to be taken into consideration when a policy is developed. Consider, for example, an adoption agency and its policy on interracial adoptions. This is a sensitive area, and whether it involves blacks and whites or children from different countries coming to this country, many considerations are involved, as well as some policy positions taken by ethnic organizations. In the process of developing a policy on this matter the agency would want to know what other groups had said on the matter, what their position was, and how the proposed policy meshed, or did not mesh, with current thinking. (See also chapter 8.)

Clearing. Knowledge of what the position of groups has been is only part of the political intelligence process. A second portion of that process involves checking proposals with those who might be affected. This checking, or "clearing," process can take several forms. One is an informal sounding out—"What do you think of this approach, or that?" Such a process usually takes place at the beginning of a policy endeavor and provides some of the parameters, as well as some of the possible acceptable solutions to problems within the political arena. (See pages 156–157.)

Checking. A second level of interaction occurs with sharing drafts and getting comments from relevant groups on the proposed drafts. Some of the time it is hard for an outside group to know what might be involved, until they actually see a proposal in writing. Exactly what does the agency plan to do about transracial adoptions? Once that point is clear, the position of outside groups can be crystalized.

Involving. A third level of political sensitivity is involvement of the affected groups in the decision-making process. This procedure has much support in American tradition—people should be involved in the decisions that affect them; for example, they should not be taxed without some representation. A somewhat less positive view of this process is that it is one of cooptation, of securing agreement through involvement, but an involvement which might cause some to lose perspective and become supporters of the general agency orientation rather than of their own special interest. Whether consideration of cooptation is the appropriate term, or part of both, the process of involvement is crucial to the policy management and guidance process.

Modeling. These other views, of course, create problems as well, since the more views on a policy one has the more likely it is that differing positions and perspectives will be revealed. One cannot simply throw all types of opinions and perspectives into a policy process and expect anything other than policy stew, in which the policymaker later is quite likely to be boiled. Some kind of systematic, structured process through which involvement can occur is of utmost importance if such involvement is to be productive, intellectually and politically. All too often, though, policy is made in a vacuum and is one that does not consider the needs of those affected. Many human service agencies even today make only *pro forma* gestures in the direction of clients. All too often, the powerless and those who have less political importance in the system are left out—for example, clients in the social service agency or students in college. It is especially important that the policy process in the human service agency reflect such involvements. For the policy process is not only important in and of itself, but also *serves as a model for the action process.* Shabby treatment of certain groups in policy often is a *signal* and a permission to treat them shabbily elsewhere.

Political sensitivity involves:
- Knowing
- Clearing

- Checking
- Involving
- Modeling

(See Exercise 5.3)

Cost Parameters

One of the primary items involved in policy management is, of course, the budget. Everything, it seems, can be done at some price. The problem is that there is never enough money to go around. The woe of budget officers, too, is the fact that needs come in endless supply. One's budget is never large enough, regardless of the actual level of that budget; therefore, it is necessary in the field of policy management to work within a set of constraints.

Relative Budgetary Constraint. One constraint is, obviously, current dollars, and the nature of the competition for current dollars. I call this the *relative budgetary constraint* because the funds available for one project depend, relatively, on what else is on the docket. The agency which applies for funds from the United Way, for example, will often receive that proportion of its budget that the overall granting agency received of its goal (assuming, of course, that its program had met with prior approval). That means that if the United Way campaign was 98 percent successful, the agency would likely get 98 percent of its request.

Subjective Constraint. There is another constraint, however, which I call the *subjective constraint*. People in general appear to have some rough idea of what things should cost and what they are willing to pay for goods and services. These two different subjective limits, A and B, are important elements in the policy management process because they affect the nature of the arguments made for resources.

The Price Limit. These two constraints are closely linked, but can and should be separated conceptually because they represent different aspects of the way in which people think about money. Budget officers and budget boards are no different. Constraint A is the "price limit" and relates to the subjective sense people have about what things should cost. Gas should be such and such a price; a clinical hour of therapy should cost between $30 and $60 per hour, and so on. If a particular policy comes in with prices that appear to be out of line, problems will develop immediately.

The Worth Limit. The second limit, B, is the "worth limit." It operates in linked fashion to the price limit. One of the two is always fixed, in essence, while the other varies in terms of thinking about the final picture. An item is "worth it" at a given price, but not at another price. Medical help is worth it at $10 per office visit, but perhaps not (or less so) at $1,000 per office visit. While price affects thinking about worth, the reverse is also true. Worth affects thinking about price. Someone may say, "The price is OK (meaning that the price is within the price constraint), but we really don't need this service in this community (or it isn't worth it at the price quoted. If we could get it free . . .)."

Relative and subjective constraints are crucial to the process of successful policy management, and one of the reasons why good policy ideas are so important. Generally, one thing that is meant by a good idea is that it is a way of achieving some goal at substantially lower cost (the efficiency criterion) or a way of achieving substantially greater impact at the same cost (the effectiveness criterion). If, for example, I could demonstrate that it was possible to counsel clients in half an hour, as opposed to one hour, I would be achieving greater efficiency. If I can develop a group method of seeing several clients at once, I would be achieving greater *effectiveness*. *Efficiency,* in this framework, links closely with the price constraint; *effectiveness* links closely to the worth constraint. Effective policy management must balance both these subjective constraints and balance them, in turn, with the objective constraints of available dollars and the political climate that makes dollars available.

Cost parameters involve:
- Relative budget constraint
- Subjective constraint
  a) Price limit
  b) Worth limit
     (*See Exercise 5.4*)

Linked to Values

The subject of constraints raises the issue of values and the relationship of the particular proposal to extant values. Some attention should be paid in the policy management process to articulating the connection the particular policy has with more general sets of organizational and societal values. Such an articulation makes affirming the policy easier, and makes opposition more difficult. It is akin to the "good idea" in which one seeks to develop policy ideas with the same features. Indeed, one not only seeks to articulate whatever links to values exist, but in fact develops policy with that idea in mind. (See chapter 12.)

Multiple Values. Such a process is considerably more difficult than one might think, in part because there are several sets of values that need to be taken into account. One set might be called core values or values central to the American culture itself. A second set is local variations of these values or variations with respect to some specific target population. A third set is the values of the people who will administer the particular policy once it is ratified. Finally, the various groups which ratify a policy may have values yet different from any of the above, making for a complex situation indeed.

Dual Structure. It appears that the core values are themselves structured in sets of opposing, dialectical parts. For example, Americans are fond of achievement and like the idea of getting ahead. On the other hand, Americans also support the idea of equality, of everybody having the "same." As a culture and as people, both values are present, both enjoy our commitment, even though one may be dominant. However, the problem develops when they conflict, as they do. One cannot have equality on the one hand and achievement on the other. Thus, over time, policies may be characterized by different emphases. Alternatively, policies may seek to emphasize one value for one group and another value for another group, at the same time. Or, alternatively, one value may come into play in one set of conditions, and another value in another set of conditions.

The central point here is awareness that the value system is dual in nature, that people in general are committed to opposing sets of values at the same time. Emphasis on one aspect of the set is appropriate, though one cannot ignore the fact that there is another, counterbalancing value with which people also agree and to which they also lend their support. The policy management process must, therefore, be aware, first, of this dualism, and second, take it into account in the development and processing of policy ideas. One example from Social Security may be helpful here. American society is committed to equity or to appropriate rewards related to one's contributions. We are also committed to adequacy—to a minimum below which no one should fall. The problem in the Social Security system is that the income one gets on the basis of equity, calculated from contributions over the years, may be inadequate. The Supplemental Security Income program (SSI) is precisely a program to bridge the gap between equity and adequacy. In this case the program has both elements, seeking to articulate the two values, each of which is somewhat in contradiction with the other.

Prevailing Climate. "Taking account" of values is an ambiguous phrase, but it has some specific referents to which I can point. First, one needs to be aware of the prevailing climate of values. Policy ideas are always evaluated within the framework of the currently ascendent value pattern. Excellent ideas, whose time has not yet come or whose time has passed, present problems from the beginning. One needs to seek, insofar as possible, to develop the policy idea in line with currently ascendent values, recalling that there is a subdominant value in the background.

Worker/Client Difference. A second problem occurs when one considers that target and administering groups do not always possess the same values and may more than likely have different ones. Thus, in human service organizations, especially, policies based upon middle-class values may run aground on the value orientations of lower-class clients. Younger people may feel that it is not too important for older people to continue to contribute to society as much as before, an orientation certainly not shared by older people. One group may think that abortion is fine; another may think it is murder. And on it goes. Workers, for example, may have professional orientations and standards which mean little to clients; clients may have world views sharply different from those of workers. For example, clients and workers may have different ideas about the kind of help the clients need. Clients may have more concrete, focused needs, such as for food, shelter, clothing, while workers may be more counseling oriented. This conflict between the professional and the pragmatic is one source of difficulty.

Another lies or may lie in the conflict between agency rules and clients' reality. Clients may need to meet at night or on weekends, but the agency may not be open at "odd" hours. The key point for thoughtful policy is an awareness of the value system in its multidimensionality. From such awareness comes an attempt to take values into account, to frame policy such that different aspects of the value system are represented.

"Linked to values" means:

- Awareness of dual value structure
- Justifying policies in several values
- Attaching proposal to ascending values
- Considering different values of administrative and target groups.

(See Exercise 5.5)

Sufficient Guides to Action

Ultimately, of course, the goal of policy is to provide role guidance and prescription; do this in this situation, avoid that in that situation. The extent to which policy can accomplish such a task depends upon many factors. In the main, the crucial link between policy and action is found in something typically called "guidelines" or sets of directions and interpretations for implementing policy.

A Policy Idea Is Not Policy. These unfortunate situations are the result of a lack of sufficient guides to action in the original set of policy ideas and the lack of an appropriate anchor in actual conditions when the policy was written. A policy idea, however good, is not a policy. In the emphasis placed on good policy ideas and good theory there lies a potential problem; people may stop there, taking the idea no further. Policy needs to be articulated with the real world and must take account of that world. It is one of the missions of the policy management process to provide such articulation, so that policy decisions are "informed" ones, informed about the actual nature of the conditions that exist, and contain guides to action that take those conditions into account. It is costly and tragic to replicate the devastation of institutional lives in a series of row houses. And yet this result is all too often the one achieved. The initial policy ideas were too loose, too lacking in concrete articulation with the real world. Policy then, as opposed to a "policy idea," should contain sufficient guides to action so that those who administer the policy have reasonable parameters upon which to base programmatic planning, design, and construction. One needs to look at the policy with an eye to at least the following considerations: specificity, implications, applicability, ease of administration, range of administrative discretion.

Bad Example #1: Community Care. Within the human service field, for example, it is not always clear what is meant by many concepts that appear in policy. What, for example, is "community-based care"? There has been a large move in recent years to locate people who had previously been institutionalized within a "community" setting. All too often however, policymakers had only the wisp of an idea, with no real concept of what "care" was to be, what community was, or how care could be based in the community. As a result, community-based policy has all too often resulted in "community institutions," row upon row of homes in which several retarded live, with none of the benefits of the institution and none of the benefits of the community.

Bad Example #2: Maximum Feasible Confusion. Another example is, perhaps, even more well-known—the idea of "the maximum feasible participation of the poor," This good policy idea created no end of mischief and wound up diverting organizational and institutional energies from a program already beleaguered with substantial political baggage from tasks of service provision. The first problem occurred in specifying exactly what each of these terms meant—what was maximum, what was feasible, and who was poor. Finally, the poverty program agencies developed some operational definitions as a *modus operandi,* focusing on a proportion of board membership. But these were challenged repeatedly and it took an enormous amount of time just to get this far. Where participation should occur was also a point in dispute—at the board level? at the operations level? Whether board membership ever or truly represented the intent of the policy planners is not known. There are many ways to participate, with board membership being only one. What is known is that almost no attempt was made to train, prepare, or otherwise take account of the special new members, many of whom were new to the whole idea.

Specificity. Policies need to be reasonably specific about the behaviors or outcomes they intend. One can ask the question, "How will we know when the policy goal has been achieved?" as one small test of specificity. Broad policies, like "maximum participation of clients," become very difficult in practice to administer.

Implications. Often the specifics call forth applications that were unintended, or they may point to embarrassing and difficult gaps. For example, in providing benefits for the poor, does one really intend to include "students"? If one excludes from the eligibility pool of adoptive parents people whose incomes are below a certain level, does this mean that some minority groups are disproportionately harmed by such a policy? Getting to specifics helps to make visible policy problems that can be prevented.

Applicability. To whom, when, and for how long is the policy intended to apply? Are there exceptions? How are these exceptions to be made? Does the policy require a "trigger condition" (you can not take this course unless you have taken that course) and will this condition be present? These are good questions to consider before the policy is placed into effect.

Ease of Administration. Is the policy easy to administer? Will it require a large apparatus to put into effect? How will compliance with the policy be achieved? Is there anything that needs to be done to simplify compliance behaviors?

Administrative Discretion. How much discretion is being left to the administrator and the administrative corps with respect to decisions about compliance, developing the rules of application, and so on? Have the crucial points been specified and ranges of acceptable behavior been defined, so that the administrator has "something to go on?" Alternatively, has the administrator been handed a "can of worms" which creates problems with respect to the actual policy decision itself? This is especially important because administrative discretion is one way in which exceptions to policy can be made. No policy can cover all instances, and administrators need ways to deal with those that do not fall (exactly) under the conditions dealt with by the policy.

Sufficient guides to action mean that the policy must be reviewed for:
- Specificity
- Implications
- Applicability
- Ease of administration
- Range of administrative discretion

(See Exercise 5.6)

Periodic Review and Refurbishment

Policy is like any other human invention; it needs care and feeding to be helpful and useful. Without that attention it becomes less useful and eventually declines into decrepitude. The typical policy process is something like the following. At some point a policy is made. That point is in a period of pressure or crisis during which, it is safe to say, the policymaking system is not operating at its thoughtful best. It is not thoughtful because there is not the time available to think through a range of alternatives. Often, too, special circumstances or special interests are in the forefront, circumstances which will not continue to be prominent in later years. But that policy is left in effect, and its use and its usefulness as a guide to action diminishes as time goes on.

Policy vs. Practice. What takes its place is "practice," as noted in chapter 1. Policy is that which is written and which serves the person, or the human service agency, as one type of guide to action. Practice is what is done, the actual pattern of behavior in a range of instances, and it also serves as a normative guide to action. Very frequently, when people say "It's our policy around this agency to do thus and so . . . ," they are

really referring to the most recent set of practices, which may be well understood by everyone, but which most frequently are *not* well understood. Indeed, by their very nature, practices are in the oral tradition, and it is usually
never clear what conditions actually mandate a specific practice. Too, specific practices are typically developed with regard to a limited range of events,
and the implications such practices may have for the total picture within the
agency, or its affect on different individuals, is usually left unexplored. Policy is not only the result of thoughtful process, but also provides the occasion
for such a process.

Applying Practice in the Agency. Much of the time of administrators,
then, is spent in understanding agency practices, trying to enforce them more
widely or to apply them or change them where appropriate. One example is
the problem of burnout faced by many human service workers, especially
those in settings requiring constant contact with clients. The typical agency
personnel policy did not have, until recently, any way to recognize this
phenomenon, and to understand the need for staff to take some time off.
Staff, using existing policy, would call in "sick," which was technically
incorrect (since policy usually required a doctor's note after so many sick
days). Yet there was no alternative and "everybody knew" what was going
on. The staff had a large number of sick days. It was not until a policy idea
of an innovative sort was suggested that the problem was resolved. The
provision of mental health days—days that staff could take off simply by
stating they needed them—was instituted. This policy has proved quite successful in many instances. It has prevented the subversion of the sick leave
policy, recognized a need of workers, created a policy environment in which
limits can be set and oversight provided, and made assessment possible. All
in all, it has been a successful policy innovation.

These criteria suggest some of the elements needed in a process of policy
review and refurbishment. Review is a term used to indicate a major over-
haul; refurbishment suggests minor adjustments. Both, of course, are done
within the context of policy assessment, which should be an ongoing attempt
to see whether the goals of the agency are being met, how, and how well,
and should spot any major problems as well. Thus, the first step in the
review and refurbishment process, and an ongoing step, is policy monitoring.

Monitoring. Monitoring is something which is actually done quite a bit,
but is not thought of in these terms. The most usual example is in the fiscal
area—monthly budget reports represent monitoring. Other reports on agency

activities—staff time lost, number of clients seen, cases opened and closed, children placed, money allocated—mean that the goals of the agency are being observed, checked. Rather, it is the performance with respect to the goals, not the goals themselves, that are being observed. That is the difference between policy overseeing and policy refurbishment.

Typically, the monitoring involved in oversight will suggest some areas where improvements are needed, and it is the role of the policy management process and the policy manager to suggest formal adjustments as they are appropriate. Such modest adjustments, made at the suggestion of the policy manager (sometimes the executive, sometimes someone else), represent policy refurbishment. The central thrust of the policy is, typically, retained. However, small adjustments are made to enhance the performance of the policy and, thus, the achievement of the goals of the agency.

Such refurbishment fills another function which is definitely nontrivial. It suggests to the clients and staff of the human service agency that the "board," or those in control, is responding to conditions and is not as removed and distant as some boards are seen to be by some clients and staff. This pattern of response is a helpful one for the agency as a whole and for the climate of the agency.

Fine Tuning. Refurbishment may occur on an ongoing basis or it may occur at some specified time, such as the end of the year, after the annual report is out. That report, which contains much information resulting from the process of policy monitoring, is a useful document to consider in terms of the changes it might suggest in agency policy. Either way, throughout the year there should be some way in which the major policies of the organization are "fine tuned," improved, "refurbished." It is perhaps useful to point out that most agencies have someone come in regularly to look at their mechanical equipment—typewriters and the like—and adjust and tune it. Almost no one thinks that such a process is appropriate for policy.

Fine tuning assumes that organizational goals remain much the same and that major events have not dictated shifts and alterations within the structure and process of the agency. However, these conditions need to be looked at on some regular basis.

Seventh-Year Review. Typically, policy review occurs under conditions of stress and such situations cannot be avoided, nor should they be, in all instances. But much conflict is a result of years of neglect and of flying by the seat of one's pants. Rather than being caused by "surprise," conflict is an eruption of situations of festering neglect. A regularized policy review process will not *prevent* all of these developments, but can be quite helpful in a range of instances. My suggestion is that at the end of each six-year period, policy be reviewed and renewed. Sometime within the seventh year the review process should go on, and in the eighth year a new cycle of policy should begin.

One way this can be assured is to place sunset provisions on each policy such that it will cease to be operative after the end of the sixth year. The board or ratifying body could continue the policy on an interim basis until a review has been completed. It must be clear, too, that the review of the text of agency policy is only the vehicle through which the mission and role of the agency, of and for which policy is an expression, is reassessed. Agencies might ask questions concerning the nature of the clientele, the nature of the technology available, the location of the agency in terms of the clients, new theoretical developments that impinge on the way in which the agency goes about its business, new patterns of staff needs and desires, and new funding patterns, among others. One assessment form, developed by David Gil, "A General Framework for Social Policy Analysis," is helpful. A second model is one developed by Gail Marker, "Guidelines for Analysis of a Social Welfare Program." Both can be found in Tropman et al (1976).

One important source of information to use in the seven-year-review process, and, indeed, in the refurbishing process as well, is a study of the exceptions to the policy. If, under administrative discretion, there has been (and there surely will have been) a sense of what the pattern of exceptions has been and the conditions and problems that generated them, these patterns and conditions could be used to rechart the policy cause.

Overall, the process described herein will emphasize proactivity rather than reactivity. Policy proactivity provides a way in which the organization can be on top of issues and developments, anticipating rather than responding. Data and information, of course, are generated as part of the monitoring activities. But policy, like anything else, needs to be assessed and improved.

Policy review and refurbishment means:
- Distinguishing between policy and practice
- Applying practice within the agency
- Monitoring policy implementation
- Fine-tuning the policy
- Refurbishing every seven years
(See Exercise 5.7)

Ratification by Legitimate Authority

The idea of review and refurbishment, when linked especially to the distinction between policy and practice, emphasizes the need for formal authority to approve policy. Policy, from my perspective, is not policy until it has been approved. Typically, something is at some point approved by a board of directors or a city council and put into "practice." After that event, many administrative regulations grow up around that policy, such regulations being the central vehicle through which policies are put into practice.

However, there is really nothing to require that these regulations be internally consistent, uniform in approach, and so on, any more than there is a requirement that an agency's ensemble of policies themselves be coherent and consistent. So the first problem that a policy encounters lies in the lack of coherence in administrative regulations. Over time, policy decay sets in. Policy decay occurs when conditions have eroded the document's utility to the point where policy/practice balance tilts well in favor of practice.

The second problem occurs with the practice itself. Practice is what people do; the actual "norms" they use to guide their behavior. These practices may vary considerably from "policy" and even from administrative regulations. This process furthers the policy decay and can render the policy, in its essentials, inoperative. Fine tuning is designed to rectify these problems and major refurbishment is designed to bring policy, regulations, and practices into "sync" (that is, to synchronize the three sets of directives).

At these key points, then, the policy needs to go back to the approving authority. Usually that process involves a number of committees and, finally, the general board will act upon the policy refurbishment. Later chapters will consider in detail what some of the implications of this process are. Suffice it to mention now that this step is a necessary one in the development of a good policy idea.

Conclusion

Human service organizations could, without doubt, spend more time and energy in the process of policy management. Frequently, *crisis* is given as the reason for failure to do so. Something is always pressing, something always needs to be done this very instant. All too often, it is said, daily routine, which is what repeated crises become, drives out policy.

I would argue the reverse. First, I would attribute much of the faulty and flawed administration of human service organizations (and many others for that matter) to deficiencies of policy guidance and management. Further, many of the so-called crises, real enough when they occur, give evidence through repeated occurrence, through their patterned occurrence, one might say, of the fact that they could have been prevented. Indeed, when a crisis comes, one of the useful exercises in policy guidance is to ask, "What set of actions, were they to have been taken, would have prevented the crisis we now see?" Proactivity stresses anticipating events and controlling them (as opposed to the more usual rule of reactivity). Even those crises that cannot be prevented may be more ably handled if policy preparation had already occurred, ideas about what might be appropriate outlined, significant information garnered, and important bases touched. Policy management then, in human service agencies or elsewhere, is simply a method, a set of ideas and approaches, to shape and structure the development of events as they unfold. I eschew the word "control" events, for that is both onerous and gratuitous. We do not, in the usual course of events, "control" these events, whether they are on the micro level of a person or the macro level of the community or society. But there is substantial interest in guiding events, in providing a government of episodes so that random elements are kept to a minimum.

Let me give one example of the kind of thing I mean. Executives frequently say they cannot avoid one type of problematic issue at board meetings (funding crises), because the federal government's funding structure, which affects human service agencies, is so episodic and uncertain. The government frequently is late in processing grants, which makes planning "impossible." In only a few cases does the board, knowing this situation, take action based upon reasonable policy alternatives, for example, approving in principle, a proposed action in advance of the federal guideline. Or, alternatively, it is possible to set up a task force that can act on an emergency basis. The question is less which way is the proper one—either may be, or some other, for that matter. Rather, it is seeking to outline in advance relevant policy options, to provide some structure for considering those options, to allow enough time so that at least some thoughtful (or semblance of a thoughtful) approach may be taken, and to proceed in that direction, rather than to let events manage the process.

The central idea here is that ideas themselves can, and should, be guided within the formal organization context. Executives, staffs, and boards of human service organizations should not simply let what happens happen, but rather should set about to shape and improve the nature of the ideas with which they work. This principle is accepted within the realm of personnel—the organization does not simply employ anyone who walks in off the street, but considers the kinds of people needed, the kinds of training and background they should have, and tries to set up a structure of recruitment that will bring them into the organization and a set of personnel policies that will improve them while they are there.

CASE ILLUSTRATIONS

THE CHILD WELFARE AGENCY

Jim began to pull together a number of the ideas that had been coming to him through a variety of sources. They covered the range from A to Z. There were suggestions that the agency follow different treatment modalities, from traditional counseling to a variety of untraditional and innovative approaches. There were suggestions that the agency engage in outreach and sell its buildings. There were other suggestions putting the agency squarely in its building, with a variety of architectural innovations to make it more appealing and a pleasant place to come to. And on they went. Sam had been collating some of these and trying to group them into categories of suggestions. Ideas had been filtering in at a slower rate from the board as well, and a suggestion or two had even come from long-time agency supporters.

Still, Jim was a little worried because of the very success of the program he had initiated. Now he wondered how he was going to choose among the various suggestions. He realized that, as acting director, he was entitled to make a choice and, in fact, should make a choice. Still, he was uncomfortable because he had no criteria available to assess the ideas and he was not quite sure how he would reply to those whose ideas were not accepted. One could, of course, always rely on authority: "I simply decided it." But he thought that that was not the right way to go. It would always come down to that in part, of course. But he wondered to what extent scientific information might be helpful. Was there anything the professors in the universities could tell us, he wondered, about some of the latest techniques? He also wondered about the feasibility, given the agency structure, of some of the ideas. In a few cases they were easy to implement and really no problem. In other cases, however, the ideas suggested would require a good bit of time, energy, and agency resources. If one looked as though it might work, it might be a way to go. On the other hand, if the probabilities were low, one should not go in that direction.

Another problem he faced was the difficulty involved in bringing the board along. While he had been given permission to move ahead, he had also indicated that he would check and clear with the board. A number of people had also talked about providing more services while spending no more than the agency was currently spending. Jim thought that that was a secondary goal. What he wanted, at this point, was to continue at least as much as they were now doing, but to pay less for it. That would give him some of the extra cash needed to repair some other holes in the organization. He thought that whatever he did, at least at this early point, should be relatively simple. He knew about a number of executives who spent most of their time checking up on their staff to be sure that the staff was doing what it was paid to do in the first place. He had no desire to spend time like that. If a staff member is not doing what he or she is supposed to do, he thought, then that is not a staff person I want to have around here. On the other hand, he recognized the need to avoid the extremely complex requirements that characterized some agencies. One thing that crossed his mind was the possibility of asking the new welfare planning council to assess the ideas and make some suggestions. They seemed to be moving from a moribund and very limited role in the community to a more vigorous and well conceptualized one. Perhaps for a small fee he could get their judgment on some of these questions.

Discussion Questions

1. Using the criteria for quality ideas in the chapter, assess the ideas this executive has been developing.

2. How might the price limit and the worth limit apply here?

THE WELFARE PLANNING COUNCIL

The executive's nemesis returned from his month-long trip around the country with a range of suggestions for possible activity. None of them seemed terribly good to her and, in fact, she was appalled by the conceptual bankruptcy that seemed to characterize many of the organizations charged with tasks of social planning and policy development. They were useful though, because they began to generate some excitement within the organization. People began to talk about the kinds of ideas that might make sense and to give some thought to the kinds of things that the agency might do. So she felt her money had been well spent, even though the results were somewhat indirect. A review with a number of other agencies had pretty much confirmed the line of thinking she had been developing, a line aimed much more at developing the agency structure in a way that articulated better with what seemed to be the emerging interorganizational pattern. She was more convinced than ever of the inappropriateness of developing plans and then trying to sell them. Rather, she began to reorganize along the lines of a policy organization that would develop assessments at the request of the organization with the authority to bring something about. The community role was one she had not completely formulated in her mind, but her thinking suggested that the organization should try to serve a policy alerting function. The problem we had before, she thought, was trying to take responsibility for some of these problems in an increasingly complex and diversified environment. Our role now should be that of a single organization that can be relied on for outstanding and interesting analyses in presentations of facts and ideas. Then we can stand willing and ready to assist other organizations in carrying those a step further. Privately she knew the council might even stimulate some work along that line, but she didn't want to lay out that kind of claim because she was sure it was doomed to failure. Rather, a more modest plan with successes that were greater seemed to her the way to go.

Discussion Questions

1. Using the criteria for quality ideas outlined in this chapter, assess some problems in the approach taken here. Some strengths.

2. Do you think the executive here is politically sensitive? Why or why not?

3. Think of an agency you know. Do you think that agency has an adequate supply of ideas? Why or why not? How could it be improved if the supply is low?

6

POLICY MACHINERY

Whether one is talking about human service organizations or any other organization or any system of organizations, the policy-making system is best referred to as the policy machinery, and one can ask how well that machinery is functioning, whether it needs repair, what kind of mechanics are important for it to function, and so on. Most human service organizations have only unassembled policy machinery, which does not really function at all or, if it does function, does so intermittently. The policy management and guidance function is to develop and maintain adequate policy machinery such that the agency can, and does, proceed in a systematic, thoughtful way to consider problems, develop policy proposals, secure ratification of the appropriate proposals, develop planning guidelines, and move toward the programming of the new policy and the revision of old policy. It is the best of *components* and *configurations* that transform (machines are always transforming one thing into something else) a loose series of ideas from the policy context into a policy agenda.

Policy machinery is:
- Persons
- Roles
- Tasks
- Processes

who and which transform ideas into guidelines
(See Exercise 6.1)

Components and Configurations

The concept of policy machinery is a processing concept, with certain components that need to fit into a loosely knit operating system. It is the system concept that is important here and the role of the policy manager is to develop the machinery so that it continually brings to the agency issues and problems, views and perspectives, which become important to the policy process. The policy context, the policy community, the policy elite, and the policy agenda represent important components of the policy machine.

However, these components do not always have the same configuration. Depending upon the issue, the policy context may well vary. The same can be said of the policy community and the policy elite. There may thus be several different policy machines that the policy manager needs to tend to, be aware of, and keep in operating order.

It is perhaps best to think of the policy machinery as a "loosely structured system" in which the elements configure to produce a policy agenda, but are not necessarily aware that this is in fact what is happening. The policy community, for example, may not know that it is the policy community. The policy manager needs to be continually involved in assessing what particular configuration is important for what particular policy area, what particular network of persons, tasks, roles, and processes link together for a specific area of policy interest. In short, two types of variations can occur within the policy machinery structure—one of components and one of configurations. Depending upon the area of policy concern, the components of the policy machinery may be different. One may need to put together different types of parts in order to have an efficient and effective policy machine. Alternatively, the configuration of components may differ. How one assembles them and the order in which one puts them together may vary as well. The policy manager, therefore, needs to be broadly knowledgeable about the policy system broadly conceived. As a particular policy problem comes up, a policy machine is specified to handle that particular problem. Like any professional, however, the policy manager needs to be broadly knowledgeable about a group of elements in the policy system. While the specifics may and should vary from policy concern to policy concern, one expects the policy manager to be aware of the policy context in her or his operating area, the relevant policy communities and important policy elites, and to be appraised as well of the current policy agendas within his or her community. It is important that local, state, and national levels be involved here as well. The policy machinery is the particular artifactual structure assembled to deal with a particular problem. However, as in other areas, one cannot simply start from scratch—call in a policeman to do a fireman's job. A particular fire will always require particular types of equipment, people, and strategies. One expects the fireman, the physician, or the policy manager to be broadly knowledgeable about what is available and what in general works and does not work in what types of general situations and to have some equipment available at all times. Hence, when a specific situation develops, that general knowledge can be applied. For the policy manager, this general knowledge concerns policy contexts, communities, elites, and agendas.

The Generalized Policy System

The generalized policy system is that loosely connected set of social structures that creates problems, identifies them, or suppresses them. It is the largest realm around and within which the policy manager works. The policy context is the collection of values and concepts relevant to the policy question. At a more specific level it is the policy community or those individuals and organizations most affected by particular problems and proposals. When we think of involving those affected we often tend to think of the negative effect. However, the positive effect is important to consider as well. Changes in agency policy, for example, should involve clients affected by that policy. It is not only that a restriction of benefits might affect clients, but an expansion might, as well. Clients might prefer an expansion in one area, while the agency might prefer expansion of benefits in another area. Clients may see themselves as needing more food while the agency may want to deliver more counseling. Funders, who may not have a great deal of substantive interest in a particular area, may however be interested in the total cost that a particular policy might involve and wish to be consulted in that area. The policy elite represents a subset of the policy community of particularly influential individuals and organizations, and it is that group that typically roughs out, at least, the policy agenda.

The Policy Context

The policy context is the broad set of values and ideas within which policy agendas are drawn. The policy manager needs to be aware of what the current and evolving context in her or his area is. Indeed, there may be more than one relevant context, and if so, those different contexts need to be known. The policy context is a phrase conveying the operational convergence of values, money, and power as they affect a particular policy realm. The policy machinery of a human service organization configures and transforms these elements into a workable policy proposal or two. Thus, the policy manager must be knowledgeable about current community, regional, and national conditions in each of these areas. Typically, her or his knowledge would be of broader scope and more detailed with respect to the local community and more specialized and focused at regional, state, and national levels. Consider someone in the field of aging who might work for an area agency. One would expect the policy manager to be knowledgeable about her or his professional field and what was happening with respect to it in the local community, and to be aware of other trends and currents within the local community—while at the levels of state and nation more focused knowledge with respect to aging would be the expected.

The policy manager needs to be sensitive to local values and perspectives, not only for the community as a whole, but also for the relevant subgroups of clients, professionals, and the various ethnic, geographic, and racial groups. Consider again the employee of the local area agency on aging. That person would need to know what the local values and value conflicts were with respect to the role and place of the older individual, the kinds of things local funders would fund, the different viewed subgroups would fund, and so on. It is hard to do what "Simon says" and link proposals to ascendent values if one does not know what they are.

Similarly, knowledge of current financial patterns and packages is an essential part of the policy context. For example, it is important for the human services policy manager to know what it is that United Way will, or is likely to, fund and what things it will not fund. It is important to know the other sources and limitations and funds, where commitments have already been made, and the like. Knowledge about foundations and their likes and dislikes is also crucial. Developing a proposal which is completely outside the terms of federal guidelines, for example, is not going to bode well for one's future influence.[1] The same could be said for people. The policy manager needs to know who is working where, what she or he can and can not do, and what her or his key skills are.

Finally, the policy manager must know who is in power, and what policies that individual, and the persons who surround that individual, prefers and will support.[2] Again, it is not a question of always going along with those policies. One may well wish to seek exceptions or to pursue different courses. But when a course has been chosen, there will most likely be opposition from certain centers of influence. One needs to take that kind of thing into account in advance.

These elements, then—ideas, money, and power—are elements that the policy manager must know while working to come up with some kind of proposal or set of proposals which have some chance of success. To ignore any component leaves a proposal vulnerable to early defeat.

The policy context contains:
- Values
- Money
- Power

applied to policy goals
(See Exercises 6.2a and 6.2b)

The Policy Community

The policy machinery touches and actualizes the wishes of the policy community or those persons, cultures, territories, and subcultures with a special interest in the areas at hand. In child welfare, for example, there are local and national policy communities made up of persons interested in the

1. The federal government in a variety of ways provides funds for social services on the basis of a state plan, and, of course, as "service providers" many private human service organizations find it a source of funding.

2. Both formal and informal power structures are important. Formal ones focus upon "office" positions; informal ones upon people said to be important. They can overlap or be quite distinct.

area, working in the area, or affected by the decisions made within the area. The policy community is not a fixed group of individuals and social organizations, but can change as time goes along. At times it is hard to enter such a policy community. There has been criticism of the private philanthropic community, for example, from minority organizations, which feel that in some instances they have not been able to secure appropriate representation and thus are excluded from the allocations process from the very beginning. Policy guidance requires not only an awareness of the character of the policy community, but cultivating it as well. Part of the informal activity of many executives serves precisely this function—finding out what some of the "community" members are thinking on a range of issues. Such activity serves not only as a source of ideas—communication from the community to the policy manager—but is also a way in which new policy ideas can be tested, "floated," made into "trial balloons " It is communication from the policy manager to the policy community. Often the communication to and from the policy community is done through the policy elite.

The policy community is those persons and organizations most affected by policy decisions
(See Exercise 6.3)

The Policy Elite

The policy elite consists of that set of groups and roles crucial in the policy community to the formation of policy in any given area. On the national scene, there are a subset of individuals whose views are a "must" on any policy in some area or another, and there are some roles whose occupants, by virtue of the role, must be invited to contribute. Often, members of the elite are possessed not with positive policy power, but with the ability to prevent what they do not want. It is this veto aspect of the policy process, in which members of the policy elite trade vetoes, that makes the policy process so often an experience in frustration. However, informal clearing, discussed earlier (chapter 3), makes it possible to hammer out some tentative agreements before the formal process begins. Such a process is, of course, open to abuse. But at the level of the human service agency, this informal process of clearing among the policy elite is very useful. The lack of clarity concerning goals, the many different interests involved, and the lack of a clear criterion, such as profit, through which alternatives, approaches, and persons can be tested, make clearing essential. It is important, too, for the policy manager to keep some kind of list, actual or mental, of who is interested in what policy realms, and to be sure that such persons are considered in the policy development phase or, if not, that their omission is deliberate, not simply inadvertent. While the board is certainly a crucial aspect of the policy elite at the agency level, crucial community professionals, important external suppliers of clients or cash (such as State Departments of Social Services or Correction, unions, client groups, or mental health, the United Way), crucial staff members, and client groups may often be important as well. While the policy elite includes those responsible for formal ratification, it is a broader group than that, and touching base with them is one way that the policy guidance specialist can see to it that political fences are mended.

The policy elite is that group of opinion leaders:
- Whose approval is most likely necessary *to achieve* positive policy action, and . . .
- Who can almost certainly *block* policy action
(See Exercise 6.4)

The Policy Agenda

The policy agenda is that set of items that can be said to form the docket of interest within the policy community broadly and within the policy elite specifically. It represents not only the items of concern to that group, but sets some priority for those items as well. Perhaps the issue is most clearly seen when a new executive takes over a family service organization. As she or he checks around the community, people will report those areas and issues that seem to be of most importance. Some will come from the policy community at large, some will come from the board, some will come from the staff, some will come from the clients, and some will be issues of personal interest to the executive. What might such issues be? Intake policy, fee policy, follow-up policy, the theoretical thrust of the agency, adoption policy, minority hiring, or parking might be among the issues typically found on such a docket.

Once the list has been established—it can be said to be the *agenda* of the *policy community*—the policy manager must rank the items accordingly to her or his judgment of which are the most important. This ranking process, which is also part of the agenda building activity, may involve a complex process of political weighting, including the executive's own preferences, or it may be a result of priority determination set by the board or by previous problems in the agency or whatever. This weighting role is one of special concern to us here and is perhaps one of the most understated aspects of the executive role.

The policy agenda involves:
- *Identifying* and
- *Setting priorities* for
- Items of policy attention
  (*See Exercise 6.5*)

It perhaps needs to be stressed that there is a long-range and a short-range policy agenda. The latter feeds into and informs the former. Items on the short-range policy agenda are usually those of most pressing concern. However, items on the longer-range policy agenda are no less important because less pressing. Indeed, frequently the "pressing" items are actually of lesser importance. The policy management process needs to pay special attention to the balanced handling of short- and long-range policy agenda setting. If one does not balance, the short-term items have a tendency to drive out the longer term ones.

Constructing the Policy Machinery

Given the changing nature of components and configurations, at least for specific purposes, the policy manager needs to have a range of skills at putting together instrumentalities that accomplish policy purposes as needed. Often such a machine is called a policy committee. It is a group of individuals who, in the judgment of the policy manager and other organization officials, have collectively good links to the policy context, represent elements of the policy community, are members of, or touch base with, the policy elite, and control, to some extent anyway, the policy agenda. It may involve people from the community, the organization, the board, client groups, and others. Indeed, it is the lowly committee, which, when assembled, becomes a crucial policy instrumentality, so much so that we need to spend additional time discussing it in subsequent chapters. These committees are sometimes more or sometimes less elaborate. But whatever they are, their essential policy function should not be obscured. They are a crucial setting for policy management.

The importance of the policy machinery concept lies in its assertion that policy is not simply a matter of coming up with a good idea and running with it to the board. That certainly has been true in the past, and human service organizations have tended to be as casual about policy development as other organizations. It is only in recent years that the concept of a "strategic" perspective within business and industrial organizations has developed, one which takes systematic account of what we have called here policy context or the external environment—how it is changing, what kinds of changes are developing, how these might affect the organization, and, of course, how the organization can exploit them to its own advantage. To a certain extent, this concept of strategic planning may become enlarged to focus on the internal aspects of the organization as well, in a more explicit and sustained way than has been true in the past. It is perhaps here that the idea of manager in the policy manager concept becomes most explicitly clear. One could think of other phrases, such as policy engineer, policy carpenter, the conductor of the policy orchestra. Policy development, ratification, and implementation is always a collective activity. This does not mean that a crucial idea may not come from an individual now and then, or that certain individuals may not have important places within the policy milieu. The American ideology of individualism still considers things as individual in their nature, cause, and cure, however much evidence is presented to the contrary. And it is certainly true that the policy manager as an individual must have certain skills, particularly with respect to the generation of ideas, their combining, and packaging. Nonetheless, it would be a great mistake for the human service executive to feel that simply appointing someone to the task of policy management, or setting up a job description called policy manager, solves the problem, under the assumption that somehow that individual can provide what is needed. What the individual provides is not only policy virtuosity in the sense of individual excellence in the performance of policy-generating and development tasks, but also the ability to construct and operate a series of policy machines.

Conclusion

The policy management process, then, is one that involves broad knowledge of the policy milieu. It includes the ability to construct a policy machine or adapt one already available relevant to the policy problem at hand, based upon and drawing from this broader knowledge. The particular policy machine, depending upon the problem, may have different components or configurations, and part of the skill of the policy manager is in sensing what particular type of configuration and what particular set of components are appropriate for a particular policy problem. Once this decision has been made and the policy machinery is assembled from what one might call the policy inventory, then it must be made to work, and, when its job is done, it must be disassembled. From a political science point of view one might call this policy machine a coalition. Assembling, maintaining, and disassembling is an important part of the skill of the policy manager. The accomplishment of these tasks, of course, is made more difficult if the policy manager does not have a sufficient inventory of personal knowledge and skill with respect to the local, state, and national communities.

For most human service organizations, the policy machinery is a Rube Goldberg rendition of a jug band. Even the concept of policy machinery is foreign to many executives. They will frequently say, "Well, I'll talk to a few people, and see what my board thinks, and then we'll run it up the flagpole and see which way the wind is blowing." Yet there really is a policy machinery in these casual observations, awkward though it may be. The ideas here will help human service practitioners to know the parts of the policy machine so that it can be started quickly and made to work well.

CASE ILLUSTRATIONS

THE CHILD WELFARE AGENCY

Jim sat in his office thinking about the ideas that were beginning to come in and sorting them out. He saw that he had three problems. One involved restructuring the internal organization, divesting it of some of its old parts and refurbishing and strengthening those that were the core of the agency's activities. A second dealt with the board. It was imperative that the ossification of board decision making and oversight activity be reversed. A vital board was absolutely necessary for the kind of agency he had in mind. A third problem lay in the environment. At the moment it was too turbulent. He had no sense of what might be happening that would affect his agency, or how he could control or shape some of those happenings.

Since the most immediate threat was external, he moved there most quickly. He established a Friends of Children Visiting Committee. He asked the executives of agencies most closely related to his to serve on it, as well as influential citizens and people who had expressed an interest in the organization. He invited about forty people and at the first meeting outlined some of his hopes, which involved revitalization of the agency with the help of the visiting committee, which might ultimately also be a source of board membership. He hoped that they would be a vehicle for interpreting to the larger community some of the things that the agency was trying to do and that they would come up with some suggestions as well. He reviewed with them the ideas that had been suggested for agency focus and asked their view on an advisory basis. The process of reconfiguration had begun.

The next step involved the board of directors. The board of the agency had ossified partly because it was so large that it could never really meet. It had sixty members and the stationery of the organization had more names than you could shake a stick at, but did not serve any real purpose. His goal, over the next year, was to move to a much more streamlined, smaller board and at the same time to move those individuals who remained interested onto the visiting committee. There, their interest could continue to be assessed, they could assist the agency, and if they wished to continue they could do so from there. For others it would simply be a way station to a graceful exit, the lack of which for many board members was one of the things that had caused problems for the agency. He envisioned now a board of maybe twenty or twenty-one who would be able to meet regularly, have some muscle and clout, and be able to cope with some of the material quickly and with thoughtfulness and quality.

Discussion Questions

1. The new executive is trying to put some policy machinery into place. Do you think he is building it well? Why or why not?
2. What other components might be needed?
3. What alternative configurations might be possible, or even better?

THE WELFARE PLANNING COUNCIL

The executive was pleased. The reorganization of her agency was beginning to take some shape. She was moving toward dividing it into sections. One section would be a social problems assessment section. The job of that group would be to monitor social trends and spot combinations of data that could lead to social problems or might themselves represent social problems. It would also perform a new version of the sort of historical problems audit that the agency had been conducting for many years. But it would be slightly converted into performance figures. The potential threat to other organizations was present, but she was determined to avoid letting that either interfere with her going ahead with it or letting it become a public way to lambaste other organizations. It would require some thought, but it could be handled.

Another section she was contemplating was a social proposal section to deal with developing and seeking out new ideas for handling some of the social problems. If necessary, individuals could visit experimental sites. They might even run research and demonstration projects in connection with the social problems division.

Since a number of these proposals would be taken to other boards, she had a small staff of two in charge of ratification. When the time came to take something for approval to a particular community board, these two would be involved. They were experts in knowing how to put things together in ways that would be most appealing and persuasive.

Then the historic social planning division would be recast. This group would swing into action only after the ratification of a piece of policy had occurred. The ratification people would also assist, and detailed planners would set to work drawing up some of the specifications for the next steps. The actual programming would, in most instances, be carried out by the agency staff, so the last area would be a social evaluation division sharing some members with the social problems division. That completed the loop that she was trying to design for the agency. People were a little bit uncertain, but willing to work.

Two studies had already been started by the social problems division with support from local foundations. One had to do with the extent to which certain individual families used multiple services and consumed far more than their appropriate share of community social services. She recalled the old study many years ago in St. Paul, done by Bradley Buell, called *Community Planning for Human Services*. In it Buell found that a small proportion of families consumed a large proportion of services. She thought that it was important to look at that problem again. A second study dealt with the whole problem of deinstitutionalization and the extent to which ghettos for the mentally retarded and mentally ill were being created in special sections of town. While deinstitutionalization was supposed to be cost effective, it was that way only if the community took up a fair share of the cost. The potential ghettoization and the need to deliver the same types of services, previously delivered in the institution, on a remote basis to a wide range of separate sites could drive the cost to double or triple that of the institutionalized cost. Furthermore, there was a question of urban warehousing. Both of these projects excited her a lot.

Discussion Questions

1. What policy community is being developed here? Is it the right one?
2. Is the appropriate policy context being shaped?
3. Who would the "policy elite" be here?

7

THE ROLES OF THE POLICY MANAGER

While the policy manager is one of the most crucial roles within the organization, it most frequently, I think, does not formally exist. The idea of policy management has not as yet become a legitimate part of the management lexicon in human service organizations. Yelaja (1975) mentions some roles for social policy practice and Mazzolini (1981) suggests a series of roles in the making of strategic decisions. The roles of the idea champion and planning diplomat have already been mentioned. Shapira comes very close in talking about "the preparation of social workers for executive positions." She says:

It follows, I hope, from the preceding remarks that our image of the executive task in a welfare system is that of an interior and innovator concerned primarily with transforming the system into a modern and effective tool for the achievement of social objectives [involving] . . . development within the system . . . by introducing greater reliance on scientific standards in the definition of the system's goals, ordering their priorities and developing means for their attainment and creation. . . .

This would mean executives tasks would—in contrast to the present pre-occupation with the immediate and the practical solutions—be primarily concerned with putting theoretical insights to use in system decisions. . . . What intellectual and personal capacities would we want for that task? I would emphasize most of all the risk taking qualities, the daring and the initiative usually associated with the entrepreneur. . . . The task obviously also requires a great deal of intellectual agility where the ability to think in an imaginative way and to cope with novel situations must be coupled with great rigor of analytic and systematic thought. This is indispensable for the use of the intellectual technologies required in the performance of those who manage and plan larger systems. (1971:65)

Shapira very clearly outlines the kinds of qualities which the policy managers should have but makes a mistake in locating them strictly within the executive. She may do that in part because there is no alternative role concept—here called a policy manager—which could embody some of these qualities and carry out some of the implied tasks on a regular basis. The executive cannot do everything. In the public service career Mark Moore raises the question of where policy managers are and uses the term policy manager. In his piece *Policy Managers Need Policy Analysis,* he speaks of the following goals that policy managers pursue within the organization:

Developing a forward looking strategy that (1) defines the goals of the organization, (2) offers a normative justification for continuing the organization's activities, and (3) gives priority to specific investments and innovations required to position the organization to accomplish its goals and keep pace with a changing environment. (Moore 1982:413)

Moore sees this as the final province of the executive. He adds:

But they are also aided by staffs with *special conceptual* and *analytic tools* [emphasis added]. These include (i) *corporate planners* who imagine alternative strategies . . . ; (ii) *market analysts* who estimate demands for given products . . . ; (iii) *financial analysts* who estimate capital requirements . . . ; and (iv) *new product designers and engineers* who seek to develop new or improve old products . . . [Emphasis in original.] (Moore 1982:414)

The human service organization may have special problems in defining the policy manager's role. Concerned as it is with people and the pressing problems they bring to the organization, it is more difficult to take a longer term perspective in the training of executives. Shapira (1971) has pointed out that executive training tends to leave out crucial components. The policy manager is one who seeks to rectify this imbalance, who seeks to bring policy management to the forefront. What is the nature of such a person's activities?

The job of the policy manager, then, involves essentially three elements. One is working with ideas. This task involves finding out which ideas are appropriate to particular problems, getting the relevant information, and pulling ideas from different sources together. (Recall the discussion of "Root Binding" from chapter 3.)

The second aspect of the job involves working with people. Blending the skills of people toward the accomplishment of social tasks is a crucial element. Ideas must be accepted, and often good ideas are not accepted because of deficiencies in interpersonal skills and technique.

Third, the policy manager needs to work with documents. Because policy is written, it is essential that the policy manager be involved in drafting the various policy reports and documents that lay the groundwork for ratification and, of course, the final proposal for ratification itself.

Three crucial tasks of policy management are:
- Working with ideas
- Working with people
- Working with documents

Role Sets for the Policy Manager

The question of how the process of working with people, ideas, and documents can be set up within the organization is an important one and best approached through the idea of role sets, or clusters of roles, with a number of important subroles that, taken together, can provide for the successful accomplishment of the policy management function. It is important to think in terms of roles rather than individuals, because, while sometimes a single individual may play all of the roles, frequently several individuals will play several roles, creating problems of policy role integration within the organization. There seem to be six major role sets involved in the policy management activity: 1) knowledge development roles, 2) interpersonal roles, 3) conflict management roles, 4) political roles, 5) organizational roles, and 6) policy group roles. In the two role set categories, organizational and policy group, there is a movement from the role to the position because, in those areas, specific assignments are frequently linked to job descriptions.

Knowledge Development Roles

As a central focus of the policy management function, knowledge development must come high on the list. This is not research in the usual sense, although a research role is involved. Rather, it involves elements of pulling together information from extant sources, crystallizing, and then compiling it, anticipating the kinds of information and evidence that might be needed and trying to bring them together.

Crystalizer. The policy manager is a "spark," a "crystalizer," one who "precipitates" ideas, one who translates "stuff" from the policy context into proposals that can be considered. She or he culls the interests of colleagues within the human service agency system for items from the policy agenda, then proceeds to combine them into material useful for her or his agency. The policy manager is an "intelligence officer" for the agency, absorbing a range of information from the policy community, linking that information with whatever information she or he has personally, and merging it with elements of the policy machinery. Then he or she brings forward ideas for consideration, ideas that look ahead, that nip problems before they become problems; in general, he or she exercises policy leadership. Policy leadership is what "good" leaders do.

Compiler. The policy manager is one who acts as a compiler acts on a computer, or as a translator acts, taking the loose set of ideas, impressions, and suggestions floating around the policy community and fashioning them into something useful for the organization. Often this process does not occur, and therefore problems develop that need a great deal of organizational energy to solve. Too, the available set of ideas for problem solution in any given instance might not be adequate for the problem's handling. The additional time provided by policy proactivity is useful here in simply reviewing possible solutions.

Time does not always permit this, however, and the policy manager, because he or she has worked along these lines, will have a background of possible solutions to problems that can be called upon in crisis situations, and upon which one can plan.

Anticipator. The policy manager's real strength lies in the ability to be proactive, to bring things together out of a complex set of activities in the policy community, to have a "synthetic" style, which can blend the many different facets of a solution into one with the potential for success. Many issues in the policy community remain latent until some crisis pushes one to the surface, or some person (the idea champion) (Daft and Bradshaw 1980) makes a convincing case. Policy leadership is the task of assisting some of these issues to surface before a crisis arises, and thus creating an atmosphere in which a solution may be sought involving less organizational energy, but more intelligence.

Researcher/Synthesizer. The policy manager seeks to be generally acquainted with scientific and research developments in her or his field and to have that information available for the policy development process. Sometimes this information is of an evaluative sort and might contain elements of evaluations, assessments, and other kinds of programmatic reviews, the implications of which could pertain to the activities of the agency in question. For example, if some other agency has reviewed adoption practices and published a study, then the policy manager would need to know that and bring it to the attention of organizational managers. On the other hand, the information may be of a more general sort that does not specifically pertain to activities the organization is undertaking now. It is useful for policy managers to do a state-of-the-research report for the staff on a semi-annual or quarterly basis, thus giving an opportunity for the review process to be shared with others and giving a certain degree of reality to the information search.

The policy manager's knowledge development role set includes:
- Crystalizing
- Compiling
- Anticipating
- Researching and synthesizing

(*See Exercise 7.1*)

Interpersonal Roles

An important component of knowledge development roles for the policy manager is the development of a set of interpersonal roles which focus essentially on the mobilization of people rather than the mobilization of ideas. Moore makes this point with respect to training in policy analysis when he says:

Moreover, emphasizing policy analysis may repel students who have institutional (as opposed to substantive) concerns, and operational (as opposed to contemplative) temperaments. The net result is that these schools produce applied social scientists who make marginal contributions to the design of policies. The much more important jobs of leading institutions in making them perform effectively are left to others. (p. 413)

The implication that there are active and contemplative postures and that these cannot be fused is also suggested by Hirschman (1982:7, 131), but this dichotomous emphasis would be fatal to the policy manager, leaving her or him in the impotent position Moore describes. Hence, interpersonal roles aimed toward stimulating ideas, refining them, and combining people in ways that generate new perspectives are an important part of policy management.

Enabler. The enabler role is one which seeks, through support and encouragement, to let ideas spring from others. The policy manager enables others to formulate and express their perspectives, their points of view, in a supportive context.

Motivator. The policy manager may also serve as an idea motivator. Idea motivation is often a group activity rather than a one-to-one activity, as is characteristic of the enabler role. As idea motivator, the policy manager seeks to set up conditions in which ideas can be shared and perspectives explored. Some organizations, for example, have a "half-baked-ideas luncheon," which allows people to share ideas and explore concerns in their beginning phase without fear of scorn or ridicule. It is of interest that the new *Journal of Policy Analysis* has a section called "Insights," in which more loosely framed and less detailed ideas can be offered for consideration. The Moore quotation above comes from a special "Insights" section entitled "Wild Ideas" about public management, edited by Robert D. Behn.

Challenger. Interpersonal roles are not always of the pleasant and supportive type however. Another role, that of challenger, frequently needs to be played. Here, the policy manager takes the position of diplomatic, but critical and questioning, adversary. The human service organization, like other organizations, is replete with organizational myths, with certainties about what works and what does not, about what is true and what is not, about what clients are and what they are not, about what is possible and what is not. It is frequently difficult to apply knowledge to these kinds of ideological and mythological statements and postures. Hence, it is important for the policy manager to, at times and again diplomatically, demand evidence or inquire how someone knows that something is true. Sometimes, based on the policy manager's knowledge of development activities, information contrary to prevailing organizational myth will be available. That information might well be laid on the table with a sense of concern about how a particular myth and the available evidence might be reconciled, since they seem to point in opposite directions. This role is not as unusual as it may seem. It is sometimes called the "devil's advocate" (Haft 1981), and people frequently announce that they are "going to play the devil's advocate role for a moment" immediately prior to raising some serious questions about a particular proposal or direction. The policy manager needs to be aware that the playing of the devil's advocate or challenger role generates interpersonal stress and has to be prepared to deal with that. On the other hand, it is useful to play that role from time to time as a counterbalance to the more positive enabler and motivator roles. If those first two roles are the only ones the policy manager plays, colleagues may feel that the policy manager lacks a critical posture.

Interpersonal roles include:
- Enabler
- Motivator
- Challenger

Conflict Management Roles

To be in an organization is to experience conflict. Differing political perspectives, differing points of view, differing personal involvements all combine to make daily life in the human service organization one of conflict and stress. Frequently, conflict emerges from a variety of sources, sometimes involving clients, staff, boards, or elements of the community. Part of the job of the policy manager is that of conflict resolver.

Solution Provider. Some conflicts exist simply because no one has any idea of how to get out of the particular conflict. Here the role of knowledge developer can be put to specific use in providing an idea for resolving a conflict. All too frequently, organizational conflicts remind us of children arguing, one saying "you did" and the other saying "you didn't," with no way to break out of the cycle. (In fairness, it should be recognized that while that perspective is likely to be accurate at a distance, conflicts that we are personally involved in rarely seem, at the moment of involvement, quite so childish.)

Negotiator. The policy manager will sometimes be asked to perform the role of negotiator or mediator, bringing disputing parties together and seeing if there are ways in which their disputes can be resolved. The negotiator role requires knowledge development skills as a central component, because new perspectives and new ways of looking at things often are the key to providing satisfactory solutions. However, interpersonal skills are required as well and the whole area of negotiating and mediating is a skill one can practice on a full-time basis. It is likely, though, that the policy manager will get involved on an occasional basis in negotiating and mediating, because most disputes involve differing perspectives about what the facts are, what the evidence shows, and what conclusions one can draw from the evidence, leaving aside interpersonal hostilities and stresses that may have generated or will surely compound the conflict management task.

Conflict management roles include:
· Solution provider
· Negotiator

Political Roles

The activities of the policy manager as so far discussed seem even-handed, balanced, and devoid of partisanship and preference. And while generally true, indeed the success of a policy manager depends in part at least on its being true, there are times when the policy manager needs to take a more focused "political" stance.

The Advocate. Policy managers at times need to act as advocate for certain groups or for certain types of solutions, especially because of their role in human service organizations. Such organizations have, as a primary part of their mission, service to the dispossessed, minorities, those of low income and low self esteem, and others who, because of personal situations, are not in the best position to advocate their own interests. Thus, the interests of the clients are in some sense taken on by the policy manager. Preparing newspaper articles, magazine articles, and leaflets and posters for distribution are some of the ways that the role of advocate is carried out. Interviews on television are another. This "other-interested advocate role" frequently has an element of self-interest and that should be recognized as well. Arguing for the support of the disadvantaged can also mean support for the agency as an instrument for serving the disadvantaged. Hence, the policy manager needs to be aware of that component of self-interest and able to deal with criticisms of it.

Lobbyist. Sometimes the policy manager works as a lobbyist, seeking to influence decision-making groups at the city, state, regional, and national levels. This role may include presentations to political figures, getting political figures involved in affairs of the organization, and presenting them with information supportive of the agency's position. The lobbyist is similar to the advocate. The primary difference is that while the role of advocate is a generalized partisan one, that of the lobbyist tends to focus on influencing government figures.

Mobilizer. Sometimes the advocate role merges into a mobilizer role or a mobilizer role develops as an adjunct to the lobbyist role. Mobilization involves the assembling of people power and money power to accomplish certain political ends. Such activities as fund-raising, the development of mass meetings, and the development of cadres of individuals involved in leafleting tend to be part of the mobilizing role. One thinks here of "mass organization" as involving fairly large numbers of people in activities like marches on Washington, marches on the state capitol, or hunger vigils. Historically, mobilization has been one aspect of what in the social work field has been called a community organization role.

Coalition Building. A fourth type of political role that the policy manager might play is that of coalition building. Because of its partisan and political history, this particular type of policy machinery tends to focus on achieving a particular goal. It is somewhat like an interest group, except that it has a sense of shortness and focus to it, whereas interest groups tend to exist over longer periods of time and have somewhat broader commitments. Coalitions often arise in response to specific types of political development and may bring together a wide range of people who may not agree on much else. Coalition building tends to focus on those individuals who have important links to other organizations and hence to have a confederated character. While all of these organizations may not agree exactly with the goals of the coalition, a sufficient commonality exists, making it worthwhile to join. Usually, coalition builders seek organizational links and organizational representations, but they also make it possible for individuals to join *as* individuals.

Organizational Partisan. The roles discussed so far tend to focus outside the organization or involve the organization with others in seeking to advance the organization's cause or well-being. However, it is also possible to play a partisanship role within the organization and seek to promote a certain type of organizational structure or a certain type of organizational policy. To an extent it is legitimate for the policy manager to also be the policy partisan. This role must be managed with a very delicate sense of balance and timing, because, as mentioned, part of the success of the policy manager's role focuses on the quality of the decision, that is in trying to get the best decision available, not necessarily the one preferred by the policy manager. If a situation arises where too often the "best decision" also becomes "the one the policy manager prefers," members of the organization will simply see the policy manager as one more focal point of political pressure and she or he becomes discredited as a policy manager. Yet it is also unreasonable to assume that a policy manager would be utterly devoid of preferences and prejudices. Hence it is the balance of neutrality and partisanship that is important—a balance that should, in the main, tilt toward neutrality.

Political roles include:
- Advocate
- Lobbyist
- Mobilizer
- Coalition builder
- Partisan

Organizational Roles

The policy manager roles discussed so far are possible assignments and configurations of assignments necessarily linked to specific organizational jobs (other than the job of policy manager itself). Within the organization, however, these more general roles may be carried out through some specific types of role assignments that deserve mention.

Special Assignment. It is quite possible for someone who has an otherwise direct service responsibility to be given an assignment handling a policy matter of a particular sort at a particular time. One example, in a human service organization, might be an accreditation visit of some sort. Sometimes human service organizations are members of larger organizations with national standards and the periodical need for review. Another example might be the annual budget preparation for a funder such as the United Way or for some special kind of funding request the agency is contemplating. These are examples of a host of possible special policy tasks which could be taken on by someone and which have the character of policy management tasks, although they will not be thought of in that way, nor will they be called policy management tasks.

Assistant to the Executive. Sometimes the executive will ask a staff member to serve as her or his assistant. This is different from an associate role in which the executive shares direction and management of the agency with a deputy. Rather, it is someone who serves the executive directly, who may act as a sounding board or perform a variety of other roles. This person can be very important to the executive as an individual who can discuss, fairly candidly and directly, organizational situations. Argyris (1982) points out that people in high positions tend to get poor information because of three organizational tendencies—distancing, undiscussability, and counterproductive advice. *Distancing* occurs as a form of denial when an issue comes up in the organization that no one wants to deal with. *Undiscussability*, which most readers will recognize I am sure, refers to those topics in an organization (or in a family or marital unit, for that matter) which cannot be discussed. It is almost as if there were a conspiracy, silent and unacknowledged but nonetheless powerfully present, to avoid touching on matters of central importance. *Counterproductive advice* seems best characterized as lying, but it has overtones of fawning and self-aggrandizement. The policy manager in an assistant role has, at times, the unpleasant task of embracing the difficult issues rather than distancing herself or himself from them, of discussing undiscussable issues, and of being a relatively straightshooter. Sad to say, all executives do not appreciate the need for those traits, but, as Argyris points out, the current situation leads to delayed and often bad decision-making.

Consultant. Sometimes a policy manager may be brought in from the outside as a consultant to the organization. He or she may be a member of the human service community. Often, policy management functions become initiated in this way. It is sometimes difficult to see people with whom one has worked in a particular way as working in a different way, or for those individuals to take on, without some transition process, different roles and functions. Hence, the outside consultant, who can assist the organization in accomplishing some set of policy goals, is frequently a good choice. Accreditation visits from national organizations are a case in point. Often, as a preliminary step, an expert in the accreditation process will be invited to spend some time with the organization and can advise the organization on the various elements involved in a particular problem. Alternatively, an organization may not be of sufficient size or wealth to have someone routinely take on policy management tasks. On the other hand, it could free a few resources to hire someone on a monthly basis to perform policy management functions, particularly those of knowledge development, translation, and synthesis. While at first this may seem odd, human service executives will immediately recognize that, at least within the clinical realm, the use of a visiting psychiatrist for selective supervision has been a long and well-established practice. Many organizations, which could not afford to have a psychiatrist on the staff full-time, can use one as a consultant. The same is true for policy management, and it is as true and as important for the same reasons that clinical consulting is important.

Organizational roles can be:
- Special assignment
- Assistant to the Executive
- Task and process split
- Consultant

Policy Group Roles

As suggested in the last chapter, policy committees, or groups, represent one of the most important instruments through which policy activity in an organization is carried out. For this reason, one of the more important assignments that a policy manager has is to these policy committees. There are several ways in which these assignments may be carried out.

Staffer. A policy manager may well be assigned to the staff of a policy committee. As a staffer, this individual is involved in assisting the committee to accomplish its purpose. Such a role typically involves all the other policy manager roles, including knowledge development and interpersonal and documentary skills (Tropman et al. 1981).[1]

The process portion of the role involves setting up the links—committees, meetings, rules for review—so that there is a relatively constant, if low level, progress on policy matters. Additionally, the process activity of the policy manager involves setting up the structures for ratification. Each of these points will be dealt with in more detail in later chapters—the process activity in the chapter on policy committees, and the substantive/task activity in the chapter on the role of the policy staffer.

1. A word about usage is important here for clarification. To "staff" a committee is to be assigned to it as an aide, not as a member. While one is often on the staff of the organization for which one is "staffing" the committee, the two uses of staff have different senses. It is for this reason that I used the Washington term "staffer" to indicate when someone is assigned to a committee to perform staff functions for it.

Chair/Member. Sometimes the policy manager is asked to chair or be a member of a policy-formulating group. In these roles, of course, there is a lesser degree of neutrality and a greater degree of substantive partisanship. Often these roles are not recognized for the policy management roles that they are. Take, for example, a program committee within an organization or a staff advisory committee. These represent important policy activities and should be approached thoughtfully and with preparation and attention rather than casually and with inattention. Executives need to recognize that these are important roles, demanding time, and must make some of that time available through administrative assignment.

The Executive as Policy Manager

Perhaps most frequently the executive himself or herself fills the policy role, using others as needed but essentially being the individual we think of as policy manager. This pattern, which in my observation is the most common one, can be either the most successful or, more typically, the greatest failure. It can be successful when the executive uses some of the functions, administratively—in terms of assignments, funds, control over material—to implement some policy initiative. Thus, such initiatives are not wasted, withering away somewhere in a closet full of reports.

The reasons for failure are more commonplace. Most executives do not see the role of policy manager as part of their job. Indeed, most do not know anything about it, have never conceived of it, do not know what it is. The management of ideas seems, to many, a very academic and theoretical phrase, with no basis in reality. Add to this perspective the press of daily organizational life, the ringing phone, the people dropping in, and the doing job becomes more complex still. In practice, many executives rely upon an executive secretary for these matters and it is here that one of the great sources of power of the secretary rests. She or he can bring ideas to the attention of the executive, save time, make contact with the board, and so on. Much opportunity for initiative is available here, which is sometimes used and sometimes not.

The executive as policy manager is often too pressed with day-to-day business to attend to policy matters
(See Exercise 7.2)

Delegation of Policy Matters

It is appropriate for the human services executive to assume some of the roles of policy management. Without that responsibility, policy innovation and development will not occur. However, it is also difficult, because of the press of daily business, for this role to become a central one for that same executive. Thus, delegation becomes an answer here, as with administrative roles generally.

One individual on the staff of the agency, given the title of agency policy specialist, will spend an agreed-upon portion of his or her time working on policy-relevant matters. In this particular case the title is important, because it must appear in the agency lexicon of duties and be recognized by the staff of the agency, the executive, and the person himself or herself. All too often the assignment of such responsibilities is casual in the extreme, if made at all. The executive calls in one of his or her staff, whom the executive has reason to believe would be good at policy-relevant work, and asks whether or not it would be a good idea to do a little long-range planning, looking at agency goals, rethinking the fee policy of the agency, or whatever. Often this occurs at a time of crisis. Some issue has come up which makes one of these questions a burning one. But after the burning question has been re-solved, there is a tendency to let the assignment drop. Without some official designation, there will most likely be no followup. It would be helpful, if regular reporting to the executive were required concerning the activities undertaken. For example, meeting for a half hour on a monthly basis in an "agency policy conference" can serve as an anchor for which, and around which, the other activities of this role can flow. A specific set of files and recognition that some small budgetary demands may be made would also be helpful.

When the executive delegates policy management roles to a subordinate, these are some of the points to keep in mind, both by the executives and by the employee. Perhaps most crucial, however, is that some regular atten-tion to policy matters can occur within the current structure of almost any agency. It is not costly, it is not a "big deal." Rather, it requires explicit recognition that this task is one that needs to be done and developing some method of doing it. It is all too often the failure of imagination, rather than the more conventional "problems with resources," which make the differ-ence. And, paradoxically enough, the failure of imagination which permits policy to lapse is the very same style and structure which lets policy proactivity lapse. The development of policy roles prefigures an organizational culture already attuned to policy problems and management, therefore one that would be more receptive to proposed solutions in the first place. The assignment of a policy role is thus a message to the organization and the staff that these are problems to which attention will be paid; it serves as both a signal and an embodiment of that orientation.

The delegated policy role:
- May begin in times of crisis, but needs to continue thereafter
- Should be long-range in orientation
- Should involve regular conferences on a monthly basis

The Policy Unit

Sometimes, and increasingly so today, larger organizations in the human service field go beyond a role and assign a few people in an "office." Essentially, these individuals and their policy unit seek to "read" the environment and develop organizational strategies for dealing with three crucial problems—*complexity, heterogeneity,* and *instability.* As these problems increase, the organization needs to develop an internal structure of management to articulate with the external pressures. Thus, when an organization is faced with a complex, highly differentiated environment of some instability, it must have an internal corporate ability to deal with problems. If it does not, the environment is likely to swamp the organization, to overwhelm it with demands it cannot react to appropriately. Many human service organizations, for example, are pressed with accounting demands from the United Way organization, from federal funders, from client groups, from a range of other state and federal organizations involving safety or environmental protection, from staff unions and other staff groups, from the National Association of Social Workers, from licensing agencies, from social work organizations of other sorts, such as Child Welfare League of America or the Family Service Society. It is hard for a human service organization of even modest size to keep up with this heterogeneity of demands. All too often, the internal structure of the organization has not been differentiated properly and sufficiently to meet these external challenges, to say nothing of developing an appropriate style of response.

One way in which some organizations have proceeded is to establish a policy unit, a group of employees with the responsibility of overseeing the organizational response to these internal/external pressures, not in terms of the actual "doing" of the relationship activities themselves, but involving several other tasks:

1. *Outlining External Pressures (Policy Context)*

The policy unit seeks to understand and communicate within the agency the overall structure of the environmental forces facing the agency.

It is at this point that the policy and planning unit will seek to make contact with external agencies to secure additional information, if not about specific demands which will be made, then about the general nature and character of demands. For example, federal funders are notorious about dates and content of specific grants one may wish to consider. Contact with them can serve to outline, at least, the parameters of their wishes, and a skeleton draft can be prepared and shared with relevant people in the organization and board approval secured on a contingency basis.

2. *Designing a Strategic Response*

The policy unit crafts an overall strategic response, for the agency, to these pressures and demands. Such a strategy may involve the development of an overall policy calendar, which lists crucial dates insofar as they are known, suggests staff allocations and personal assignments to correspond with the calendar, to give people some sense of the upcoming events. In this case, knowledge is power, in that the more in advance events are anticipated, the less stress it will take to deal with them.

After a response strategy has been developed, the policy unit begins to look at the substance of each issue and to develop substantive, as opposed to procedural, strategy. Substantive strategy relates to the content of a response to an external or internal pressure, rather than to matters of timing and location in a sequence of events. For example, having established the fact that there will be a certain grant deadline and that work must begin in June in order to meet the funding requirements of October, one needs to consider what one will say in such a grant, and how the text of that grant, which must be written in any case, may be used elsewhere and serve several other purposes as well.

3. *Working With Key Policy Committees*

The policy unit, in addition to assisting the executive, works with key policy committess within the agency to secure their inputs within a relevant time frame, as well as to acquaint them with the problems and difficulties ahead. This process also alerts them to some of the upcoming issues and the specific nature and content of the ideas with which they will be dealing.

4. *Developing Policy Documents*

As is already clear, the policy unit develops the basic outlines for style and contents of the various policy documents and involves other relevant staff and consultants as well as appropriate board members, outsiders, and the executive. Each policy element here will eventually be reduced to a draft of something—for example, a grant proposal, a new board policy, or a statement that can be used by a review team. As developer and custodian of all policy proposals, the policy and planning unit is in the best position to seek what else the agency has done that might be relevant, to pull that material together, and assign someone to coordinate the particular proposal or document. Once a draft has been developed (and this involves, by the way, contacting many people for information and using the intellectual resources of the community and nation as well), it is circulated to relevant individuals for comment and review.

The policy and planning unit, then, contains within itself the three central skills of the policy manager—working with ideas, working with people, and working with documents. The ideas need to be blended with people and reduced to documents, which are then shared with people and revised to meet their suggestions and to incorporate new ideas as they come into the field from external sources. Often the policy manager will be an "expert," especially knowledgeable about one field of interest or one policy arena, but sometimes not. In any event, these three components are essential for the unit, whether each person has all of these skills or whether two or three different people in the unit have them.

Two other points deserve stress here. One is that the unit works both on short- and long-range elements of the agency's operation and sets up a schedule dividing the work between the two. A great danger to the unit, which usually resides in the office of the executive, is that it becomes captured by the rush of business flowing through that office and thus becomes sort of an extension of the executive. When this happens, it is no longer a policy and planning unit in the terms I have described. Short-term work is always possible, but it should be done within the context of a longer-term agenda.

The second point of importance is the need for policy and planning staff to work both inside and outside the organization. Too often, one of these is forgotten; often it is the need to work with inside staff. The policy and planning people come up with good ideas, then find they have no support inside the organization. Time must be spent both in building relationships and in sharing ideas and perspectives.

The policy unit performs the key tasks of policy management by:
- Outlining external pressures
- Designing a strategic response
- Working with key policy committees
- Developing policy documents

The Part-Time Policy Manager

Most of these activities could be carried out well if the policy manager were assigned this task on a full-time basis. Unfortunately, in human service organizations, most are not, and the roles are often shared with another task assignment.

One Issue, One Time. It is not uncommon for someone who has some direct service responsibility for clients or some other responsibility to be asked to look after another area of concern to the agency, for example, an upcoming accreditation by a national or local body. Thus, one way part-time can occur on a single-issue basis.

Sounding Board. At other times, the executive will use an individual as a sounding board and, for a portion of the day, an assistant. In this capacity, part-time policy management is limited in time, but the issue is general, as opposed to the above example, which concerned a specific issue.

Task and Process Split. Still a third pattern is for two persons to play two subroles within the policy framework—one handling task items and one handling process items. One person in a child welfare agency, for example, may handle the task of alerting the executive to emerging developments in the child welfare field, while another may handle the arrangement of meetings and the liaison with the board (other than that done by the executive).

Any of these approaches can work well if the executive provides a policy coordination leadership role. Unfortunately, all too often the executive does not provide this leadership and coordination, and because those to whom various tasks have been delegated are subordinate, policy matters cannot be brought to the attention of the boss in any authoritative way.

The part-time policy manager is one who takes policy management on:
- A one-time, one-issue basis
- A sounding-board basis
- A task/process-division basis

Role-Set Integration

The foregoing material suggests the complexities involved in the roles of the policy manager. Sometimes these roles belong to a single individual and must be merged with each other as well as with other ongoing roles in the organization. That is one type of role integration problem. A second occurs when a single individual is fully assigned to the policy management function. In that case the individual has to be able to maintain a policy management capability while at the same time entering to some degree into the daily life of the organization. For reasons of interpersonal prestige and reward, as well as the excitement of daily on-line activity, it is not infrequently the case that policy planners and policy planning units find themselves fighting fires instead of designing new equipment. There is an excitement to fire fighting that the rather more placid new equipment finds hard to match.

Hence, constant pressure erodes the policy planner and the policy planning unit. (The same pressure, of course, is present with a part-time policy manager, although the press for demonstration of organizationally approved competence in on-line duties is perhaps not as great there.)

When the executive performs the policy management role, there are other types of difficulties. For example, the inherent need for time and exploration involved in policy management tends to conflict with the rapid breaking demands in other aspects of the executive role. The call of the concrete often results for many executives in the victory of the visible, leaving undiscovered and better alternatives for other organizations at other times.

In the larger human service organization, the large bureaucracy or megabureaucracy where policy planning units exist, the same pressures are compounded by the need to integrate within the unit itself its perspectives and activities. This is often made more difficult by the lack of systematic training for policy managing professionals and the likelihood that individuals with limited or inappropriate backgrounds may be assigned policy management functions. The problem is, of course, only potential; it does not always occur, but is one to be aware of. In addition, there are the tensions inherent in dealing with task and process activities and in dealing with a number of emerging activities at the same time. Special attention to integration needs to be given. How might it be done?

There are no good answers to this question, but some procedures might be helpful. The first is simple recognition of the types and dimensions of conflict and the nature of the pressures they bring. While recognition is not itself a solution, it tends to lessen some of the pressure, which may at times build up to a very serious level. We have all experienced the rush of relief when a problem is "recognized." At least that gives us something to work on.

The first kind of recognition, of course, is self-awareness. The policy manager needs to be aware that there is a problem, or an issue, of role conflict, and whether that conflict is among different aspects of the policy manager role-set or between that role-set and some other aspect of organizational activity, such as a clinical role. Other types of conflict might occur as well. The distancing that the policy manager needs to maintain to be effective as a scrutinizer of the current agency process may cause problems with colleagues in the agency. Then, too, the role of devil's advocate or some other similar role can, in the long term, build up some negative reactions.

Inherent in the policy manager's activity—looking for new and better solutions to the organization's activities and even changing (or proposing change in) those activities—lies a threat to current staff. Even in the mildest form, proposing new approaches implies criticism of those using, and advocating, current approaches. Even in a benefit-benign setting (one in which someone is using, but not especially benefitting from, a current approach or procedure) the threat of change is likely to generate resistance. Sometimes (more often than many of us care to admit) situations are benefit-malignant; that is, individuals are personally gaining in some way from a particular procedure or approach, and change means loss of some important benefits or perquisites. Whatever the reason, policy managers are likely to be in a position of potential, and frequently actual, estrangement from their colleagues. Recognizing this likelihood is important for the policy manager. It is also important for the executive to recognize it. The executive is able to provide some concrete assistance to make life easier—through making time adjustments, picking up costs, shaping the assignments of the policy manager to a reasonable number. The policy manager can brief the executive on policy progress through regularly scheduled meetings. These meetings are an important part of the work of policy management, because they not only serve to educate the boss to the issues of policy relevance, but give the boss some feel for what the policy manager is doing and educate her or him to the function of policy management itself.

Conclusion

In the human service field, the time has perhaps passed when a few individuals in one organization can do policy and planning work. There is too much complexity within the human services, too many differing expectations, too great a series of problems and difficulties, for this to occur. Each organization should develop its own policy and planning capability, however modest such an effort must be. The establishment of a role, a person, or a small staff responsible for policy and planning is, in today's society, essential for the very survival of the organization. I should like to stress again that such activities are not to be confused with administration, the daily decision making about problems that occur and the daily management of events. Rather, policy management is the development, ratification, and implementation of ideas, using the pressures upon the organization to advantage as a lever for improvement and progress. The policy manager is one of a new breed of organizational executives who will help the human service organization do a better job, and a more effective one, who will design measures to test these claims, and who will make it possible for the agency to continue functioning in a complex environment.

CASE ILLUSTRATIONS

THE CHILD WELFARE AGENCY

Jim sat back in his chair and felt fatigued but pleased. The first three months of his acting directorship had gone far better than he expected. When he had taken over the president and he had gone out for a drink, the president, who had only recently begun to find out some of the problems and difficulties, had told Jim that, frankly, he was an undertaker and the board would see to it that he got a little extra compensation for performing this unpleasant role. The board did not expect that anything could be done. The board seemed to feel that the agency was like a 1927 car that had suddenly been pulled out of the garage. While it had been a champion once, it could not now compete with the best and, in any event, the lack of attention and the deterioration over the years made the board too tired to want to even think about giving the race a shot.

But that was not the way things had turned out. The funders had agreed to a moratorium. They did not have many alternatives anyway, even though they were dissatisfied. The agency friends' group had started to function and already twelve people had left the board of directors and moved to the friends' group. Another ten were scheduled to move fairly soon. The most difficult problem was the internal restructuring, and that was not yet complete. The substance abuse section had been closed and files and activities there turned over to the substance abuse agency in town, with a pledge to cooperate. That agency was delighted. The Winnebagos had been sold and several of the outlying offices had been closed. The cash flow situation was actually much better than one might have thought and Jim had one ace up his sleeve: he had been informed that a will had recently been probated which left the agency $500,000 in cash and an estate up north. It wasn't an estate, really— it was sort of a hunting and fishing lodge with about a thousand acres and several lakes. There were some upkeep problems, but he had already talked to the recreation foundation and was able to get a small grant to handle some of them while the agency decided how to proceed. They could, of course, sell the property, but he thought that that would be not the way to go. Rather, it might be a site for a camp operated by the agency. If the site would permit, and it looked very much as though it would, the lodge could become a hideaway meeting place. There might be ways to organize professional conferences for parents while their children were at the camp in the summer. In any event, the interest from the funds invested in bonds at 10 percent would now provide an income of at least $50,000 a year to the agency. While that certainly would not resolve their financial problems, it would provide a substantial rebalancing of their endowment and the income could be used for a variety of useful purposes. None of that would be finally and officially settled for several months, so he had the virtue of that security without necessarily having the news dull the edge of crisis still present within the agency. One idea he had was commissioning the Welfare Planning Council to do a small study. It would be an organizational/environment assessment, taking some of the ideas he had developed, which had come from the agency and the committee, and it would also take a look at the demographic and the emerging demographics and make some suggestions about future directions.

The council was really picking up some steam. What pleased him the most, though, was Sam. Sam had really begun to fill out as an assistant to him and was operating beautifully while still carrying a caseload. He had completed the task of securing and assessing ideas from a number of individuals in the organization and a pattern was beginning to emerge. Sam was working back and forth between the organizational members and Jim's office and was also taking on some of the responsibilities of briefing the board. In addition, Sam had come up with a number of useful ideas himself and had fed those into the process. What was nice, too, was the sort of enthusiasm that Sam had for the organization. For the first few weeks after Jim had taken over, going to work was like going to a showing of "Night of the Living Dead"—people stood around and automatically went through the motions. They had been certain that the axe was going to fall and that it was only a matter of days or hours. But gradually it had dawned on them that the axe was not going to fall, that the axe wasn't even in the barnyard. Here and there throughout the organization hope began to spring up. Sam had had a good deal to do with that. His own enthusiasm was infectious to some extent. He acted as a sort of spark, but he was also receptive to what people wanted to say. The older director had increasingly closed himself off and for that reason staff had stopped making suggestions. There really was no point. He had always found reasons why a suggestion could not be carried out or was a bad idea. Sam, on the other hand, was good at getting ideas from people, because he always found reasons why they were good, even if they might not actually work.

Discussion Questions

1. What are some of the roles you see the executive playing here? Are they policy management roles? Who else plays these roles?
2. Could a policy management role be institutionalized here? How?

THE WELFARE PLANNING COUNCIL

As she saw it, the executive was fashioning the Welfare Planning Council into a social policy organization that would serve the whole community. The organization would be smaller and more streamlined than it had been in the past. The quality of staff would be higher. It would work in relationship with United Way in a five-year tenure contract, which would provide some base funding. United Way liked tha idea because it did not commit them to ongoing funding and the amount of the contract would be somewhat less than at present. Further, this organization, in its newly emerging shape, had been able to specify the kinds of claims that could be made. Hence, both organizations felt a little more comfortable and relaxed about their relationship with each other. The executive was convinced that if the service was good and the study products appropriate, there would be no difficulty in renewing at least some level of funding. If, on the other hand, that should not be the case, there was the real question whether the organization should be in existence anyway. Their new small contract with the child welfare agency was a case in point. It was only a $5,000 job, but it represented the kind of thing that she felt was appropriate.

Discussion Questions

1. Compare the policy management roles of the planning council with those of the child welfare agency. What are the similarities? What are the differences?

2. Of the policy management rules, some are suggested here and some are omitted. Which are left out? How could they be worked on?

8

POLICY COMMITTEES

For the policy manager, meeting management is as crucial a skill as the ability to interview is to the more clinically trained individual. Policies, as I have argued, are essentially ideas about courses of action which have been systematically put together in ways that allow them to guide future action and have been ratified by an official body. It is the ratification process that changes the proposal from a set of suggestions or options about the way things ought to be into a set of proscriptive activities that have binding force. It is partly this focus on ratification that calls our attention to the policy committee. By and large, ratification occurs within a group context. Some kind of official body—a board of directors, advisory committee, or special task group—becomes the official ratifying center. The policy manager's attention is drawn to an analysis of how groups make decisions, but the focus here is, and should be, a policy focus, not an interpersonal one. Thus, in thinking about how groups make decisions and how to manage the decision-making process so that decision quality is increased, one needs to think more about structure and roles than personalities. But more on that when boards of directors are considered.

The whole emphasis on decision-making groups can be extended beyond those that provide official ratification—here called boards to indicate they have formal legal authority for purposes of ratification—to an even broader collection of committees. These are groups set up to make various kinds of decisions and process various kinds of information that often is of a pre-policy or post-policy nature, that is, committees involved in analyzing data and coming out with reports suggesting guidelines for future action to communities as a whole, to organizational entities, and to the nation. These documents are not formal and legal except to the extent that they meet the committee's charge taken in and of itself. They are not formal prescriptions for our behavior. Hence, committees make official recommendations that do not have the force of policy (but are sometimes called policy recommendations). In a sense, then, the policy manager must take as within her or his compass the whole matter of committees and boards—how they function and how they should function. A great deal of the effectiveness of the policy manager evolves upon the ability to manage group decision making in a way that enhances his or her own skills, supplements them, and enriches and augments the proposals the individual policy manager seeks to make.

On the other hand, groups sometimes work on post-policy matters. Once a policy has been established, there needs to be additional work to detail the operational implications of that policy, set up operational decision rules, and put it into effect. Planning committees are often involved in this, and indeed, it is what we mean by planning.

The Garbage Can

Whether one "likes" to work with decision-making groups and committees or not is beside the point here. They are with us, and their number and importance will increase. As Cohen, March, and Olsen (1972) have pointed out, decision making in organizations is all too often a "garbage can" or potpourri of disparate elements. They point out that all organizations have a series of streams running through them—choice streams, participant streams, problem streams, and solution streams. These must all be combined if an effective solution to an organizational problem is to be developed. Frequently, they are more or less randomly combined, causing mischief within the organizational framework. Policy managers need to give some thought to orchestrating these organizational streams so that the requisite information, ideas, skills, and resources are available to handle particular tasks.

Cohen, March, and Olsen have touched an important chord, and one that needs a bit more comment. When people think of decision making as a garbage can, it nearly always rings a bell. If we stop and think about it a bit, it strikes us that most of the comments people make about decisions and decision-making groups is negative in nature. Boards, people say, are "dead wood," "committees take minutes to waste hours." The general tenor of references to decision-making groups is a negative one. In some respects, this attitude is quite odd. One does not expect therapists to take such a dim view of the counseling interview. And yet, from another point of view, it is understandable. There are a number of reasons why, as an introduction to considering how to manage policy meetings more effectively, we need to try to explain this attitude.

Latent Functions

The first reason is that policy groups perform latent functions for society as a whole and in a sense carry a greater burden than might be expected. What are some of these functions?

Representation

Policy group members carry the burden of "representation" from their different constituencies or sectors. In a democracy, the policy committee is one of the central vehicles through which the democratic spirit is given institutional expression.

Participation

A second function relates not to representation, but to participation, not who is involved, but how much they are involved. American society values participation, stresses it, and to a considerable extent, rewards the active participant with extra "points of power or influence" in the complex negotiations involving "who rules." The policy committees carry the burden of participation. And participation helps express intensity or "quality" of preference in a society where numbers and quality of preference are seen as a rule.

Pluralism

Policy committess also carry the burden of pluralism. In a society as diverse as ours, with so many different points of view, representation is not a totally satisfactory solution to the problem of participation and yet we encourage people to become involved under norms of participation. We encourage more formal legal structures to bring people into positions of power and call it representation. However, there is also a large informal network of people not in representative positions who are nevertheless influential with respect to particular issues. They cannot be ignored and the committee is a good place to secure their involvement, a good vehicle to "touch base" with them.

Equality

The committee is also characterized by its apparent emphasis on equality. While it is well known that there are status differences within decision-making groups and that often these distinctions are made very early in the life of the group, there is, nonetheless, a sense in which all members are equal. In this important sense, committees represent "the egalitarian way."

Information Cluster

To these larger social functions, we must add some more practical ones. Among these, certainly, information ranks first. The day is largely past when a single individual in any complex organization can know all that needs to be done, can probe the environment for all the requisite intelligence, and handle the flow of paperwork. Information must be brought in from several sources, codified, organized, synthesized, and presented within a decision-making context. This is not a task for the individual anymore, even in the mechanical sense. There simply isn't time. But the problem is not only one of mechanics, but one of perspective too. As information becomes more complex, a single individual may engage in inappropriate simplification through selective information-securing and selective interpretation. Policy committees are useful not only in providing "many hands," but also the additional perspectives necessary to adequately interpret and distil information. This information can be (and is) both technical in nature and political. Both are needed if the decision is to be a good one.

Formal and Informal Power

There is also the whole problem of formal and informal power structures within the organization. Everyone who has studied organizations knows that there are both formal and informal structures of power. Rather than seeking to answer the question of which is the "real structure of power," let us take the position that both exist, that they sometimes touch and sometimes stand apart from each other. The policy committee represents one important and unacknowledged vehicle by which the formal and informal power structures come together. For this reason, the construction, operation, and dissolution of organizational or interorganizational policy committees represent one way in which influential and knowledgeable people are brought together with those who hold positions of authority and responsibility, whether or not those two sets are completely concentric. In fact, it is our best guess that they are certainly not. To the extent that they are not, the craft of committee composition is all the more important.

These are all hidden functions the policy committee must perform over and above the management of whatever task happens to be immediately at hand. The policy manager must be aware of these omni-latent processes because they can not only affect the nature of the decision process as it is ongoing, but can also erupt and intersect, derail and ultimately destroy the ongoing process of the committee.

Intensity of Preference

Finally, committees are a way to express the intensity of preference within the American political system. We like to give people wide latitude in expressing their feelings, even though that may be counterproductive for purposes at hand. Most of the time our preferences in certain matters are expressed extensively. One man, one vote is an example. The fact that some people may be much more involved, concerned, and affected than others tends to be disregarded, and yet as a practical matter the political system recognizes that intensity of preference cannot be disregarded for long any more than extensity of preference can be. Some structure for processing strong feelings as well as breadth of feelings is necessary for a stable system. The committee process is one way in which the depth and strength of people's commitments can be expressed. Sometimes, perhaps quite often, we are swayed by those presentations. In any event, it is important to provide a vehicle for that kind of expression, and committees, boards, advisory groups, and other policy decision groups tend to be such vehicles. Managing that expression, while at the same time proceeding with the tasks at hand, is a complex and difficult assignment.

In human service organizations, state bureaucracies that offer human services, and other organizations of a social welfare nature, these latent functions, are important, because it is the special commitment of the human service field to deal with those who have been disadvantaged. The disadvantaged are sometimes defined as those who are unrepresented, who suffer from inequality, evidence low participation in community affairs, and are excluded from the formal decision-making structure, even though they may possess a great deal of informal knowledge and power. While a number of organizations may be able to successfully ignore the pressures from this group, it is less easy for those of us in the human service fields to do so, nor do we wish to. However, having recognized the pressures, additional management skills and planning are needed to take them into account.

Latent functions of policy committees are:
- Representation
- Participation
- Pluralism
- Equality
- Information cluster
- Formal and informal power
- Intensity of preference

Negative Concepts

The fact that policy committees perform a range of functions, many of them latent, which are part and parcel of the manifest ones assigned to them through their mandate, is not the only source of trouble. There are a number of other points that need to be understood before prescriptions for improvement can be offered.

Activity Contrary to American Values

Committee activity, to say nothing of policy activity, tends to be contrary to American values in an important way (although supported by American values in another way). American society is individually oriented and we define work as that which is done by the individual. Solo performance and solo excellence are highly prized. Collective performance is harder to assess and less cherished. Perhaps that is because it is more difficult to identify key star individuals. The fact that a star sports team, for example, needs all of its members because of their different contributions and the intermeshing of those differences is something only grudgingly recognized. Hence, policy committee activity tends to be defined as non-work, and for that reason we tend to ignore it, to not prepare for it, and generally to set it to one side. Work thus treated is likely to be ineffectively performed and that ineffectiveness is then taken as evidence that the original hypothesis was right. Zander says it well:

However, readers face a dilemma . . . [we] are not all that interested in explaining or improving group life . . . individuals feel that the organization should help them; it is not the individual's prime job to help the organization. Basic values . . . foster this formation of groups that put the good of the individual before the good of the group. In Japan, in contrast, important values foster interdependence among persons, courtesy, obligation to others, listening, empathy, self-denial, and support of one's group. (Zander 1982:xi)

Blaming the Victim

Policy committees are, in a sense, something of a victim within American policy machinery; important, present, needed, and yet downgraded and downplayed. One can view them as sort of a corporate victim and, from that perspective, one would expect them to be blamed for their own failures. Indeed, they are. Blaming the victim has a long tradition within society, and the tendency to blame committees for the failure of committees is well within that tradition, and convenient to boot. It is convenient because it displaces the blame from the individual who might feel some residual discomfort at having failed in performance. But to locate the "fault" in "the committee" not only extends it beyond the person, but depersonalizes it completely as well. Thus, no specific individual, unless the fault is egregious, is required to take responsibility for committee failure. Thus committees fulfill an important scapegoat function which should not be overlooked for its utility in displacing attention from role performance and rule enforcement which could indeed improve group decision making.

Lack of Training

Another reason that committees seem to bear the brunt of such disesteem and perhaps the cause of some of their ineffectiveness as well is the lack of training in group decision-making methods and behaviors. I refer here to both formal and informal training. Some people argue that team sports prepare people for the kind of activity that group decision making involves. Perhaps that is so to some degree, but it is also true that a very competitive stream runs throughout that training with an eye toward individual accomplishment and distinction. Less attention, informally, may be paid to collective satisfactions derived from membership and participation in a successful group effort. On a more formal level, the policy committee is not thought of as the appropriate vehicle for training, or even the appropriate target for influence. We tend to think of policy makers and decision makers as if there were specific individuals located in specific places who could, if they wished to, make decisions fall our way. There certainly are influential individuals, but the idea that these individuals are solely the appropriate targets belies what we know about the policy process. The policy process is a collective process that involves important collective action at points of crystallization. The idea that somehow individuals are the custodians of decisions tends to divert our attention from the communal interstices where decisions are really made or not made.

Overload

We have a tendency to overdo a good thing when it comes to committees and decisions. While separable points, these tend to be joined together. Committee overload relates to that instance when a committee begins to function well. Capable functioning of policy committees tends to make them a magnet for other tasks, and soon a committee will find itself with a large number of additional assignments. Unless very careful about "mission intake," this committee will soon find itself with more tasks to accomplish than it actually can accomplish. At that point, its functioning will begin to falter and it will take its place with the other policy committees who have not "lived up to expectations." The policy system takes that as evidence that policy committees never "work anyway" and conveniently ignore the role that the policy context itself had in pressing for overload.

Decision overload is a similar type of phenomenon, but relates to a particular decision instead of to the functioning of an entire policy committee. In this case, the decision tends to become itself overloaded with parts added to it. Thus, instead of a relatively parsimonious decision relating to X topic, people begin adding elements to the decision, so there's X_1, X_2, X_3, X_4, and the decision becomes increasingly complex and politicized. It becomes complex because it is very difficult with so many parts to keep them all together in a coherent way. It becomes politicized because the large number of parts means that a large number of interests are affected. And the more interests affected by a given decision, the less likely that decision is to be made at all (or, to put it another way, the greater the likelihood there is of retaining the status quo). Decisions, therefore, do not get made, and the policy committee's reputation for effectiveness declines apace. These two processes can work singly or together, but they are important reasons why things go wrong.

These reasons, then, can conspire, singly and severally, to negatively affect the functioning of policy committee activities. There is, of course, a self-fulfilling prophetic element here. The more we believe that group decision making is ineffective, the more we act in ways that make it so. Then, seeing that, we use it as evidence for the correctness of our original proposition. The problem we face is not one of eliminating group decision making, because that cannot, and indeed should not, be done. Events are too complex, decision makers too biased and of too limited a perspective and focus to be the decision makers within a policy framework. Too many actors are involved in any event. Thus, the policy manager needs to find ways to improve group decision making within a policy context, focusing more on the improvement and structuring of information flowing to the individual, rather than improving interpersonal relationships, though the latter is certainly helpful and appropriate on its own terms. I stress the improvement of information and its structure, because information is crucial to the making of good decisions. Without an appropriate information structure, even the group that gets along best will not be able to make high quality decisions.

"Policy" Is Not Action

Somehow dealing with policy, because it involves ideas, does not seem to be "doing anything" and hence does not satisfy American values' appetite for action. This, of course, is doubly unfortunate, because both the committee and policy instrumentality and the policy itself are more negatively viewed than they should be, thus creating a double reason to avoid focusing on them and improving their activities.

Negative concepts that burden policy committees are:
- Activity contrary to American values
- Blaming the victim
- Lack of training

- Overload
- Policy is not action

High Quality Decisions

The job of the policy committee is to make decisions and, it is hoped, to make them of high quality (Haft 1981; Moore 1982). All too often committee activity is seen as an odyssey of nondecision, avoiding opportunity here, tabling it there, failing to seize it in some other place. A decision is, of course, (1) a choice (2) among competing alternatives, with both components required. Without alternatives, choice is nonexistent. Without choice, alternatives are useless. The policy manager is crucially interested in facilitating, intellectually and interpersonally, the work of the policy committee.

The policy committee must:
- Make a decision (vs. no decision)
- Make a decision of high quality (vs. poor quality)
(See Exercise 8.1)

Consider the five-phase system outlined earlier (chapter 3): problem identification, policy options, policy ratification, policy planning, and programming. Committees operate during each phase of the process. The policy manager, in the role as committee staffer, works with the committee and across different policy committees, depending upon whether the same committee has a continuous policy responsibility or policy responsibility moves from one committee to another. And planning committees—groups that work on laying out operational plans—abound. Many human service organizations are going to administrative teams (teams of administrators) to run the agency.

Phase I: Problem Identification

The first role policy committees play is one of problem identification. It is usually within the committee framework that initial decisions about the policy agenda are made. Policies are designed to solve problems either current or anticipated. But all problems cannot be looked at nor all difficulties addressed, therefore decisions must be made about which problems are most pressing or might be, and these need to be selected from the wider range of possible problems that could be considered.

In Setting Priorities for the Policy Agenda the Policy Manager:
1. Works with policy committees to scan the policy environment
2. Identifies current and future trouble spots
3. Sets priorities for the items, working with policy committees and policy elites.

Setting priorities is a complex task involving several dimensions. One, of course, is the urgency of the item; items of an urgent nature usually get high priority. However, urgent items are not always the most important, though they frequently drive out more important ones. Sometimes, somewhat less urgent items are really of greater moment to the organization. Thus, decisions have to be made about balancing urgent problems and important problems where these are not identical. A third dimension, besides urgency and importance, has to do with resource allocation. Among the array of urgent and important problems, as well as some both less urgent and less important, decisions must be made with respect to how much and what kind of resources are needed to develop options. The policy manager assists policy committees in this task.

In setting priorities a policy manager takes into consideration:
- The urgency of the problem
- The importance of the problem
- Resource allocation

Phase II: The Generation of Policy Options

The development of policy options falls heavily on the interaction between various policy committtees within the organization and the policy manager. There may be an executive committee of the board, a program committee of the agency, various review committees of one sort or another, an informal or a formal staff committee. Some or all of these may have essential or peripheral roles (or no role at all) in the development of options surrounding a particular policy idea. The course of policy development is like a spider's web. There are committees and collectivities at various junctures of the intra-organizational system and that system extends, of course, outside the organization. It is often unclear which committee, or set of committees, needs to be involved and one job of the policy manager is to think carefully about what committees require involvement and how that involvement can best be accomplished.

But there is a dilemma here too. In touching base with various committees, the policy manager needs to think through the nature of the presentation. On the one hand, the presentation of a problem with some tentative options should not be so brief as to provide a paucity of information that really does not permit the committee to do its job of review and suggestion. On the other hand too detailed a report has the same effect. What can one say when the job (it may appear) has already been done? The policy manager needs to think through the spider's web of committees and come to some preliminary decision about which ones are appropriate. Sometimes this information will already be available. It will be standard practice to check with the executive committee or the planning committee, since these committees usually consider such matters. However, because the extent and the varying ways in which organizations use committees it is likely to be a matter of organizational practice, and hence one with vague, rather than specific, norms attached to it.

In option development the policy manager:
1. Thinks through which committees lie at the junctures of the policy's spider's web
2. Considers the best way to present new ideas to the committees
3. Assists committees in developing the policy agenda items.

(See Exercise 8.2)

Option Elaboration

The purpose in working with policy committees varies considerably depending upon which stage of the policy development process one is in. These initial phases involve policy committees in matters of environmental screening and scrutinizing, assessing organizational potential, defining problems, setting priorities for the policy agenda, and thinking through the kinds of options that might be reasonable to consider, depending upon the problem involved. Once a problem has been identified and begins to move through the policy committee process, the policy manager takes initial responsibility for a series of options that might be reasonable for solving that particular problem. It is usually these options, to a greater or lesser degree, that are shared with the various policy committees. And, not incidentally, it is very important for one set of policy committees to know what other policy committees think. Thus the staff advisory committee in a human service organization may be very interested in knowing what the board thinks about a particular problem and the structure of its solution. Conversely, the board may be very interested in having some idea of what the staff would want. Hence, part of the policy manager's job is to take information from one group to another. This process of sharing perspectives should not be confused with the process of policy clearing. In working with the policy development process in its preliminary phase, the policy manager should view any suggestions for solution as also preliminary. One of the things policy groups are good at is spotting the problems in potential solutions and offering improvements. The virtue of policy committees often lies in their ability to review proposals that policy managers have made, find the flaws in them, and improve them. Policy managers should expect that there will be flaws in their initial proposals, because they are perhaps the worst people to review their own initial suggestions. It is through the suggestion of options, their revision, the provision of fresh suggestions, their revision, and the combination of all these suggestions that the process of policy shaping occurs.

The process of policy shaping involves:
- The presentation of preliminary options by policy managers to policy committees
- The review of those options and their combination and improvement
- The reduction of the range of options to a reasonable few

Policy Clearing

Once the various policy committees have gone through the policy-shaping process, and the policy manager has identified the problem and reduced the number of options to a reasonable number, then a more sustained process of policy clearing can go on. Typically this occurs as the policy is in the middle phase of its odyssey toward ratification. The clearing process is one in which interested policy committees are given an opportunity to comment on a proposed policy or series of policy options. Sometimes these may be the same groups that participated in earlier discussions and they now have the opportunity to see the shaped result of those discussions. At other points, the series of discussions the policy manager generated results in a need to check with yet additional policy committees which might have an interest in the proposed policy. Generally speaking, the clearing process is with people who are thought to be generally friendly toward one's point of view. Clearing with those who are likely to oppose a policy only gives the opposition more time to organize. (See page 90.)

There is an exception here, however, and that is with formal authorities, typically bosses and those in superior positions. Sometimes this process is viewed as too time-consuming. And in America, where time is money, this charge is a serious one. And there is no question that some of this clearing is unnecessary—there are such "adverse effects" as backlash or the development of opposition. On the other hand, the benefits of such a process, not only in terms of neutralizing the complaints of noninvolvement but also in terms of securing useful and constructive comments, should be considered. Seward makes this point when he talks about a Japanese process called *ringi*. It means: "in effect that a proposal drawn up usually at the middle management level [is] passed both vertically and horizontally until a sizeable group has studied it *and concurred in it*" (1972:249–50; emphasis added)

The process of clearing, then, essentially involves three groups. One is the policy elite of the organization—that group of executives and managers who must give the go-ahead before policy can be finally put into operational form. This is not necessarily the decision point. The policy may still go to a decision point group. However, this does allow one to can get a sense of what the policy elite has to say about the proposal. A second group has to do with the vertical structure, as Seward mentioned. This has to do with parallel groups, which may again be involved in aspects of the policy and for whom advanced knowledge of what is being considered is crucial. A third group, and one most often ignored, has to do with those below the level at which the policy is formulated. This group is important, because those below may be among the ones who will have to implement aspects of the policy.

Let us consider who there might be in a human service organization. A policy manager might be in that role at the associate director level. Here he or she would perform clearing tasks at the executive level, possibly with the permission of the executive and some of the committees that intersect between organization and board. These might include the finance committee, the personnel committee, the program committee. There may be other levels parallel to the associate director. Many, in fact, may be outside the organization. Other organizations, a coordinating committee, a policy-sharing group of one sort or another may well be interested in what the organization has in mind. There may also be groups of formal authorities and elites whose understanding and cooperation would be imperative in the carrying out of any policy. And the staff and clients need to be consulted. The information and perspectives garnered from such a round of activity may lead to a higher quality proposal and decision.

Policy clearing means involving:

- The policy elite
- Other interested policy committees on the vertical axis, both in and outside the organization
- Those below the level of the policy formulator whose cooperation will be necessary in order to carry out the proposed policy

Proposal Revision

Committees control the process of policy proposal revision. Typically, after the clearing stage policy proposals go through several drafts. Often the policy manager will work closely with members of the ratifying committee to secure a draft close to the known needs and wishes of the ratifying committee membership. Sometimes the policy will have received "in principle" ratification, and this process is one of working out the details. At other times a problem with a list of policy options needs to be made available to the group. Whatever the actual course of the policy document, the policy manager needs to coordinate the flow of drafts to the policy committee members, secure their feedback, and develop new drafts. Sometimes the same committee reviews a second and a third time, as in some aspects of policy clearing. At other times different committees propose revisions with regard to their own special expertise, such as budget or personnel, and make their own comments. The process of policy revision is different from the process of policy clearing. Clearing is informal and unofficial. It is a process by which policy committees are made aware of items under consideration by other policy committees and are invited to share their views. Policy revision, however, is a formal process in which groups are asked for official views. It is at this juncture that one can see the importance of policy clearing, because it gives people a chance to look informally at something that in many cases, though not all, they will have to look at formally.

There are a number of specific problems the policy manager has to face in the policy revision process. One has to do with the simple mechanics of keeping track of the sequence of drafts and incorporating (or rejecting) the comments made by various individuals. While a mechanical task, this job is fraught with political difficulties, because people become very sensitive about having their suggestions being appropriately considered. Thus, accepted suggestions need to be incorporated, those which cannot be accepted for some reason need to be diplomatically handled. A numbering system for drafts is useful at this stage in order to simply keep track of which pages have which comments on them. Sometimes there are alternative suggestions, both of which cannot both be incorporated. If that is the case, more diplomatic work by the policy manager to resolve those differences is needed, either at private individual sessions with those who made the suggestions or by listing them in such a way that the committee can decide which of the opposing approaches it wishes to select. The final thing the policy manager needs to be particularly sensitive to in terms of policy revision is checking the flow of drafts with committee schedules so that the requisite draft is available when the committee meets. Otherwise problems will arise when the committee meets and the draft is not ready.

In policy revision, the policy manager:
- Monitors the progress of policy drafts
- Checks on the appropriate sequence of drafts
- Resolves conflicts in language
- Links draft and committee schedules

Phase III. Policy Ratification

Once this prior work has been done, a policy proposal is passed along to the group or groups whose formal approval is needed before the policy can be legitimized. In a human service agency, this is the board of directors, but it is not always *only* the board. Sometimes there are external groups whose approval is also needed. For example, if a child welfare agency wants to convert a residential home to group living, its own board may (and will) wish to approve the action. The local planning commission, and perhaps the local city council, will need to grant approval as well. These are all decision-making committees of one sort or another, and the policy manager has, as a key responsibility, the task of "dealing" with the presentations to these groups and conferring with the executive director at critical junctures. This process involves not only informal intelligence-gathering activities, but preparing the required documents, in the required style and format, and appearing with the agency delegation when the time is right for action.

Often there will not be acceptance the first time. The policy committee may want information about other options considered, or the agenda may be too long and the item in question will not come up, even though it has been scheduled. In all of these cases extra work will be required of the policy manager. She or he will have to go back and do what is required, which can range from starting almost all over again, if the formal approval meeting was a disaster, to making only minor adjustments and taking the document back for review. This process is among the more difficult ones, because the policy manager needs to contend not only with additional work, but with the disappointment of defeat, and perhaps the guilt of responsibility as well, if the lack of action, or the negative action, was the result of some error.

In policy ratification:
- Formal documents are presented to the board and/or official groups which must approve them
- Revisions are made if necessary
- Some rejections must be expected

Phase IV. Policy Planning

Once ratification has been achieved, the planning committee typically becomes involved. This committee is usually a group of people internal to the organization who sit down and develop the operational definitions required to shape the approved policy into workable and specific terms. This process can be brief or long, but it is usually necessary. And, frequently, continuing work for a while at least is required to get a good set of action guides. In research there is the concept of a "pretest" or questionnaires, in which the initial formulation of questions is "pretested" on a group of people to spot hidden problems or difficulties and to test the time of the interview. In almost every instance problems develop that can be rectified if found in advance. A similar procedure is appropriate for the planning committee. First, it is important to pretest the guidelines so that they will not be put into effect before one has a chance to get some feedback and make adjustments. The pretest process should be in two parts. There is the initial discussion, within the planning committee and with others, just mentioned. Then there should be some period of trial implementation, involving some segment of the organization, but not the whole organization (using, perhaps, a field office or one division), so that operational problems can be spotted.

In planning, the policy committee:
- Drafts operational guidelines
- Performs a pretest
- Develops a trial application

Phase V. Programming

In programming, committees play a less powerful role, although, as noted, many human service agencies are moving to the concept of an operating, or administrative, team, which includes the executive director and her or his top associates, the associate director, and heads of major programs or departments. This group will often meet on a weekly basis, or perhaps twice during the week, to review problems and make decisions about what to do about upcoming difficulties—the waiting list, the client who fell down the stairs, the personnel policy revision proposal. These groups will become more popular, because executives cannot hold in their heads all the information they need to make even an apparently simple decision. Decisions have requisites and implications, which need to be explored for informational and political purposes before going ahead.

The administrative team can always make ongoing adjustments in the policy implementation process. Sometimes, however, more systematic problems develop, and the team needs to go back to the planning phase and do some systematic redesign of the operatinal guidelines. At other times, even redesign is not enough, and supplemental recommendations need to be made to the ratifying body, and policy changes made. And these problems and adjustments in time initiate the policy loop.

Conclusion

The policy committee is one of the central vehicles for policy accomplishment. It is the building block of the policy machine. There are whole ranges of committees important to the human service policy manager for approval, review, comment, and information. Sometimes it is not clear to the policy manager and the committee itself which is which, and committees become confused about their roles and responsibilities. This confusion presents special problems for one crucial committee, the *primus inter pares* group, which affects the life of the human service organization—the group responsible for organizational governance. Often this group is the board of directors, but it may also be a public body, such as a city council. It is to a discussion of this group that we now turn.

CASE ILLUSTRATIONS

THE CHILD WELFARE AGENCY

The problems that beset the Child Welfare Agency were beginning to seem more manageable, even to the staff. The crisis, however, was perhaps most acute at this point, Jim knew. Everyone had been willing to chip in and make a range of sacrifices when it seemed that the agency might simply shut its doors. There was a sort of "wartime" mentality. However, as the transition to "peace" began to develop, people were less willing to make those sacrifices and, indeed, became more insistent that their way be the one followed. There had been a change in the agency character and climate. The old executive had been sort of the lone ranger of child welfare. He and he alone knew what was right. He and he alone told people what to do. He and he alone had the custody of the agency's mission, role, and future. The unfortunate deterioration of responsibility in recent years had so changed the agency character that there had been no corporate or collective sense of the agency itself.

However, the need to pull together during the recent crisis and the sense that everyone had contributed directly or indirectly, primarily or secondarily, began to create a climate of community. It was this climate that the executive wanted to encourage. Jim thought that it would not be appropriate to move from an autocratic to a completely consensual administrative structure. He was firmly committed to the notion that individuals have to make some decisions and that he was one of the key decision makers. But now that the large number of associate directors had been reduced, he had a vacancy. He had one associate, not four, and so thought he might form a staff advisory committee that might make some recommendations about who could fill the vacancy as well as act as a catalyst for the developing community feeling.

Advisory committees, he knew, could have a number of problems. In order to make this one work he set down some guidelines he thought would be helpful. First, it would not be chaired by him. A staff member would be elected to handle it. He would meet with the committee occasionally, but not all the time. As he pointed out in his note, it is very difficult to give advice that someone may not want to hear if that person is sitting next to you. He asked the committee members to write giving him their suggestions and promised to read and consider every one but not necessarily to implement each one. He would, however, reply, so that the advisory committee would know his thinking on each particular point. He pointed out that while they might respond to his requests, they should also feel free to initiate pieces of advice to him. In this way, he felt that the different sectors of the agency would talk things over in a legitimate way, passing some of their thoughts on to him and keeping the flow of reactions and comments coming. It was perhaps a dangerous route to take, but one he felt necessary if the energy that had been developed was going to continue.

Discussion Questions

1. Is the new agency making effective use of policy committees? In what ways? How might its previous problems have been prevented through a more judicious use of committees?

2. What future committees might the agency need?

THE WELFARE PLANNING COUNCIL

With things beginning to pick up a bit more momentum the executive turned toward the problem of the community and how it might be more effectively represented within the planning organization. She had very little trouble with particular contracts where the requests were clear and straightforward. In each case there was a particular client as well, with specific points the client was interested in pursuing. Two things bothered her. One had to do with the absence of the ability to provide a community component to those specific studies. She might want to bring some things to the attention of the organization from a community perspective that might be quite different from the original concepts. Yet that might take some additional resources and input. She might also like to provide a community perspective on the more narrow confines of the study. That was one thing that could be added over and above expertise. But the question was, of course, how to do it. She hit upon the idea of forming a community concerns advisory committee with about thirty members. Great care would need to be taken to get representation from all segments of the community. It would not be a board of directors but would guide the agency with respect to its community focus. It might undertake such jobs as reviewing studies for community view, suggesting needed community studies, or highlighting community deficiencies. Her community was so diverse that it was probably not going to be possible to get every group represented satisfactorily. However, it was certainly a start.

She talked to some foundation people and was able to excite them about this concept. What she wanted from the foundation was a small budget, maybe $15,000 or $20,000, which could be a sort of "community" budget. It could be used to pay for specific committee-initiated studies or for adding components requested by the committee to other ongoing studies. This, she thought, would add depth and thoughtfulness to the work they were doing while making it possible for them to retain their policy planning focus.

Discussion Questions

1. Outline some of the ways that "hidden factors" of the committee are displayed in the council's developing committee structure.

2. What is the sequence of committees needed to deal with changes in the council? Are enough present? If not, which ones are needed?

9

POLICY GOVERNANCE:
BOARDS OF DIRECTORS

Policy management has both an internal and an external focus. On the one hand, it looks inside the organization and seeks to improve the development of the governing principles which guide the organization as well as to provide ideas which are improvements in the operational definitions and patterns with which the agency has come to be familiar. On the other hand, it also looks outside the organization at the policy context, the policy community and policy elites. These contextual and communal elements can be at national, state, or local levels, and require a good bit of attention from the policy manager. Hence, the policy manager has somewhat of a dual focus. This is nowhere more true or important than in the human service organization, because the activities of that organization are less specific, less measurable, and have less demonstrable results than those of some other organizations. The ''success'' of counseling, day care, or even welfare grants, is not something that one can evaluate with ease and clarity. Hence, for reasons of ''product,'' human service organizations are more vulnerable to criticism and attack from the outside than other organizations might be.

It is also likely that the larger policy environment within which the human service organization acts is, perhaps, somewhat ambivalent about the human service organization itself. On the one hand, that environment wants to provide necessary and useful social services to segments of the population. On the other hand, there is a certain amount of suspicion that these services and assistances may not be necessary, may be abused, and hence, the environment is more turbulent, more questioning, than may be true for a business. And, as Peter Drucker has pointed out, there are some differences between the human service organization and "business" organizations. Most businesses get their income from the sale of a particular product. Hence, the performance of the product and the generation of the revenue can be tied reasonably close together. That is less true for human service organizations. Let us look carefully at the first part of the idea already quoted in chapter 2: "The one basic difference between a private service institution and a business is the way the service institution is paid. Businesses (other than monopolies) are paid for satisfying the customer . . . service institutions are paid out of a budget allocation . . . from a general revenue stream not tied to what they are doing" (Drucker 1973:49).

He is certainly right in the large sense. However, even he may misunderstand how much of the human service organization's income is generated from fees, even though these fees may be heavily subsidized by the revenue stream which he notes. There is, nonetheless, an important client satisfaction component in the human service field that many people overlook. Withal, however, Drucker is right, and the vagaries and influences that affect that income stream of which Drucker speaks are likely to be quite different from influences that satisfy or do not satisfy particular subsets of clients.

For these reasons, the governance of the human service institution is more difficult and presents more problems than many people realize. The board of directors, the central policy instrumentality of organizational governance, stands at the crossroads of external pressures on the organization to restrict services, tempering services, providing minimum services and, on the other hand, receives pressures from the internal environment, which seeks to expand services, to provide more services, and so on. Tensions between fewer and more services are only one of the types of tensions that the board of directors has to deal with. Others involve the balance among various types of services from the individual on the one hand, to more political and advocacy types of service on the other; from providing direct grants on the one hand, to providing training programs that enable people to earn their own money on the other; the list goes on and on. One crucial role of the policy manager is to assist the board of directors in coping with these multiple problems and in developing an integral sense of the mission and role of the human service organization. The board of directors accomodates these conflicting pressures in different ways. These accomodations are decisions made by the board of directors, and because this decision stream represents the collective policy of the organization, it represents one logical place for policy management activity, and one important reason for the policy management interest.

Implied in the above is a second reason: the quality of decisions (see chapter 8 also). Decisions made by boards of directors are necessary, but are not sufficient for the functioning of the human service organization itself. In other words, it would be very hard for the human service organization to function well if the board of directors made a poor decision after a poor decision after a poor decision. The reverse is not always true, however. Just because a board makes good decisions does not mean that they are well carried out and implemented. Nonetheless, it is very difficult to work with poor basic material. Hence, ensuring the quality of board decisions is a matter of the highest policy importance and of great interest to policy managers. This represents a second reason for policy management interest in the board.

The third reason, of course, lies in the legal responsibility that resides within the board itself. Like it or not, the board of directors of a human service organization is legally responsible for the activities of that organization. Hence, its decisions and actions take on more importance than they otherwise would. Inaction, for example, in providing appropriate insurance coverage can lead to potential liabilities on the part of the directors themselves.

Last, policy managers may be asked to serve on the boards of directors of other human service organizations as knowledgeable professionals from the system. Policy managers thus not only assist the functioning of boards of directors in their own organization, but may, as members, become directors of other human service organizations. Hence, the board and working with the board become very important components of the policy manager's role in assisting the board.

Boards of directors are crucial because:
- They are at the juncture of internal and external pressure
- They need to make high quality decisions
- They have legal responsibility for the organization
- Policy managers often are asked to serve on them

Board Responsibility

When the policy manager has, as part of a job, an assignment working with the board of directors, what might this involve? Basically, five responsibilities are important aspects of such an assignment: first, one assists the board to recognize its legal responsibilities and to prepare for them in an effective and efficient matter; second, one helps in the recruitment of new members (always a problem for boards of directors) and in their training and development. There are ways that this process can be structured that will assist the actual operation of the entire organization, not simply improve the board itself. Third, the policy manager needs to assist the board in developing its own organization, setting up subcommittees and subgroups within it to carry out its responsibilities. Here the policy manager needs to assist the board to develop good decision procedures. Fourth, the policy manager needs to assist the board in a decision audit and decision autopsy procedure in which the board seeks to assess itself with respect to its activities over a one-, two- or three-year period. Each of these requires a bit of comment.

Four areas of important responsibility are:
- Legal
- Recruitment
- Board organization and decision procedures
- Policy refurbishment and review (Audit)

Legal Responsibilities

Part of the human service organization operates as a corporation, under a charter granted by the state in which it gives its service. Some states, like California, have not-for-profit codes, which specify the nature of the board's structures and outline its responsibilities. One of the first jobs of the policy manager is to find out what set of legal requirements and restrictions operate with respect to not-for-profit organizations in his or her state and to see that the board is informed of the requirements and complies with them. This typically involves, and should involve, consultation with an attorney who is familiar with the laws of the particular state. It should be unnecessary to point out that lack of compliance can result in substantial legal liability, and yet many directors are unaware of the potential liabilities they may incur by accepting board membership. The historical notion seems to be that if one were trying to do good, one would be immune from liability even if one did wrong. A number of doctors who have tried to provide on-site accident help and later been sued have found that there is less support for this old idea than had been hitherto thought. Similarly, within the human service field, it seems odd that one could be sued for "malpractice" if one provides a free service. Yet this is a distinct possibility, and one made plausible by the fact that a number of clients are now on a *fee-for-service* basis. Malpractice insurance has become a standard feature for many private practitioners and there is now directors' insurance available as well.

If one can step back from the specifics of a particular state requirement, however, there are three general legal requirements that the board should think about—diligence, avoidance of harmful effects, and prudence.

Diligence

Diligence in the accomplishment of organizational purpose means the board members must attend to matters for which they have accepted responsibility, such as attending meetings. Zelman's article on "Liability for Social Agency Boards" is worth quoting on this point:

Although few agency board members may be aware that . . . accepting a board position obligates them to be diligent in looking after the interests of the membership they represent. Throughout the years and at different locales, three different standards have been used to determine the degree of diligence a member of the board may be reasonably expected to display: that of an ordinarily diligent man acting under similar circumstances; that of a reasonably diligent man acting under similar circumstances and a like position; and that of a reasonably diligent man acting in a like position under the same or similar circumstances in the conduct of his own affairs. (Zelman 1977:271)

The specific interpretation may vary by state, and it does. The policy manager can invite an attorney to speak to the board about how standards of diligence might apply in their area. Nonetheless, diligence is one responsibility of the organization.

Avoidance of Harmful Effects

Avoiding harmful effects is the second responsibility of boards. The board must see to it that the organization's mission is carried out in such a way that people who come in contact with it are not harmed. Purham, in his article "Non-Profit Boards Under Fire," comments on the difficulty hospital boards face.

When we started to raise room rates or put a new wing on the hospital, or just relocate, or provide a new service, we just went ahead and did it. All of that changed beginning with the Darling Case (a 1965 court decision in which a hospital was found liable for a physician's negligence), which put the hospital boards on notice that they, along with the medical staff, have the legal responsibility to assure that quality care is being rendered (Purham 1979:110)

The fact that clients may contemplate taking the social agency to court is something that boards have to consider.

Prudence

Directors are also required to avoid self-serving conduct for personally enriching activity. Zelman calls this the standard of prudence, and he is worth quoting again:

The exercise of prudence as well as diligence is associated with the satisfactory performance of board duties. In contrast to the concept of diligence, which involves positive action, prudence involves the avoidence of acts demonstrating lack of loyalty and good faith. In this context, loyalty refers to refraining from acting in one's self interest in any manner that may interfere with the corporate business. Good faith refers to the exercise of honest and reasonable judgment to perpetuate the best interests of the organization. To avoid liabilities resulting from a lack of reasonable prudence, board members should bear these definitions in mind as well as the following precept: they may not gain private profit in their official position and may not deal with the organization from an adversary position acting as or for a competitor. (Zelman 1977:272)

Diligence, the avoidance of harmful effects, and prudence represent the fundamental legal responsibilities of board members. Yet many human service board directors have no sense of these responsibilities of the fact that they could be liable if they failed in carrying them out. The policy manager thus needs to work with the board to assure a full understanding of the legal implications of board membership.

There may be other legal requirements the board has to meet and it may well be the policy manager's responsibility to assure that it does. For example, some states have laws that govern the degree to which meetings must be open and notice given. There may also be laws relating to the acceptance of certain types of federal contracts, affirmative action laws, access for disabled individuals, and so on. These cases may not result in personal legal liabilities. They, nonetheless, can embroil the organization in legal complexities that are best avoided by preventative action.

Three legal responsibilities are:
- Diligence
- Avoiding harmful effects
- Prudence

Recruitment of Board Members

A second responsibility that evolves upon the policy manager is the development of a capable and competent board membership. Typically, boards have a nominating committee, which the policy manager may assist and which is responsible for beginning the process of securing people to replace outgoing board members. This process should be a very thoughtful one and should involve the introduction of knowledgeable people from the agency circle of acquaintances and friends through some kind of previous service to the organization or the board itself. Unfortunately, this is often not the case. Two types of problems are systematically found by human service boards of directors. One problem involves lack of foresight and lack of planning, which results in a last minute scurry to secure nominees for posts that have become open. Often, these are individuals recommended by other board members, and thus the board is open to the charge of "cronyism." Sometimes, if the bylaws do not prohibit it, current board members are renominated for second, third, and fourth terms. Neither of these things is bad in any given instance, but as a *pattern* of recruitment, it does not represent the kind of knowledgeable and informed seeking of individual members that would be appropriate. Furthermore, it often produces individuals who are acquainted only in passing with the agency in question and with the board of directors in particular, or they may be too involved; neither is an objective posture. Not only may they be unaware of their legal responsibility, but they may be unaware of a good bit of what the agency does. Hence, this is a problem to be avoided.

A second problem has to do with the desire agencies have of seeking a "prestige board," that is, a group of notables who, in effect, lend their names via board membership to the organization, but really do not participate at all. We have all seen examples of this type of board when we get a letter from a human service organization listing a board of directors of fifty or sixty individuals in the left hand margin. In no way can it be a working board, yet it creates a problem because expectations are unclear. Roles and responsibilities are unspecified and a different type of structure needs to be developed.

Advisory Board

The policy manager can assist the board in recruiting new members by following a two-step process, a process which, incidentally, will also help the structure of the board itself. It is my recommendation that each of the human service agencies have a fairly large advisory board, visiting committee, or board of delegates, which may have up to fifty or sixty members. This group can form an outer circle of support for the agency. It can meet perhaps once a year. It can receive communications from the organization. It can be the source of individual members for particular committees and for other particular purposes the organization may wish to accomplish. Through this interactive process a stable of individuals who know about the organization and about whom the organization knows something can be developed. This advisory board concept suggests the perfect place for local notables to lend their names if they wish to do so. Responsibilities here are minimal. They can, by membership, indicate their support over all of the agencies' goals and visions, and yet they do not need to become involved in the legalities of board membership, which, as mentioned above, can occasionally become liabilities in a very literal sense. From this advisory board of possibly fifty to sixty members, the actual board of directors of the agency can be drawn. A number between eighteen and twenty-four in conventionally accepted as a good working number.

The policy manager then has the job of seeking to enhance the quality of decisions of the board of directors via enhancing the quality of the membership. Quality here is defined in terms of background, interest, commitment to the organization, and a willingness to accept the responsibilities attendant on board membership.

A Diversity of Interests

During this process, the policy manager also seeks to assure a representative "balance" of interests, ethnic backgrounds, gender, racial, and religious orientations on the board. It is impossible, of course, to have actual representation from "the Jewish community," "Catholic community," "labor," "business," although this is frequently discussed as if it were possible. What is useful, however, is to have individuals from diverse backgrounds and points of view, with special care being taken to have those points of view represented on the board of directors that are of crucial import to the organization's tradition or mission. This means that, if possible, it would be useful to have some clients or ex-clients on a board, if it is a counseling agency. It means it would be useful to have some representation from major funding groups and so on. The exact mix is not something that can be given by a formula, nor should one lie to a potential candidate in order to get a particular kind of member. All too often, problems of diversity and board heterogeneity are ignored until someone raises an issue, and then there is a tremendous scurry to find a black or a woman, usually accompanied by loud complaints that "they" aren't available; "they" don't want to participate anyway—not surprising, if one asks only a week or two in advance. In any event, good representation needs to have this kind of heterogeneity and performing the task of recruitment is certainly a first step.

Members Have Special Needs

There may be other things with particular subgroups that would make membership possible that the policy manager might be sensitive to. For example, for some individuals transportation assistance is an absolute necessity. For others, some kind of child-minding assistance is important. Still others may have other needs. This is not suggesting a wholesale questionnaire to board members, but rather asking for sensitivity to the fact that some individuals do not have the kinds of resources that permit them to absorb the range of expenses involved in board membership. Also, one needs to be sensitive to the level of board experience. Simply bringing a person from a minority community onto a board does very little good unless that individual can participate effectively and efficiently, and unless the board is willing to accept that person's participation. The two-step model of board recruitment provides a possible way to engage in some degree of board training well before any member gets to the board itself, and this is important whether or not the members are from a minority group.

Let me reiterate the purpose of a vigorous recruitment and development plan. It is to provide heterogeneity, various points of view, and a well-functioning board. But one wants this because of the central role the board plays in policy ratification. The policy manager's work can be of the highest quality, but if it is routinely voted down by the board for this reason or that, the work is to little avail. Quality decisions, therefore, not only require quality input from the policy manager from the substantive side, but require a board of directors usefully informed, capable, and competent in assessing and deciding.

In recruiting members:
- Use advisory board concept
- Secure diversity of interests
- Be sensitive to special needs

Board Organization

The policy manager's task with respect to board organization frequently lies in assisting the board to develop a set of structures that help it do its work. Often the new social agency board or the new human service organization board meets as a committee of the whole. Frequently, on that early board will be some members of the cadre that founded the organization itself. It might have been a crisis call-in center, for example, where the board members were the actual individuals on the phone, and then funding became available, grants were developed, and staff was hired, requiring the founding members to shift from actual operating rules to policy rules. This transition is frequently difficult and requires assistance, so that the board members undergoing it do not undertake those activities now carried on by paid staff and alternatively do attend to the important series of policy decisions that will come before them. As time goes on, however, boards find they usually operate best via a committee structure. It is not possible, given the time available to most board members, for each board member to review in detail all of the matters that will come before it, nor is it even wise. A number of those matters will be of a technical nature and require attention from a technical point of view. Thus a subcommittee structure permits detailed attention to specific sets of problems, followed by a recommendation of some alternative ways to proceed, from the subcommittee to the full board. While the nature and number of subcommittees are quite varied, many human service organizations have a typical cadre that includes the executive committee, the finance committee, the program committee, and the nominating committee. There may be a variety of other special committees, such as a resource development committee or a recruitment committee, but the ones mentioned are certainly among the most common. Let me say a word about each.

The Executive Committee. The executive committee consists of the officers of the organization and perhaps one other member. It is typically empowered to act when the board cannot act as a full board, and it sometimes deals with a number of very sensitive issues. Often the executive committee is the one that reviews the executive and makes a recommendation to the full board on salary increments for the executive. Furthermore, the executive committee is frequently an agent of the "clearing process" used by the executive when matters arise on which there is uncertainty concerning the extent to which they should be brought to the full board. The executive committee also serves as a sort of integrating system, pulling together perspectives from the finance committee, the program committee, the nominating committee, and many other committees. Some executive committees have members or chairs of those other committees as members of the executive committee. A problem, of course, is that there can get to be too many meetings for particular individuals. Care needs to be taken with respect to the full board to clearly outline the duties and responsibilities of the executive committee, because in many instancs the full board is suspicious of the executive committee, feeling that decisions are really made there and that they, as members of the board, do not really have the opportunity for input.

The Budget/Finance Committee. The budget/finance committee is what one might call an oversight committee. That is, it oversees in some greater detail than the full board the expenditure of funds within the agency. It checks on the monthly flow of cash in and out of the agency and may make a number of minor decisions of a judgmental sort to keep cash input in line with cash output. The finance and budget committee will typically be the group which, based upon its expertise, develops and recommends to the full board, with the support of the executive, a budget for the fiscal year. That could be spoken of as a fiscal policy role. The oversight role comes into play once that budget has been approved and there are expenditure categories with funds attached ready to be spent. It is a good practice to have more than one group involved in overseeing the expenditure of funds. Hence the finance committee, often headed by the treasurer, performs this role. In a number of human service organizations the treasurer, along with the executive director, signs checks. The two-signature requirement for institutional checks is a good one, and is a good protection against the potential misuse of funds. Sometimes the finance and budget committee also dips into resource development. But my view is that that task, dealing as it does with the generation and soliciting of funds rather than overseeing their expenditure, is best left to another group. Overseeing the outflow of funds is a complex enough task for a volunteer group to undertake, and the skills that are needed to oversee are quite different from the skills needed for fund generation.

Program Committee. The program committee tends to focus upon the service structure of the organization. What are the services it should offer and how are the services it does offer actually working? In this respect, the program committee is similar in its oversight role to the finance committee, because it concerns itself intimately with program activity and the problems and prospects attendent on it. Typically, the program committee will make a yearly recommendation directing the activities of the organization for the coming year—how much counseling should there be in this particular agency? How much drop-in service? how much free food? While the finance committee may use those board members who are fiscally knowledgeable, the program committee may use those who have a human service background and who can contribute the more technical expertise needed in program design. In both cases, however, it should be stressed that the composition of the groups should not consist *solely* of those individuals. There should be other individuals with fresh and perhaps even divergent perspectives who could add a certain degree of yeast to the discussion.

Nominating Committee. The nominating committee is of great importance to the organization and often appears to be very much underrated. Typically, a month or two before board elections a nominating committee will rise up from its usual moribund state and rush around the community looking for nominees. This is the helter-skelter process described above. A more appropriate role for the nominating committee is an ongoing one in which the community is continually scrutinized for possible individuals who might join the advisory board. The nominating committee would keep a list of possible individuals who would have been suggested to them, who have expressed interest and willingness to help, or who have appeared in the public press and the public media and have indicated a skill and confidence that the organization needs. The first nomination, following the scheme outlined, should be to the advisory board. Then, from that pool, the nominating committee can select candidates for the board itself. That is a big job and is certainly not one that is episodic in nature.

Boards Need Structure

Any kind of board organization that works and that the board likes should certainly be given a try. Boards, however, tend to like a structure in which they all come together and discuss everything. Unfortunately, as time goes on, as agencies grow, and the complexities of issues increase, this procedure is neither wise or fruitful. Without adequate preparation in the form of sub-committee reports, discussion of topics, especially technical ones, tends to be highly general and unspecific. It frequently wanders, letting people who moments ago participated in that meandering criticize it, often with a phrase like "this board never does anything," as if this board were an entity, divorced completely from themselves, and they were observers rather than participants in and contributors to the problem they criticize. The policy manager thus needs to make available to the board what is known about board structure. The subcommittees I have mentioned are certainly typical and would serve as a good start. There may need to be *ad hoc* committees of various sorts and for various purposes. Structure should create a facilitating climate, not an imprisoning one.

Board organization involves:
- The executive committee
- The finance committee
- The program committee
- The nomination committee

The policy manager not only needs to assist the board in establishing a good working structure, but also in helping it to function. Involved here is a diplomatic process that seeks to move people among the various subcommittees. Once subcommittees are established, they frequently encounter the problem of becoming "member-fixed," that is, the same people always serve on them. Thus, new members never get to be on the finance committee, and members of the finance committee never get to grapple with problems of program or with the difficulties of securing and recruiting individuals. For more points of view, some degree of flow among members of the subcommittees is important.

Policy Refurbishment and Review

The material discussed so far—legal responsibilities, recruitment of members, board organization—is really the means to the end of high quality policy and high quality decisions. But one might well ask, "how can we tell if a policy decision is of high quality?" The answer, as I have said before, is "one cannot." If the information is good, the discussion good and the decision taken in a timely fashion, the likelihood that the decision will be an adequate one will certainly be high, but it may not be, and it is doubly and triply likely that we will not spot our own errors, at least at the time. Sometimes the quality of a decision can be ascertained only after some time has passed. For these reasons, we need to expect that there will be problems in the policy decision we made and that we will need to undertake appropriate and regular policy refurbishment.

Policy Refurbishment

Policy refurbishment means that all organizational policies of an important sort are assessed on some regular basis—I suggest once every three years—with appropriate amendments and adjustments made to keep the policy functioning at a high quality. Several things can happen that are worth mentioning. One has to do with the erosion of policy by practice. (Recall the discussion of policy and practice in chapter 1.) At a certain time a policy is passed and at that time it meets the agency's needs. However, the situation to which that policy addressed itself may change, at first slightly, and then more as time goes on. The individuals who administered the policy may change—one may retire, another may take another job—and new individuals may be brought in, slight differences in need, or in application may occur. Hence, a year or two later one looks at the policy and looks at what is actually going on and finds a great degree of difference. There will always be some degree of policy/practice difference. But when that gap becomes wide, it means that the policy is no longer that made by the board, but rather has shifted completely into the executive office. This does not fulfill the legal responsibilities of the board, nor does it represent the combined wisdom of the board members applied to a particular issue. Hence, the policy manager needs to engage in a structuring of policy reviews so that the organization can take a look at such situations in more systematic detail.

This process may sound easier than it actually is. Part of the problem is that once a decision is made, people no longer want to look at it. "If it's not broke, don't fix it" is one of the common phrases heard in situations like this. There is a lack of urgency, since the policy is not really under the gun, and on the countervailing side, there are a number of issues, frequently quite urgent, pressing the organization. In fact, the sloppier the procedures of the organization, the more likely it is to be faced with "emergencies." The more it is faced with emergencies and the need to make decisions quickly, without adequate information and without adequate time to digest the material, the more likely it is that those policies will be of poor quality. To the extent that the decisions are of poor quality, it is more likely yet that they will not solve the problems to which they were addressed, or not solve them well, or solve them on a superficial basis, thus generating still more emergencies. There are yet other problems. Decisions made under emergency conditions tend to be among those for which the information available is inadequate. Furthermore, under those conditions emotions are likely to run high, and decisions involving topics where emotion runs high are less likely to be as thoughtful and cogent as they might otherwise be. Hence, the very situations that work against policy review and refurbishment make them even more necessary. Because, without systematic attention to policy in more tranquil times, turmoil is high. (See pages 98–101 and Exercise 5.7.)

Policy Review

Refurbishment, however, is no substitute for review. It is good to dress up a policy periodically to deal with some specific problems and difficulties, but one should not ignore the need to look more systematically at policies. A regularized process of policy review, about every six years, is certainly a good idea. While the refurbishment process may take a point here and a point there and pass an amendment or an adjustment, the policy review process looks at the whole process and reaffirms. Indeed, my strong recommendation is that policies contain sunset provisions, so that they expire after six years, and thus force the board to take a look at something they might otherwise put off. (See pages 98–101 and Exercise 5.7.)

The Decision Audit and Decision Autopsy

A quite common process is to consider the decision audit and the decision autopsy as analysis options. In the review and refurbishment process one looks at particular decisions or particular policies scheduled for review well in advance. That longitudinal view might be supplemented as well by a horizontal one. The decision audit or planning audit looks at the decisions made over a given year and tries to come to some overall characterization of their thrust, quality, and import. It is useful for a board to ask itself, ''what decisions did we make this year?'' to list them, and to spend some time considering what action they took and the degree of satisfaction, based on retrospective knowledge, they had with the results. The decision autopsy represents a more focused analysis of decision errors and mistakes. We are all going to make them. The difference is between those of us who learn from them and those of us who repeat them. It is imperative that, when a bad decision has been made, it be looked at in terms of seeking to explain what happened. Was there inadequate information? Was the problem incorrectly formulated? Were there some important unknowns that later materialized? Were there problems in the decision process itself? Were possible alternatives suppressed because of interpersonal conflicts within the meeting when it was discussed? And so on and so forth. This will not happen too frequently. And the more, of course, the planning autopsy is done, the less likely one is to repeat the same kinds of problems. The seven criteria developed by Janis and Mann (1977) and contained in Exercise 2.3 are one way to assess the decision process.

Policy refurbishment and review should:
- Assess and adjust policies every three years
- Review and revise every six years
- Develop decision audit and autopsy procedures

Conclusion

This chapter is focused on the role of the policy manager as a board facilitator, seeking to acquaint the board with its legal responsibilities, recruiting good members, setting up an appropriate organization and a systematic process for reviewing and looking at decisions and policies. Without such activity, the board is likely to languish and either become a rubber stamp or take off on a course quite on its own (Goldberg 1980). One other responsibility of the policy manager, however, needs to be the subject of an entire chapter: the development of good meeting procedures.

CASE ILLUSTRATIONS

THE CHILD WELFARE AGENCY

The plan that Jim had developed for slimming and trimming the board of directors was continuing to work well. The board was now almost half its former size. A third of the members' terms had come up during the year and they had been transferred to the agency friends' group. Some Jim wanted to retain and he spoke with each one privately, indicating that for political reasons a little time would have to elapse but he would be able to use them in this other capacity. In all instances this seemed to work out quite well. Other members had resigned or had never shown up, so they were diplomatically reassigned to the agency friends' group. From Jim's point of view two things were essential with respect to this board of directors. One was pro-activity and the other was oversight. The board needed to look ahead and try to anticipate problems the agency might face and provide guidance and decisions that would move the agency in useful ways toward coping with the anticipated problems. Second, and perhaps most importantly for this board given its background, was the need to move in a sustained and systematic way to oversee what the agency was doing, including overseeing the executive operation. Jim ruefully thought he had not got off to a terribly good start in that department since he had used the emergency situation to continue an "autocratic" agency model, but that had been for a fairly brief period of time and he did not want it to go on. Perhaps the best way to begin, he thought, would be to involve the board in an assessment of what had been accomplished during the first nine-month period.

Privately, Jim thought that the board was a major cause of the agency being where it was. People in town now seemed to blame the former director and, indeed, a number of his patterns and activities were an obvious cause of the agency's problem, but one had to go a bit deeper than that. Why had these patterns and activities developed and why were they permitted to continue? It was nowhere written that the board had to sit idly by and let things go on year after year and not be informed about them. Anyway, the board was the legally responsible party, not the executive, whatever the executive may have thought or however the executive may have acted. As difficult as evaluation was, it was more concrete than thinking and planning ahead. Jim sat down with the president and together they worked out an evaluation plan that seemed to be satisfactory. With some modification it was approved at the next board meeting. In essence the plan consisted of an in-depth review of the current pattern at the organization and a concurrent evaluation of the executive's performance. The executive was asked to put in writing the goals he would try to achieve during the next year, which the board could modify as appropriate. These goals would then form the basis of a sort of loose contract both board and executive could use as a guide for activity over the coming year. At least, thought Jim, it's a start.

Discussion Questions

1. How did the board get in such bad shape? It could not have been "only" the executive. He was just one person. What else could have been involved?

2. What are some of the steps used to refurbish the board? Do you think they will work?

THE WELFARE PLANNING COUNCIL

The executive of the Welfare Planning Council turned her attention to the board also. Her problem was a bit different, however. Under the old community influence model the welfare council's board had sought to involve the "power brokers" of the community, women and men who could "make things happen" and who "had clout." Under the new view, one in which the welfare policy and planning council was more an idea-generating and idea-effecting organization, with ratification and the force for implementation coming from the agencies themselves, this board was not the most appropriate group of individuals. Rather, it seemed that people with more technical and substantive skills, who were respected not so much for their community power but more for their academic, intellectual, and technical power, would be the way to go. She realized that one could not change a board overnight, but the kind of expertise and directions needed were now coming to be different. How might they begin to move in this direction, she wondered? And then, it hit her. The nominating committee! We should begin with the nominating committee and seek to use it as a vehicle not only to nominate officers but also to recruit new members. She telephoned the chairman of the nominating committee and arranged a time to get together to talk about the upcoming replacements.

Discussion Questions

1. Do you think that the executive's strategy for board change is correct? Will it work? Are there other strategies that could work too?

2. Think of an agency board you know. What are some of the problems it has? Why? How can it be improved?

10

MANAGING EFFECTIVE MEETINGS

The policy manager constructs policy machinery to accomplish policy tasks. As I mentioned above, policy machinery tends to be policy committees for groups of people assigned to undertake various policy tasks. For this reason it is imperative that the policy manager be well acquainted with the structural necessities involved in running a good meeting of a decision-making group. Much of the policy manager's time will be spend in decision-making groups of various types. Further, the board of directors activity, with which the policy manager is likely to be heavily involved, also has requirements for good meeting procedures. Without such procedures it is impossible for boards to act effectively. The interlinking skills of managing ideas, people, and documents require that skill and the management of policy groups be a part of that because, without the ability to manage policy groups, it is impossible to effectively carry out the first three tasks. Documents typically come before policy groups for various kinds of action. One needs to know how to prepare these documents and how to process them in the decision-making group itself. People are crucial to decision-making groups too and the policy manager needs to be aware of the way in which people are likely to interact and the way in which roles, or views, oppose each other within the decision-making situation. All too often, because of the interaction of people and the lack of preparation of documents (or the preparation of documents in the wrong way really), ideas become submerged rather than surface. The decision group is a powerful tool for improving the quality of the policy decision, but, like all tools, it can be used against that goal as well as for it. Skill at meeting management does not replace skill in the concept and research areas, diplomacy in dealing with individuals and groups, and the ability to write clearly and well. However, without the additional craft of meeting management, those skills are likely to be less effective and less influential.

How to Make Things Go Right
in Policy Meetings

One of the essential roles of the policy manager is to make things go right. What is crucial is a set of skills that help to guide policy committees in a more policy positive direction. I will briefly present eight rules, which will help to make things go right and which represent an important part of the skills of the policy manager. It is important, though, to keep a couple of assumptions in mind before discussing these rules, because they stem from a particular perspective on the policy decision group.

Information Is Essential. The first assumption is that information is absolutely crucial to high quality policy decisions. Thus, the system that I will briefly sketch out here is predicated on securing and providing information to decision-making groups in a timely fashion and in a form that takes advantage of the skills and capabilities of the group rather than works against it.

Structure Is More Important Than Personality. The second assumption is that the structure of this process is more important, all things considered, than the personalities involved. Many of the materials available on how to run good meetings focus on ways to deal with personalities—hostile Harry, angry Arthur, silent Sue, and so on. Dealing with personalities, however, without providing a good system for providing information, specifying goals, and developing decision rules, is not likely to be much help. Hence, our focus is on rules and roles rather than the personalities involved. The best way to think about the roles is to think of the policy committee as an orchestra with a conductor, a score, various virtuosi performing on their various instruments, uniquely skilled, yet combining to do something that none alone could do. It is to get the orchestral sound—the high quality policy decision—that the policy manager works hard. There are some rules which will be helpful to the policy manager in seeking this goal.

The Rule of Halves

The Rule of Halves is simple. It says that all material for an upcoming meeting shall be in the hands of the agenda scheduler one-half of the time between the meeting dates. That means, for example, that if a monthly meeting is scheduled, at the two-week point the agenda scheduler should have all the material available to be considered at the upcoming meeting. These candidate items are reviewed by the agenda scheduler in a number of dimensions.

Item Screening. The items are screened for appropriateness given their content and the amount of information of people available. Items which cannot be decided because of inadequate information are not useful ones to place on the agenda. This does not mean they will never be placed on the agenda. It does mean, however, that a process of screening for adequate information should go on.

Item Scrutiny. Items are scrutinized for completeness as items. Frequently, items come in ways which are only partial. That is, if item X is to be considered, then item X plus one must also be considered because of its linked implication. Hence, there needs to be agenda augmentation so that the item can be usefully considered in its appropriate context. Sometimes agenda decomposition needs to occur, an item is suggested which is in too large a lump, has too many implications, and needs to be broken apart in its subsections so that appropriate intellectual digestion can occur.

Item Sifting. Sometimes items thought to be appropriate for the agenda of a policy group are best handled in someone's office or on the telephone. The suggestor will not always be aware of this. S/he may not have thought about it, or events may have developed which make other items more urgent. The opportunity to look through items ahead of time is therefore useful.

Item Ordering. One of the important processes permitted by the Rule of Halves is the ordering of items. In fact, this is so important that it has its own rule—the Rule of the Agenda Bell, which will be discussed below.

The Rule of Three-Quarters

One of the reasons for the Rule of Halves is, of course, the Rule of Three-Quarters. The Rule of Three-Quarters requires that at the three-quarters point a packet of material goes to the members of the group, giving them time to look at the material (contents of that material will be discussed under the Rule of Reports). Without that opportunity, it is difficult to approach a matter thoughtfully. The policy manager should try, if at all possible, to avoid handing out material to be read at the meeting itself. People simply do not have the time to look through the material during the meeting and comment on it, if the comments are to be anything more than off-the-cuff reactions.

One last point concerning the actual language used in the material sent out for the agenda needs to be made as part of the Rule of Three-Quarters. Frequently, agenda language is casual and lacks specificity. Words like "minutes" or "the Jones-Smith Report" often appear as topic headings. If possible, these kinds of phrases should be avoided, and specific, more directive headings should be used, containing action verbs that focus the reader's attention on the action desired. Thus, rather than "Minutes," the phrase should read "Approval of the Minutes." When a report comes up for action, it should be "Consideration of the Smith-Jones Report" or "Approval of the Van Purchase Agreement." Without that kind of specificity, part of the purpose of the Rule of Three-Quarters is thwarted. One wants to alert people in advance to the expected course of action. One does not want to prejudge the outcome of that action, but rather to emphasize its nature. In addition to action phrases, include below each item a sentence or two about the nature of the action. Thus, under the item "Approval of the Van Purchase Agreement," a sentence could read, "Approval is requested for the expenditure of $2,000 to lease a van." This gives agenda readers and skimmers a taste of the core of the topic and is likely to encourage them to take a look at the copy of the Van Purchase Agreement included as an attachment.

The Rule of Thirds

The Rule of Thirds says that the meeting of a policy group is typically structured in three parts. The first part represents a developmental stage, in which the group assembles, catches up on past events, handles minor business, and generally gears up for the middle section. In the middle section the most important items should be handled. Once they are decided, the task phase of the group's responsibility has, in important respects at least, been completed. The third phase is a decompressing and distancing from the material and moves the group to discussion items. The items and the flow of items need to be organized consistent with this flow of expectations. Very few meetings are structured according to this principle, but it links very much to the bell-shaped curve structure.

The Rule of Minutes

Minutes are among the most mischievious of policy group documents because they frequently invite, by their very structure, discussion of last week's meeting again this week. This often occurs because of the way in which the minutes are written up, and for this reason, the policy manager is better off preparing content minutes rather than process minutes. Process minutes are of the "he said/she said" variety and policy managers invariably find that once people see what they said, they argue they never would have said that. The issue is not one of accuracy, and getting a tape recording to prove to somebody that he said something which, upon reflection, he finds embarrassing and offensive will not solve the problem. Rather, the minutes should be of the content variety. Content minutes are those that contain a brief summary of the item, followed by a discussion of the different points on the item, followed by the *decision* on the item, highlighted and in different type. This last point may seem like a small one, but it is important nonetheless. If human service organizations are going to do policy audits and policy autopsies with a special focus on key decisions, then they need to have very quick access to the decisions made over a three-month, six-month, and twelve-month period. If one can review the minutes of the group and quickly pick out decisions by virtue of their being listed in this special way or special type, the process is immeasurably shortened and for that reason made possible. Tossing somebody a stack of old minutes and asking him or her to dig out the decisions is a task, which, because of its difficulty, is likely to encounter resistance and not be completed.

The structure of minutes should be agenda relevant. Agenda relevant minutes are those that have the same numbering system as the agenda itself, making it easy to move from the agenda to the minutes and back again, finding out what was on the agenda and what was decided.

The Rule of Reports

Reports are discussed in more detail in chapter 11, but a word here is appropriate. For most committees, information underload is "corrected" through information overload. When committees do not have enough information, staffers sometimes try to correct the situation by providing too much information. We are all familiar with the "fat" report which cannot be digested at all in the time available. What is needed, alternatively, is the *Executive Summary,* which is a brief, one- or two-page report that gives members the essential information in terms they can get through in the time they have. Basically, executive summaries that go to policy-making groups should be in three parts as an *Option Memo.* The first part should contain a restatement of the problem. The second should present reasonable options for dealing with the problem. The third should present the preparer's recommendation. The policy manager is often the preparer or architect of the policy document, and thus has the opportunity to say what she or he thinks would be a reasonable solution. However, the policy manager needs to be aware that the purpose of including options is to let decision-making groups come up, to some degree at least, with their own ideas. Thus, the recommendation section should always be headed *preliminary* or *tentative,* and the policy manager should expect the final decisions to be somewhat different, although perhaps not very different, from the original recommendations. Following this set of procedures also militates against the policy group's feeling as if were a rubber stamp. If all the policy group gets is a single recommendation, its decision options are reduced to two—approve or reject—closing out the most creative options available and often generating resentment within the membership of the decision-making group. Hence, providing options and directing the group's attention to a range of possible solutions is good. That range, incidentally, may be quickly expanded by the group as other options are thought of, since the policy manager or subcommittee is not likely to have thought of all the possibilities—at least all that are reasonable. We are not suggesting here that every single possibility in some kind of "maximizing" way be listed, but rather a satisfactory number of reasonable ones. Nonetheless, there may be more satisfactory ones than have been thought of thus far.

Rule of the Agenda Bell

The Rule of the Agenda Bell provides a set of directions for structuring the agenda in such a way as to facilitate the consideration of items by ordering them in a way consistent with the flow of energy within the group. Let us consider a seven-item agenda and think about how our process of setting agenda priorities has identified those more important and those less important. The agenda should then be structured something like this.

Item 1: Minutes. Item 1, minutes, should not take a great deal of time, especially if content minutes are used. The purpose of minutes is to provide a record of the previous meeting, not provide an occasion for rehashing it.

Item 2: Announcements. A few announcements of a non-controversial sort may be made here. This is not the time for progress reports of committees. In fact, this agenda contemplates no such reports. If there is business to be done, it should be listed as an item. If there is no business, the committee should not report. If a subcommittee wishes to discuss something, it should come as a later item.

Item 3: Modestly difficult item. Item 3 should be an item selected from the agenda priorities discussed under the Rule of Halves. As an item of only modest difficulty, it should be a short item, basically one that can begin to get the group into decision-making activity without necessarily throwing the book at it the first time.

Item 4: Moderately difficult item. After Item 3 has been completed, Item 4 should come up for discussion and decision. Item 4 should be one of moderate difficulty, not the most difficult, which will appear as Item 5, but certainly more difficult than Item 3.

Item 5: The most difficult item. Item 5 is the most difficult item and should occupy that place in the meeting between about the 40 percent point and the 60 percent point, or the middle of the meeting. It is not quite the middle third and it can be expanded to fill the entire middle third, if it is very difficult, or, if it is a difficult item, but not of overwhelming difficulty, can be shortened to 45 percent to 55 percent. There are many reasons for scheduling Item 5 here, among them the fact that attendance is usually highest. Late arrivers will have come and the early leavers will not have slipped out yet. Also, the group is at the high point of its physiological and psychological energy. After the midpoint, and most especially after a period roughly approximating the seventh-inning stretch, interest and energy for the task at hand begin to decline. Hence, one should already have completed the most important aspects of the task at hand. Item 5 is expected to be controversial, therefore to locate it too close to the end of the meeting may well embroil it in the psychology of meeting termination. Locating it too near the beginning may find not everyone psychologically prepared, or even present, and thus effective handling is made more difficult.

Item 6: Discussion only. Item 6 should be labeled explicitly for discussion only and serves several purposes. First, of course, it serves as a break. The big issue has been decided (it is hoped) and the group does not want to, and should not, move directly to another decision issue. It is time to give people a chance to unwind a little and take a break from the hard work of decision. A discussion on some other topic is a useful way to structure this. The policy manager might even want to schedule a short stretch after the completion of Item 5 as a physiological release from psychological tension, but the discussion of an Item 6 certainly serves as a good way to do the same thing. Then one does not run the risk of pushing people too far in the decision-making process.

Item 6 has a number of other merits that need mention. One has to do with the problem of bad judgment on the length of time Item 5 will actually take. While it seems legitimate to focus it during the middle third of the meeting, it may explode unavoidably and take longer. If that happens, one can use Item 6 as a cushion. Since it is a discussion item, it can be squeezed into a smaller time frame, thus making it possible for Item 5 to be completed during the meeting. Otherwise it might have run to the end of the meeting and been prematurely aborted.

Item 6 is a good time to discuss proposals in a preliminary way too, and it is here that we can introduce the Two-Meeting Rule. The *Two-Meeting Rule* suggests that most items moderately to highly controversial be introduced first in Item 6, then at a subsequent meeting in Item 5. The Item 6 discussion period should prohibit decision-making, giving people time to think through an item without the need to act on it immediately. It is very difficult to have to act at the same time one receives an item, and an intervening period of time often is a positive force. If one follows the Two-Meeting Rule, one might also assign the role of devil's advocate. Frequently, in board and policy committee discussions, the reigning ideologies and myths prohibit thoughtful and serious exploration of alternatives of even modest change from current practice. It is very difficult, in an interpersonal situation without group support, for individuals to undertake the necessary argument appropriate for bringing out the positives and negatives. In the devil's advocate role an individual is asked to offer arguments contrary to the proposal being offered for discussion, specifically to look for and raise problems or to propose more controversial alternatives. If asked to perform this role, it is likely that someone would be willing to carry it out. It becomes a standard operating procedure in the organization and raises no comment, and creates the conditions for greater clarity and vigor of discussion. On the other hand, one can also use the pro/con advocate model. In this model, an individual is assigned to argue the merits and another the demerits of a particular proposal. Here again, the intent is to bring out subtleties and complexities that would not emerge in a discussion without this kind of structure. I need to inject a word of caution here. The devil's advocate model and the pro/con model are not ones to use on every issue. They can become stereotyped and tired. However, if used judiciously and for important matters, they can be very helpful in bringing forward various points the board needs to consider.

Two other possible vehicles can be used in Item 6: the *in-principle technique* and the *straw-vote technique*. The in-principle technique is a conscious attempt to divorce the ''principle'' matters at hand from the more detailed matters of application. Frequently, if an item is complicated, important matters of principle as well as difficult matters of detail become involved in the discussion. It is difficult for these two levels to exist simultaneously, and, if a discussion proceeds too far along that path, it suffers from intellectual oscillation that destroys the utility of either type of discussion. Item 6 is most useful for discussing matters of principle—do we want to go this way in principle or do we want to go that way? While it is true that subsequent details may change, once used, the question here is not one of detail but of overall perspective in judgment. If one can limit discussion to that, it is quite possible to deal fruitfully with matters of high policy without getting bogged down. One should be aware of the in-principle technique and use it.

A straw-vote technique is a way of setting priorities for alternatives essentially useful to staff within the organization. It should be kept in mind that the development of information with respect to alternatives is a fairly complex task and not one which is, by any means, costless. Thus, the executive and the deputy may well wish to have some information about the relative priority of preference among particular alternatives from the board and from other policy committees so that they can assign staff to work up alternatives in an order that meets the general wishes of the decision-making group. A straw-vote technique simply sets priorities for a number of alternatives that may come up for discussion and permits the most economical assignment of staff.

The Item 6 area then, as can be easily seen from this discussion, is one that serves a variety of crucial needs within the organization. Hence, the items there should be thoughtfully and carefully scheduled; it should not be a dumping ground. If an organization needs, for reasons of its own tradition, to have reports from committees that do not require action, they can be placed at the end of the Item 6 period and very brief oral reports can be presented.

Four techniques for Item 6 are:
- Two-meeting rule
- Devil's advocate
- In-principle technique
- Straw-vote technique

The Rule of Agenda Integrity

The seventh rule focuses on systematic efforts to make worthwhile the time that people put in going over the material they should have received under the Rule of Three-Quarters. All policy managers frequently send out material in copious detail and then become upset when people have not read it. Under the Rule of Reports we discussed the options memo and the executive summary to help people get material more palatable to them. However, the utility of getting that material must be reinforced within the meeting itself, and the policy manager, through the Rule of Agenda Integrity, must seek to structure that reinforcement. *The Rule of Agenda Integrity* simply stresses the necessity of covering all the items on the agenda and not covering those not on the agenda. If one is to ask people to make investment in preparing for a meeting through review and thinking about the material to be covered, then that investment of time and energy must bear fruit in the meeting itself. If the material is not reviewed, as promised by the agenda, then the message members will receive is that it is not worthwhile to bother reading the material. This message may be reinforced if policy managers give a fairly extensive oral review of the material, which also makes it unnecessary to invest time reading and studying. The more one seeks to rectify lack of preparation on the part of members by adding material in the meeting itself, the more one creates the very situation one seeks to overcome.

Why, though, should one object to discussing new items? Isn't new business "a historical part of many agendas?" Indeed it is, but it should be handled very gingerly. There are reasons for avoiding new business or for handling it in such a way that it becomes a suggestion for the agenda next time rather than an agenda item this time. As policy managers are aware, the quality of the discussion is related very positively to the amount of information available on the topic. New business items are typically those that have the least amount of information available. Hence, discussion tends to be ill-formed and not very productive. This alone would be sufficient reason for limiting new business items but there is a second reason—the introduction of these items tends to drive out those previously scheduled. Therefore, if one is to discuss new business at all, it should be at the end of the meeting as a conclusion to the Item 6 section. It is more useful to invoke the Rule of Halves and have such items come in, in advance, to the agenda scheduler or policy manager.

A final point about agenda integrity is in order and it relates to attendance decisions. Members make attendance decisions based upon their understanding of the items up for discussion and those not up for discussion. Most of us have more committee assignments than we can comfortably meet in a single day or week, and therefore we set rough priorities for ourselves and plan to attend those meetings which appear to be most important to our concerns. If I decide to attend a particular meeting and find that the item in which I was extremely interested is never discussed, I tend to develop a rather negative feeling toward that particular committee, and may lessen my participation. Similarly, if I do not attend a particular meeting, based on the announced agenda, and find matters of interest to me did come up and were discussed, I may be similarly upset. This is not to say that such events will never occur, but rather, the policy manager should consider the agenda a rough sort of contract among the committee members and seek, insofar as possible, to have that contract honored.

The Rule of Temporal Integrity

Temporal integrity means three things: begin on time, end on time, and follow a rough internal order within the agenda itself in terms of the amount of time spent on particular topics. It strikes home to readers as they think of the endless times they have wasted before meetings begin and the frustration they have experienced while trying to leave one meeting to hurry to the next one. The policy manager needs to take this small problem seriously and make every effort to begin on time and to end on time. The importance of this lies as much in the attitude of the members toward attendance as anything else. If people have a sense that their time commitments will be honored, they are much more likely to be willing to come to the meeting. Hence, it indirectly aids the quality of the decision.

The second point, internal time allocation, is important as well. We have all experienced the "runaway item" that suddenly develops a great deal of interest and controversy. An unusual case, but one to be expected and avoided. The reason, of course, is that the more time spent on one item, the less time there is to spend on another. Small and relatively unimportant items can drive out discussion of more important items simply because time has run out. One of the easiest ways to handle this problem is to put suggested times beside the item on the agenda. This lets people know about how much time would be appropriate and gives them some guidance about how much meeting time they should devote to a particular topic.

Eight Rules to Help Meetings Go Right:

- Rule of halves
- Rule of three-quarters
- Rule of thirds
- Rule of minutes
- Rule of reports
- Rule of agenda bell
- Rule of agenda integrity
- Rule of temporal integrity

Conclusion

Policy managers spend a lot of time in meetings and the need to have them go well is essential to the development of high policy decisions. Thus, policy managers need to be aware of ways in which meetings can go well and in which the creative potential of a number of interacting individuals from different perspectives can enhance rather than retard the quality of the policy process. The system discussed here is information driven. It sets up a structure for funneling information to committee members, asks them to spend time discussing the implications of that information, and then to make a decision on the basis of it. When information is not available, an item is set aside.

There is another element important to the policy manager in the committee process. Policy is certainly ideas, but it is also politics, and the ability to develop quality decisions and to carry them out depends very heavily upon the quality of cooperation and the degree of agreement among those involved. The committee represents one, perhaps the central, locus within the organizational framework (intra-organizational system) and within the larger set of other organizations with which the policy manager's agency interacts (inter-organizational system). The bringing together of people within the human service system and linking that system to other systems is an essential part of the political job of the policy manager and deserves attention. Hence, from two perspectives the policy committee is a crucial target of policy manager intervention—from the intellectual and conceptual point of view and from the political and interpersonal point of view.

CASE ILLUSTRATIONS

THE CHILD WELFARE AGENCY

While things at the board level had moved swiftly, they had not always moved smoothly. Part of the problem was the truly chaotic board meetings that had characterized the agency for many years. Part of the reason the board had done what it had done, or actually not done the things it should have done, was that the previous executive had become increasingly arrogant, demanding, and assertive. People said that in earlier years he had worked very well and smoothly with the board, but perhaps over time he had lost patience. Anyway, there seemed to be a sense in the community that as time passed the man had felt that he knew what needed to be done and was not terribly willing to listen to new board members and new perspectives. For the past ten years at least, the board meetings had been legendary battle scenes, in which the executive had literally intimidated the board into submission through table pounding, shouting, and threats to resign at almost every meeting. Jim wondered why the board had not simply accepted the resignation or fired the executive on the spot. But he didn't spend a long time on that question, since he had never really heard that anything like that happened. Still, the legacy of those behavior patterns continued. In particular, it was very difficult to plan for board meetings. Members would not follow the agenda. They came and went at will. The list of difficulties went on and on. One of the things Jim thought was needed was some board training, especially if the board was to move from a position of hangdog reticence into one of vigorous pro-activity. He realized that his own behavior during the transition period communicated this kind of role to the board. Therefore, he thought he would try to get an outside person to come in and begin to work with the board in some training sessions to develop their sense of competence and to provide them with some suggestions about the ways to go.

Discussion Questions

1. Think of some meetings you were at recently. Do they seem to have the kinds of problems discussed here? Why should so much conflict have erupted? What could be done (could you do) to change it?

2. How can the executive keep from becoming too powerful (or too dominating) a figure? Are there some techniques discussed here which could help?

THE WELFARE PLANNING COUNCIL

The executive had spent a lot of time recasting the board, and it had begun to look quite good. Their meetings were running so smoothly that, in fact, they had lead to the development of a new task for the agency. Several board members had commented that because their meetings were running so well they had used some of the techniques in their businesses. She began to think that if the materials and structures that seemed to work well here could be packaged and made available to others, they might benefit as well. She thought that one of the great problems of good decision making, whether at the agency or the community level, was not so much lack of power, but rather lack of a reasonable and sensible process for getting information together and assessing it. Power, she thought, was often used as a substitute for intelligence. Therefore, she began to think about ways in which her organization could provide some training in good decision making—and perhaps market it as a service to the community.

Discussion Questions

1. Think about some committees or boards you know about or are on which seem to run exceptionally well. Ask yourself why this is so. What are some of the policies and practices that make it so?

2. Pretend you are a participant or observer at the next meeting. Make a list of the tactics that help to strengthen the process of group decision making and make it good.

11

POLICY WRITING

Much of the policy manager role involves writing—preparing reports and summaries, communicating with other sources and resources about information, and pulling together research information and technical perspectives. It is in the written document, most usually, that the policy manager's many lines of work come together—academic research, personal communication, policy and program history, and political information. In addition, of course, the manager's own perspectives are important here.

The fact of the matter is, in human service organizations, as well as elsewhere, that policy is written. If it is not, it is the *language* of a proposed policy which is approved, however much intent is meant, or "we assumed this and that," it is the *language* one must attend to, refer back to, and consider when considering policy.

But language is more than the form of the end product. Language structures the alternatives, facilitates or hinders consideration, and makes the processing of ideas easy or hard. Since policy is simply the writing of ideas, the language in which those ideas are expressed can make all the difference, especially if some of the ideas are new.

However, I am not going to focus here on the language itself. Others have done that already, and better.[1] The focus here is on a slightly "larger" aspect of style—the knowledge needed in organizing and presenting written work, on (1) an organizational level within the agency, (2) a personal level, within one's own time, and (3) a psychological level within one's own feelings and attitudes. This perspective is not meant, in the least, to imply that a word-by-word analysis of style, and its improvement, is not important. Quite the contrary. But, it is also the case that such analysis is perhaps better done within the overall knowledge of the type and nature of the document under consideration, its intent, purposes, and audience. It is to this end that the chapter here will focus, seeking to lay out the different types of documents required of policy managers, the special purposes these documents have, and the nature of these types of documents individually, however, let me sum up and share a few hints that policy managers might find helpful.

When organizing and presenting written work, one needs to consider:
- One's own agency
- One's own time
- One's own feelings and values

Communicate Ideas

First, of course, is the communication of ideas. The essence of policy management is the orderly discussion of ideas, the spawning of new ideas from that discussion, and the subsequent consideration of those ideas in the process of policy development. Whatever else the document might do, it should help that process. "Help" here means special structure, one that prunes the documents of unnecessary, unwelcome, unhelpful redundant repetition (for example!), and goes straight to the heart of the matter. Many policy documents are obese, and one cannot find the idea at all; it is buried in pounds (sometimes literally) of documentation and extra copy. One group I served with brought their reports in stacked high on secretarial chairs. The only reason they did not use wheelbarrows was that they could not order them from the office supply catalogue!

1. See, for example, William Strunk, Jr., and E. B. White, *The Elements of Style* (New York: Macmillan, 1959).

Put Conclusions First

The purpose, then, of the policy document, especially in its early phases, is to communicate ideas clearly and crisply. This criterion applies whether the document is a letter, a memo, an executive summary, or one of the several kinds of reports one might prepare. The key in communicating the idea is first to state the central premise; then, and only then, add elaboration; then, and only then, add possible problems and benefits; then, and only then, add evidence. (Very complex supplements to evidence can be in an appendix.)

This point might sound strange, since we are all taught in school to do the reverse. And there are times when the policy specialist needs to use the academic approach. The academic approach usually states the problem, then discusses the problem, then discusses the discussion of the problem, then goes into a long discussion of methodology, then discusses findings, and then, and only then, reaches conclusions. The process is one designed, among other things, to bring the reader along with the writer to the conclusions. In policy research, this process is too cumbersome, too long, and loses too many people along the way.[2] More successful is a technique that states the solution to the problem or suggests several alternative solutions, based upon research done and information gathered. After the reader has had the opportunity to see what is proposed, the policy specialist can suggest some pros and cons of the solution or solutions. Then, after that information has been digested, the writer can explain how the information was gathered and how that process might have affected the results.

It is in this way that policy writing and thinking differs from that of the academy. In policy, the idea is central; the ways in which the information is generated become secondary. In science, the methodology, the ways the information was gathered, becomes central; the idea becomes secondary. This difference is, of course, overstated. Nonetheless, the policy specialist and the policy maker cannot spend time looking for the "optimum" methodology. They must find, in Simon's terms, "satisfactory" ones![3] If a source

2. See, for example, James A. Jones, "The Researcher as Policy Scientist," in I. Spergal, *Community Organization: Studies in Constraint* (Beverly Hills: Sage, 1972).

3. J. March and H. Simon, *Organizations* (New York: Wiley, 1958) pp. 140–141. They argue that "An alternative is satisfactory if: there exists a set of criteria that describes minimally satisfactory alternatives; and the alternative in question meets or exceeds all these criteria." They should add: "within available time constraints." Time is a third factor here, as point 3 below suggests.

of information is so questionable that it invalidates the data, it should not be used. Or, if used, it should be noted in some way as highly questionable. Many ideas are lost or buried under an avalanche of material with which the intelligent nonscientist has neither the background nor the time to cope.

Work to A Decision Point in Time

Time is a third central point; policy-relevant documents are usually produced under great pressure. The staffer needs to be able to develop a set of techniques to secure information and get it down on paper rather quickly. Here, information delayed is information denied. The more leisurely pace of the academic researcher, however justified in terms of science, has a rough go in the policy process. Policy life is marked by crucial junctures— the senate is voting, the hearing is being held, the allocations committee is making a decision, the board is meeting. Each situation represents one of the crucial junctures for the policy manager. Rest can come after the vote; not before. No effort must be spared to get the information there, in the appropriate format, on time.

Get Ideas on Paper Quickly

What are some of the techniques for getting things down fast? Policy managers have their preferences, but several of the following are popular. One, of course, is simply typing it out. Some people can compose on a typewriter, following an outline, while others cannot. Agonizing hours over the perfect opening sentence is not going to do much good. For those who use the typewriter, the knowledge that the first draft will be a private one, revised by you before anyone else sees it, is helpful in getting those initial thoughts out. Most people who write a good deal "cut and paste"—using sections written in one place for another. It is necessary to be aware of the fact that words can be changed so that one feels free to put them down in the first place.

Then, there is dictation. Many recording methods are available, and they have the advantage of being able to record thought quickly, on the spot. However, they are not the panacea that the salespeople would have us believe. One reason is that people sometimes have verbal constipation or diarrhea just as those who write do. This, though, can be worse, because someone has to type it and then you have to read it. It is often shocking to see just exactly what you said, in the same way it is to see yourself in a video. The key here, of course, is the same as for the written draft: *use an outline*.

Rewrite

After the initial draft has been completed, an additional technique is useful, if available. Sometimes the smallest things cause infinite trouble, and in the case of policy papers, which often go through draft after draft, that "small" thing may well be the secretary who simply cannot stand to do one more draft. What is helpful here, whether the initial draft is on paper or cassette, is a memory typewriter that allows considerable revision with modest retyping. There are even more elaborate word processors that make substantial revision much easier. It may seem, and it is, a small point to talk about how to make a draft, but, as noted before, drafting and drafting again is one of the most important aspects of a policy manager's writing responsibilities. Thus, one needs to think not only of how to do it physically, but how to prepare the structure of the text so that revisions are in fact facilitated, and the actual paper and structure on the page can handle it. Additionally, one needs to prepare oneself psychologically for this kind of "revisionism."

Prepare Psychologically for Review and Revisions

One of the more difficult elements of the policy manager's job in the writing phase is to think about the many people who might review the document and to prepare for that review. The document writer is the crystalizer, the point person, the "lead dog" of the policy process. Thus, much criticism might well come to that person simply by virtue of being first. It is a sort of analogy to being the first child in a family. Drafts will be torn apart. Revisions will be requested. As the manager will find, suddenly everyone is a writer, eager to display (though not write) expertise on the meaning of this word or that and provide insight on the meaning of this passage or that, often at random. Some of these comments will be helpful in terms of the written text, but many will not, or will have to be used to satisfy an individual's political orientations, which are expressed in a grammatical mode. The manager should remember that policy documents, preeminently, are an example of the "symbolic politics" and "political language" that Murray Edleman wrote about.

It should be clear, then, that beliefs and perceptions based on problematic categorization are not the exceptions. In every significant respect political issues and actors assume characteristics that are symbolically cued. From subtle linguistic evocations and associated governmental actions we get a great many of our beliefs about what our problems are, their causes, their seriousness, our success or failure in coping with them, which aspects are fixed and which are changeable and what impacts they have on which groups of people. (Edleman 1977:41)

It is this politically evocative function of policy language that makes the writing process in policy so difficult. One has to consider the intended audience. The staffer needs to recognize the likelihood of political necessity for approaches and language that might not otherwise make sense and be aware of the fact that some policy participants will need to criticize for that purpose only. A strong ego is needed, but even more, is recognition of the complex political process in language itself, a crucial aspect in determining the reaction one gets. Too, the early draft is likely to be the first time many policy committee members have seen, and thus are likely to be somewhat shocked by, the concrete expression of what they have been talking about. Knowing these things can help the policy manager understand the process of draft critique, interpret the criticisms, produce fresh drafts, without becoming too involved in the process as an author.

Know the Audience

All writing pays attention to some intended audience. In the case of policy writing, there may be several audiences, each of which is partially different from the others, and each of which brings in some new people, people who have not had the benefit of participating in the previous round of discussions. This problem of changing audiences means that time will be well spent by having the staffer brief newer members about what has happened. Often such courtesy will save time later, when objections which have been handled in an earlier phase are raised.

The audience "problem" is best thought of as a series of concentric circles of people in the policy context who must be satisfied with a document, who will read it and comment on it. Time spent initially in outlining that process, that series of concentric circles, in terms of what groups and individuals are involved, will be well spent. One can think a bit about the nature of the language and the need for certain types of language based upon the nature of the audience. Each profession, each specialty, has its series of code words, and the staffer needs to be aware of these, using or not using them deliberately as appropriate. Edleman, in his section on "professional imperialism," notes how language is used by professions to advance their own point to view and offer their own solutions to social problems (Edelman 1977:101). The policy manager must be aware of these possibilities in others, and in himself or herself as well.

Because language is such a multileveled cuing system, the manager must be aware of its potentials, even if many facets of its operation are hidden. The policy manager should seek to avoid the more blatant elements of political language, that which Edleman calls bureaucratic incantation, quoting Kenneth Burke about language that "sharpen(s) the pointless and blunt(s) the too sharply pointed" (1977:101), that inflates all proposals as historic, all achievements as "the first time in recorded history," etc. Because of the job, the policy staffer is likely to be partially responsible for "bureaucratic language"—manuals, booklets of instructions, bylaws, public announcements, what I will call "exterior language," that is, language designed for exterior consumption.

The manager should seek to avoid the worst of the linguistic sins of exterior language in policy documents. It is perhaps as hard not to overclaim as it is not to over-budget—everybody's doing it. But there can be linguistic inflation, just as there is grade inflation and financial inflation, and it can be prevented to a degree by good judgment on the staffer's part.

There is a counterpart, of course—"interior language," that language designed for "internal" use only, in letters, internal reports, and so on. These two kinds of document have different functions, even though exterior documents are usually based on early drafts of interior ones, where the initial definitions of the problem are shaped and the initial frameworks for solution are considered. A powerful first draft can have impact, and it is here that the staffer has the greatest impact.

The policy manager, in writing policy documents should:
- Communicate ideas
- Put conclusions first
- Work to a decision point in time
- Get ideas on paper quickly
- Rewrite
- Prepare Psychologically for review and revision
- Know the audience

(See Exercise 11.1)

The KNOWER System

All of these observations may be well and good, but how is one to put all of them into practice? If one has the appropriate sensitivities and the appropriate background, how can they be translated into something useful? That task is a complex one, but the KNOWER system has been helpful and can provide an overall guide to policy writing. It is not the only possible guide; it is good enough to be helpful though and hence meets the "satisfying" criterion already mentioned.

KNOWER stands for *KN*owledge, *O*rganization, *W*rite, *E*valuate, and *Re*-write. Each phase is part of the drafting process, and if the production of a draft can be viewed as a process, then the staffer can have some sense of the whole.

Depending upon how involved one gets with the process, there are volumes that can help. Perhaps most useful is a volume by Mary-Clair van Leunen (1978), *A Handbook for Scholars*. The second, more complex for purposes beyond those here and hence, less useful overall, is the *Chicago Manual of Style* (1982). The *Handbook* gives one most of what is needed in putting together reports. The *Manual* is most useful as one moves toward publication.

For most purposes the KNOWER system provides a useful way to think through the issues and touch all the proper bases. As one becomes adept at such production, one will modify these rules and develop his or her own. This system is outlined below, followed by a detailed discussion of each point. The discussion can only be illustrative, because too much detail is as harmful as too little. This discussion is aimed at providing one guideline that might have some beginning use. Each of the five parts—Knowledge, Organization, Write, Evaluate, and Rewrite—will be considered in turn.

The KNOWER System for Policy Writing

I. Knowledge
  A. Define Problem
  B. Secure Information About Problem
    1. Academic information
      a. the library
      b. computerized data banks
      c. reports, fugitive documents, available from agencies
      d. use the phone to secure information from around the country
      e. personal informants
    2. Political information
      a. talk to key individuals

        b. touch base with key groups

        c. check any formal requirements

    3. Historical information

  C. Redefine the Problem

II. Organization

  A. Make an Outline

  B. Place Summary First

    1. Problem

    2. Options

    3. Your recommendations

  C. Abstracting the Summary

    1. Problem

    2. Findings

    3. Options

    4. Recommendations

  D. Details of Findings and Methodology

  E. Physical Considerations

III. Write

  A. The Draft Idea

  B. Political Language

  C. Writing Hints

    1. The Phsod Effect, and the You Tendency

    2. Quick period

    3. Vary language

    4. Anchor with illustration

    5. Write to press release

IV. Evaluate

  A. Consider Action Desired from Document

    1. Formal outcome

        a. receive

        b. accept

        c. approve

    2. Informal outcome

        a. review

        b. comments

        c. in principal

  B. Send Document Out

  C. Review Comments/Reactions

    1. Formal

    2. Process

V. Rewrite

I. Knowledge

All writing, not just policy writing, begins with knowledge. The staffer needs to know what kinds of knowledge will be important and where to get it. It is for this reason that staffers make it a point to read national and local papers regularly and to look through book ads and journals in their general field. Because of the pressures of time, it is often too late to get all the information when the time comes. Generalized preparation is appropriate and helpful. (The Notations here follows the outline and are indicated for informational purposes. In a finished report they would not necessarily be present.)

(IA) Define Problem

Once the initial assignment has been made, the problem to be considered will have to be further refined and defined before work can begin. It is useful here to make a list of the different ways the problem could be approached and to keep it available. The manager, in consultation with the committee chair will have to make a decision about the breadth of the topic, the range of information to include, and so on. As important as that is, it is also important to understand that this point is one of the first decision points. Political elements can enter here, in terms of whether one does or does not touch upon certain matters. For example, in an adoption study is the sensitive matter of interracial adoptions to be considered or excluded? Once the general parameters have been set, the process of information gathering can begin.

(IB) Secure Information About Problem

There are at least three broad areas of information needed in thinking about any problem. One is what I call "academic" information, which deals with facts, figures, and so on. The second is political information: which groups feel what ways here, whose interests are likely to be advanced, and who has held back from different courses of action that might be taken? A third is historical information: what has been the practice in the past on a matter? what is its background and how is it imbedded in the fabric of concern which confronts us today?

(IB.1) Academic Information. The main sources of this information are institutions: a) the library; b) computerized data banks; c) reports, fugitive documents, and statements put out by firms, institutes, or the government

that might not be in general circulation. It is in these places that much of the raw information for reports can be found. The computerized data banks are especially helpful and contain information compiled on many different bases. *The New York Times,* for example, maintains a data base that allows access to newspaper activities by topic or day. More than these, however, may be needed. Thus one might need to use sources such as the following: d) the phone, to secure information by calling around the country to check key facts; e) personal informants, who can be professors or key people in key places, and who can lead one to sources of information as well as comment upon its accuracy and authenticity. It is important for the staffer to have available a bank of information sources on hand for quick access.

(IB.2) Political Information. Rather than facts and figures, political information depends upon who is winning and who is losing in particular policy encounters, what they want, what they would settle for, what their aspirations are, and so on. It also brings to light the positions of key individuals and groups on emerging issues. Finally, it touches bases with any formal requirements that a policy must meet, perhaps made by other levels of government, such as an affirmative action guideline or a production quota. Thus, the following are general sources for political information: a) check with key individuals; b) check with key groups; c) check any key formal legal requirements that might be important. These touchstones mean that the staffer must have some idea beforehand of who these individuals are, what the groups of importance would be, and which formal policy requirements would be germane.

(IB.3) Historical Information. One needs more than simple data and political rundowns, however. These pieces of information must themselves be placed into a perspective, one that locates the issue and the information in its historical context. Where are we now on this issue with respect to where we were? Such a question means that both the historical information and the political information need to be put into some perspective of change, of difference. Thus, the information needs to be processed a bit—rates of change computed, and the general development of a change perspective, things were this way then, they are now this way.

(IC) Redefine the Problem.

The original problem definition provided a way to get going and to organize the search for information. However, that definition was developed in relative ignorance of information. After getting information, there will almost certainly need to be some change in the problem definition, some redefinition adjusting to the new pieces of information that have now come to light. To retain the original problem definition is almost always a mistake; it is always one if such retention is mindless, a simple continuation of the original formulation without some thought about it. If it is to be retained, it should at least be as a result of a conscious decision. Such retention is rare though. Usually the problem will need to be reformulated and recast once information is available.

II. Organization

Once the information has been assembled and the problem redefined, that redefinition is used to reorganize the information into a report that will convey the information in economical and readable form. The organization phase is a transformational one in which masses of information are transformed into something that can be used by others. This phase is crucial for that very reason; all too often the staffer/writer acts here as a conduit or wheelbarrow, simply moving the masses of information from several different papers into one paper, called a "report." That kind of activity is a buck-passing of the worst sort. At this point synthesis occurs, and the staffer/writer needs to have a framework for organizing ideas, which can be used to categorize and summarize the raw information. The key focus here is the outline.

(IIA) Make an Outline

The outline is a multipurpose document. It is the endoskeleton of the work, and its key headings and points represent the key points the outside reader is to remember. They represent the main threads in the warp and woof of the argument. Most of the problems report writers have come from lack of an outline. It is useful to think of writing as involving at least two aspects: intellectual and artistic. The intellectual—the ideas and the structure—is in the outline. Once the outline is done, one can concentrate on the central aspects of saying something well. It is very hard to do both at once however. For that reason, an outline is one of the great necessities. It provides one with the opportunity to see the skeleton of the argument, to arrange the branches of the leafless tree, without worrying about how the leaves can be arranged. Then, after an initial working, and only then, should one begin to write.

Additionally, it is helpful if the outline can be woven into the structure of the argument, using heads and subheads, much as I have done here. The outline as shown has become the working outline for this section of the text. The items are organized in a series of levels: the roman numeral items represent the main division of the piece; the lettered items are the infrastructure of the argument, the main subpoints, with numbered subdivisions below. Thus:

<u>CENTER HEADING, UNDERLINED</u>

Side Heading
 Paragraph heading. Text . . .
 Paragraph heading. Text . . .
Side Heading
 Paragraph heading. Text . . .
 Paragraph heading. Text . . .

This system brings the outline, which is also the table of contents, into the text itself, and provides an easy way for a reader to scan the material.

(IIB) Place Summary First

What, then, should guide the internal organization of this outline? The summary of the whole report should come first and be about 10 percent of the report. Hence, if there is a twenty-five-page report, a two-and-one-half-page summary would be the best way to go. A one hundred-page report would have a ten-page summary. Why? There are several reasons for the summary. Policy writers are addressing people who want answers, not reasons and evidence, although they typically want those, too, but in the background. Those individuals need to know the problem, and, immediately, what you are going (or proposing) to do about it. The main argument follows later.

Also, there will be many people who will not read the whole report, who are not interested, who do not have the time, or whatever. For them, a summary is useful, because it provides them with the main conclusions based upon evidence, but without all the baggage that evidence and more detailed consideration brings. Central here is an understanding of the *problem of aggregation*. That problem refers to the large pile of reports policymaking people typically get. Each report seems necessary to those who issue it. However, from the receipt side, many reports, perhaps most, go unread, because there are just too many things to read, all sitting on the policymaker's or the executive's desk. Thus, I recommend sending out the summary and keeping the full report for those who ask for it or for those for whom it may be essential. And while paper and reproduction costs should not be the overriding consideration, they are important, and the summary can be useful especially when the report is a long one. What goes into the summary? It recapitulates the report as a whole, in terms of problem, options, and recommendations.

(IIB.1) Problem. A brief statement of what the problem is, the effects of the problem, and the predisposing and precipitating conditions that brought it to the attention of the group. Any essential history of the problem with respect to the group considering the report should be mentioned.

(IIB.2) Options. This section presents possible actions based upon investigation. It represents the conclusion of the report in terms of alternatives. Usually a brief statement of positive and negative results is given with each of the alternatives.

(IIB.3) Your Recommendations. The reader would usually like to know whether some of the options are preferred or recommended. If it is appropriate at all, that recommendation can go here. I say, "if appropriate," because in some instances the policy board or executive does not want to be influenced by recommendations. In that instance, of course, they can be left out of the text. However, it is useful and usual to have some thoughtful notes about recommendations, because the policy writer is almost certain to be asked about them during a meeting, when it is better not to have to consider an answer for the first time.

(IIC) Abstracting the Summary

The summary, with the parts given above, is the introduction to the report and is self-sufficient in terms of writing and conclusions. If someone wants more detail, it is given in the main body of the report, which is written first. It is from that main body that the summary is abstracted and it consists of four parts: the problem, the findings, the evidence for the findings, and the option/recommendations section.

(IIC.1) The Problem. This initial section gives the history of the problem in much more detail than in the initial summary. The political and intellectual antecedents of the problem are outlined, as well as any attempts to work on the problem that have failed over the years. Academic references and footnotes can well be used here to anchor the points made and to cite other literature.[4] Different scientific perspectives on the problem are discussed and the weight or "standing" of these perspectives given. Overall political dimensions are added, crossrouted with the political perspectives. The total

---

4. It is useful here to use footnotes, not to prove to the reader that one is scholarly, though some may be interested in the evidence, but rather as a simple method of keeping records. Many times key pieces of information become lost in the process of putting a report together. Anyone who has ever tried to check references and sources knows how useful it is to have them there.

picture embodies a complete scientific and political picture of the problem at hand, along with any financial or technical elements.

(IIC.2) Findings. This section reveals what the staffer's research uncovered about the problem. The actual findings themselves are placed in the next section. Here a consolidation of the evidence is given in sufficient detail to let the reader see the full implications of what has been found.[5] Nothing is presented here that could not be backed up by the findings section, but the findings themselves do not detract from the overall presentation.

Evidence. Sometimes the findings are more of an "evidence" sort, reasoning based upon a series of pieces of information connected by logical threads. These types of information are also "findings," in the older sense of "When you looked, what did you find?" They should be presented in full.

(IIC.3) Options. This part of the report is the one most often left out. Managers review the evidence and then give their recommendations. That closure means, often, that many other possibilities may be overlooked or that options become so interlinked with recommendations that it is difficult to separate them. The staffer, therefore, should write a special section detailing what might be done in the case at hand. Most options, including doing nothing, should be here, even some more radical alternatives. The full range of information comes to play here, and sometimes these options need to be phrased in an "if/then" way. However, the key point is to be sure to develop a set of alternatives. Without this section a policy might be made with an extremely constricted view of the process of idea development and the ways in which particular problems might be handled.

(IIC.4) Recommendations. Finally, the staffer can outline recommendations, whether his own, or those of the policy groups working on the problem. The important point is that there be a distinction between the options and the recommendations. When these become merged, there is a mix of person and preference that does not lend itself to sensible discussion. Rather, it makes identification and approval of some option tantamount to approval of the policy manager, which infuses the discussion with emotion and creates a situation in which it is extremely hard to think about possibilities separate from people. This section should indicate why the recommendation has been made, what makes the proposed course of action superior to others (those listed in the options section), and what disadvantages, if any, the course of proposed action has. This last point, the listing of disadvantages, is essential, ethically and politically. It is professionally inappropriate, es-

5. Some prefer to integrate the actual display of the findings (tables, charts, quoted from information sources, whatever) here. It certainly can be done. My feeling is that it represents too much of a crush.

pecially within a human services context, to have a situation develop in which errors of omission—the omission of giving possible consequences—lead to a policy being adopted with less than the available knowledge. We would not expect a physician to withhold potentially bad consequences of a procedure just to get us to have that procedure.[6] Similarly, the policy professional should not withhold information, even if it goes against his or her recommendation. Politically, too, it is important, because once lack of candor is discovered trust is gone.

(IID) Details of Findings and Methodology

The policy audience, as opposed to the academic audience, is typically not too interested in actual findings or evidence, except in an illustrative way. For this reason a special section on methodology and findings is placed in the back of the report, sometimes as an appendix. It should be understood that the differences in audience interest in no way affect the need for scientific accuracy, and the same canons of inference and logic, the same rigors of proof, apply here as in an academic paper. However, the policy relevance of the findings may be quite distant from their scientific import, and if there is any of the latter it should be in the findings and methodology section.

(IIE) Physical Considerations

The last part of the planning and thinking about the organization of the report lies here. What kind of physical structure should the report have? How long should it be? How much money is involved in reproducing it? How many copies will be needed? These questions are among those which should be considered, tentatively at least, in the beginning, because they influence how one will write and organize the report.

The organization of the report is also influenced by "report graphics," involving layout and thinking about how to present data in ways that are maximally illustrative. Even though most of the data will be presented in the findings section, attention should be given to making it understandable and readable. Then, too, there are times when it is important to present some data earlier, and sometimes reports will have accompanying presentations, such as slides or graphs. There are ways to present complex constellations of data without simply giving an off-putting cluster of tables and numbers.

Perhaps the best example of attention to such matters is in the annual

---

6. Although this has surely happened, it is not "professional."

reports of some large companies, where designers work on the format and a "slick" production is the result. We are not at that point, and those reports are for mass public consumption. Nonetheless, there is much that could be done, without considerable additional effort, to attend to issues of report graphics.

III. Write

After attention has been given to knowledge development and organization, the time has come to write. Note, though, that it is not until the middle of the system that writing begins. Premature attempts to put things on paper make the process of writing very hard, a problem many people attribute to the writing itself. Often it is a lack of knowledge (what to say) or of organization (how to structure what is said) rather than the writing itself (how to say it).

(IIIA) The Draft Idea

Reports for the human service field are no different from reports in any other field. The first problem is to get something down on paper. Once that hurdle is passed, things become much easier. For this reason, one should develop the habit of getting a first draft down quickly. As easy as this idea seems, it is extremely difficult to do, because all of us write for "hidden audiences," and it is the image of those hidden audiences, sometimes hidden even from ourselves, that make it difficult to put words on paper. This sentence is started and stopped, as is that one, and another, and another. If one realizes that the initial draft is for the writer's eyes only, the process becomes a little easier. You know that you will have a chance to revise, to "cut and paste," and, indeed, must have that chance before the initial typing for distribution.

Making yourself the first audience is psychologically essential for this next suggestion to work; set a page-time limit for yourself. For example, you might say that you are going to do three pages a day every day. That may not sound like a lot, but at the end of a month, there are thirty times three pages or ninety pages. What is essential is to get something, almost anything, down and revise later. Many people seek to write and revise at the same time, a process that can not be successful, since the orientation for writing is different from the orientation for revision. One involves a loosening up, a willingness to let go and let words come on the paper. The second involves the careful sculpting of the work, sentence by sentence.

One is rough carpentry; the other finished carpentry. The former must precede the latter.

The draft idea, then, implies the following: 1) an initial audience of the writer only; 2) letting oneself go in terms of getting words on paper; 3) then, and only then, revising; and 4) setting up some kind of page-time schedule to assure production of text. If these suggestions are followed, report writing will be much easier than it has been in the past. (See the section earlier in this chapter on getting ideas on paper quickly.)

(IIIB) Political Language

During revision one can look at the text for the appropriate political language. Several considerations are involved here. As Edleman has pointed out, the words themselves have certain meanings, which pluck certain strings in the reader. People need reassurance that the proper incantations have been mentioned, as if that meant that the proper things would be done. While what is said and what happens are two different things, it is nonetheless necessary for the writer to check to be sure that the right language and phrase bases have been touched. Being sure of this reaffirms values in the reader-writer relationship. What might some of these be in the human service field? Attention to minority groups, equal opportunity, and touching base with all relevant individuals are some examples. Even more generally, mention of saving money, of a wish to reduce expenses (even in a proposal that suggests an increase in expenses!), suggestions for excellence and quality improvement, and similar themes appropriate to the specific text will "resonate" well with the reader. Failure to touch these bases can lead to criticism and make the whole draft suspect. The writer then either has to argue that she or he erred, which looks bad, or that those things are unimportant, which looks even worse.

Similarly, certain types of references should be avoided. In the initial cover memo (of drafts) care should be taken to downplay the role of the writer and credit should be given, by name, to everyone involved and everyone on the list of readers. The writer should seek to portray himself or herself as a simple midwife for ideas and thoughts really developed by others. This process is especially hard for academics, where writing credit achieves almost the level of a form of psychic compensation.[7] This process of generalized attribution not only makes criticism more difficult, but makes

7. See John E. Tropman et al., *Strategic Perspectives on Social Policy* (Elmsford, N.Y.: Pergamon Press, 1976). The chapter on policy implementation by Tropman and Dluhy is important here. Perhaps I have overstated the "simple midwife" notion. However, the central point is how credit can be generalized rather than monopolized.

acceptance by readers easier. And there is a certain accuracy to it in the largest sense. Many of us have indeed "drunk from wells we did not dig" and are all too eager to grab credit. This process of generalizing credit, of looking for ways in which credit can be extended more broadly, reminds us of our interdependence.

A report is in many ways like a budget. One may well include in it things that will, in the final analysis, be struck in the heat of compromise. This is most likely to occur in the recommendation phase and can provide one solution to the dilemma often faced by report crafters when they get to that stage. Almost always two possibilities present themselves. One is to present some recommendations sure to be accepted, but which for that very reason might be less than radical in scope. The second possibility is to present more radical recommendations, to "tell it like it really is," even if it means that they will have more limited effect and perhaps be rejected.

A possible solution here is to structure the recommendations from the more specific, less radical, to the more general. Then the more radical ones can be used to set the farthest point at which the discussion of compromise can begin.

This use of different levels of recommendations suggests another purpose of the report. Sometimes a report is not really intended for the policy committee, but rather for the general public. In this case, the policy manager is not really developing policy proposals for committee consideration, but proposals for the public agenda, which the committee passes upon on its way to the more general forums of discussion. Sometimes, the policy manager feels that "her" or "his" committee will be negative on something that she or he feels strongly about, and the policy staffer writes the report essentially for other audiences, to whom the report will be leaked, and who will, the staffer feels, be incensed when the central initial committee rejects the proposals. This game is a dangerous one and should be avoided.

(IIIC) Writing Hints

Here is not the place to go into a detailed exposition of writing and, as already indicated, there are places where this has been better done anyway. There are some details, however, which bear attending to, some errors that crop up so continually that they should be mentioned as checks for the report writer.

(*IIIC.1*) *The Phsod Effect.* I once received a paper with the phrase "and the organizational phsod collapsed . . . ." I could not figure the word out until I read it aloud. That's right—facade! Check your words to be sure that you are not guilty of malapropisms, misspellings, and the like.

The You Tendency. In the previous sentence I used a common structure that it is best to avoid—"you" in some generalized plural sense. There is no such "you" around. It is better to use one, such as "one should . . ." "One should check words carefully to be sure that there is no malapropism, misspelling, or the like."

(IIIC.2) The Quick Period. Sentences with many subordinate clauses, sometimes called complex sentences, and those using "and" or other conjunctions, sometimes called compound sentences, are generally to be avoided, although there are times when longer sentences are useful, which, by the way, is not always easy to determine, although there are some good rules one can use, but if you (oops) use the quick period rule they won't be necessary. Avoid sentences like that one. Short, snappy ones are best. A quick period means crisp sentences with a minimum of "ands" and "buts," "whiches" and "thats."

(IIIC.3) Vary Language. Some reports contain a dismal amount of repetition of language, with the same word cropping up in sentence after sentence. Sentences should be avoided that begin with the same word that ended the previous sentence. A thesaurus will give synonyms so that repetitive repetition can be avoided. (Oops again!)

(IIIC.4) Anchor with Illustration. If it is possible, anchor the point with an illustration. The very word "anchor" suggests the kind of thing I mean here. If there is a case example or a calculation that can give meaning and vitality to the point, it is useful to include it. Is there a computation? Then perhaps an example could be given. Is there an especially appropriate policy application? Then perhaps a case example would serve. These illustrations need be only a sentence, although they could be longer. The purpose is not to become involved with the illustration, but to use it as a signpost or street light along the way.

(IIIC.5) Write to Press Release. One important principle in constructing paragraphs is the "press release" principle. It suggests that an editor could cut from the bottom up; thus, the material is self-sufficient, sentence by sentence. It means placing the most important material first, followed by less important material throughout the paragraph, the page, and the section. Following this principle means that the skimmer will still get some of the crucial points.

IV. Evaluate

Once the document is finished in draft form, place it in a drawer for a few days and let it sit. Reworking it immediately is likely to be a nonproductive enterprise. One is not fresh enough, free enough, to take it on immediately. Scheduling should allow time for this. Also, one needs to do some intellectual reconnaisance, to see what others think of the draft (it should be the second draft), and what the various policy committees are up to.

Once the initial period has passed, look at the draft again. Polish it up a little, and have a circulating draft prepared. The circulating draft is the one you share with friends and colleagues. (Alternatively, if there is a secretary who can do minor polishing, she or he can take your draft and work it up into the form of a circulating draft. The important point is that, while the circulating draft is a preliminary one, it should look crisp, fresh, and accurate. Writers do not control the secondary circulation of drafts, as mentioned above, and they may be sent to others less sympathetic.)[8]

(IVA) Consider Action Desired from Document

As the document is being prepared for circulation, consider what kind of action is desired on the basis of this document. What is it that you as the writer are seeking?[9] Generally, there are formal and informal outcomes desired.

(IVA.1) Formal Outcome. Formal outcome relates to the action desired by the relevant policy committee(s). Such groups can (a) receive, (b) accept, or (c) approve the report. Each action is more serious than the preceding one, and each therefore demands a more rigorous, more thoroughgoing draft.

For committees to approve a draft proposal usually requires more detailed work than is true for acceptance or receipt. Keep this in mind as the draft circulates. Sometimes it is a good technique to circulate a draft for receipt only, secure feedback, and then use that feedback to prepare something for approval.

(IVA.2) Informal Outcome. It is well to think, too, about what kind of informal outcome might be desirable. For example, one might (a) like someone to review the draft for overall compliance to standards required by a particular group. Alternatively, one might (b) ask readers for comments on the text of the draft. Or, finally, one might (c) ask readers for an assessment of whether, in principle, the report seems adequate, either in writing or in ideas. Here the reader is not asked for a detailed critique; rather something

---

8. This process assumes that the original draft was written or typed by the policy manager. If not, if it was dictated, there may be a circulating draft after transcription, or there may be another draft after review of the original transcription.

9. I know I just violated one of my rules. One can do that occasionally (the "you" tendency).

less than that, something relevant to the overall thrust of the document is the target of review.

(IVB) Send Document Out

After the purposes and persons appropriate to the review have been ascertained, send the document out along with a note indicating what the reader is being asked for and with a time deadline attached. About half way through the time limit (the period between the time the document went out and the time it is due back), call and ask how things are going. This call will provide some informal intermediate feedback and serve to jog those who have not yet read it.

It is useful to make a list of those who should get the document and to whom it was sent. Often, people who might provide useful feedback are overlooked and not included in the initial review list. A little thought here saves much time in soothing miffed feelings later.

(IVC) Review Comments/Reactions

Once the comments and reactions have been received, review them in detail. Try to get some overall sense of the reaction to the draft. Was it positive or negative? Was the writing criticized or the substance of the proposals? What will be needed to fix it up? Great care should be taken in going over the criticisms, because they can often be misleading. Some people have a tendency to respond positively, yet couch serious reservations in terms that sound quite praiseworthy; others do the reverse, praising in a negative context. Therefore, comments cannot be taken "as is," but need to be interpreted and seen within a larger light. Here, too, the staffer needs to remember the "strong ego" requirement. Often criticisms will be harsh, and it is hard not to become angry, especially if the report has taken a lot of work, as most reports do. One should always keep in mind that it is better to get criticism on a preliminary draft, which can be repaired, than in a meeting when there is no chance to do much.

Sometimes certain individuals, often key persons in an approval process, will not have time to look the draft over carefully. Thus, the staffer may need to meet with those persons and share the general idea, testing the waters for reactions, comments, and advice. These comments can prove to be very useful, even if not as detailed as written ones.

Overall, then, comments will fall into two general types: (1) *formal ones,* aimed at the text, and (2) *process ones,* aimed at the politics of approval. Both are needed; both need to be taken into account in rewriting.

V. Rewrite

After looking over all the comments, one can begin revising the draft. It is useful to sit with one master copy and enter the changes suggested by each draft on that single master. Do not, at this crucial juncture, toss a bunch of copies to a secretary and ask him or her to "clean it up." This job of preparing the master draft is one for the manager. Often there will be conflicting points of view, conflicting suggestions that need to be harmonized, or a decision may need to be made as to which way to go on a matter. It may not be possible to harmonize all suggestions.[10]

The formal revision must be based in part on suggestions received from the *process* of consideration of the draft. Feedback may indicate that the report is headed for smooth sailing. More than likely, though, comments may indicate that certain sections are offensive, or a certain recommendation might not pass, or that a pet reference of committee member Smith is not mentioned, and so on. One needs to do more than rewrite in most cases; it is more a job of recrafting, fitting the writing to the political process of consideration and approval.

Conclusion

This system of writing reports—the KNOWER system (*KN*owledge, *O*rganization, *W*rite, *E*valuate, *R*ewrite)—is designed to make report managers write more effectively in communicating the ideas they wish to convey. And one should keep in mind that the goal of writing "good" reports is not a literary one. Rather, it is an attempt to convey ideas, to develop and communicate them in the policy process. And, in turn, the purpose of this process is to improve the quality of ideas that are developed initially and flow to policy deciding committees. This quality is improved through better and more systematic search for knowledge, through improved organization of ideas, through greater clarity in putting down ideas, through systematic procedures in evaluating early drafts of the written report, and through rewriting to take into account the information developed in the evaluation process.

Like all other human activities, good ideas, of high quality, will benefit from systematic treatment that takes a planned, reasonably ordered approach

10. It is useful to drop people a note of thanks for their reading and to tell them, in that note or personally, what you did about their most important suggestions.

to the gathering of data and its presentation. Most of the time ideas are thought to lie in the realm of "creativity" and "everyone knows" that creativity cannot be forced, cannot be pushed. It either occurs or it does not; there is either some result from the creative process or there is not.

While there is an aspect of spontaneity in the creative act, that analysis provides little one can do except sit and wait for "it" to strike. Meanwhile the clock on the policy process ticks on. And even the most brilliant idea needs work, shaping, structuring, and blending of other elements into it. Indeed, in the world of policy, the fact that an idea is brilliant is no guarantee that it will be successful. So even that flash of insight needs to be fleshed out, dressed up, and presented to the appropriate policy ratification bodies.

The KNOWER system for policy report writing involves:
- KNowledge
- Organization
- Writing
- Evaluation
- Rewriting

(See Exercise 11.2)

A Word of Caution

This chapter has strongly emphasized the importance of the policy report and the importance, therefore, of paying close attention to it. The rules I have suggested here, and even the KNOWER system itself, should be used in a way that meets the working style of the policy manager and her or his setting. Perhaps using these suggestions is a good way to begin; after all, we get very little training in writing reports or in communicating ideas in report form to policy-relevant audiences. The point, though, is to be thoughtful, not rigid.

A Word of Encouragement

Writing it down, almost everyone says, is hard. Perhaps the panicky feeling is not exactly close to that generated by math, but "writing" anxiety and "math anxiety" have at least one thing in common—a set of concrete proposed answers that others can look at and for which we can be criticized.

In the human service profession, this tendency, if it is that, becomes exacebated by our oral tradition. Somehow putting things on paper seems an exercise in the overconcrete, something that destroys flexibility and receptivity.

This note of encouragement is aimed at recognizing these problems and appreciating their significance, while urging forward movement anyway. It is hard to write. Yet the fact still remains that policy is written. Thus, it has to be written by someone. And following the prescription of proactivity that is a theme of this volume, better that it be written by "us" (whoever we are) than "them" (whoever they are). The point here is a serious one. If human service professionals do not take the initiative here, then it passes to others, whose policy preferences and loyalties may be far from ours. It is worth it, for this reason only, to give it a try.

CASE ILLUSTRATIONS

THE CHILD WELFARE AGENCY

Jim wanted to begin to improve the internal functioning of the agency and turned to the whole problem of the agency's policy descriptions and program outlines. As one might have expected, they were quite inadequate. The board of directors had no specific manual with bylaws, the legal requirements that affected it, or the policies and procedures it should follow for its operation. Similarly, while there was an agency manual, it was a very large antiquated volume that, everyone agreed, had no relevance to the current situation and, in fact, had never had relevance. The agency had been run by "word of mouth," and so "everyone knew" what to do, but what "everyone knew" was often different. It would be necessary to develop systematic written policies from the board level down through agency operations. There should be a coherent and well-written personnel policy, he thought. Futhermore, each program should have a description that could be revised periodically if necessary. There should be a manual for staff and one for the board. These were major jobs, which could not, of course, be completed all at once. But Jim set about constructing the machinery that would get them rolling. As a first step he reviewed a list of needed documents with his assistant and passed the proposed list on to three groups. One was the newly formed staff advisory committee, the second was the board of directors, and the third was a group of "friends of the agency," women and men who were executives of other organizations. He asked whether the list seemed reasonable and whether they had any sample documents that could be assembled. He similarly asked national agencies for suggestions. At the same time he asked for information on some of the best agencies in the country and telephoned the executives of those organizations to find out what they did in this area and what examples they could send. He talked to the local university to see if he could get a student from the School of Social Work who might welcome the opportunity to do some drafting of policies, procedures, and program descriptions. That person could at least begin to get some things down on paper.

Discussion Questions

1. How do you think the reports and materials your agency develops can be improved? Can you think of ways that ideas can be presented more adequately? More succinctly?

2. How can agencies develop a more focused role with respect to policy? Writing? What steps would be needed to do this?

3. Do you think the executive here is taking the right course? What else should he do? What should he not do?

THE WELFARE PLANNING COUNCIL

The new executive thought that a more systematic approach was needed for the reports and documents that the council was beginning to develop at a fairly vigorous rate. Until recently there had been no common format for these documents nor had the quality of writing been as clear and simple as it might be. Part of the problem was that the audience for these reports was so diverse. It included professional people in professional fields and lay individuals without much professional expertise. Great care had to be taken with the use of "jargon." Systematic attention was needed to the entire problem. Her first thought was to get some professors from the university to come and do some training with her staff, but she was afraid that the professors would not always represent the best kind of perspective for the writing that her staff needed to do. As an alternative she called the publisher of the local newspaper and asked whether one or two journalists might like to earn a little extra money by instructing a class in the techniques of writing under pressure and for a fairly diverse group of people. That, at least, would be a start. And, she thought, they might help with thinking of a new name for the agency. Welfare Planning Council represents an old function and approach. That's gone now.

Discussion Questions

1. Can you design a common format for reports and written documents at your agency? Try laying one out and see how it works.

12

VALUE DILEMMAS IN SOCIAL POLICY

The policy manager in the human service organization exists in a turbulent environment. As one who has responsibility for the supply and shepherding of new ideas that govern the solutions to problems facing the agency, the community, and the society itself, the policy manager will almost always find herself or himself in a matrix of conflicting claims, assertions, demands, and requests. It is often never clear what is the most appropriate way to go. And in addition the policy manager may well feel personal conflict, wanting to move in one direction and yet also wanting to move in another direction. The human service organization is, perhaps more than all other organizations, subjected to difficult conflicts because of the wish and need to use itself as a policy model. How, for example, can a human service organization have a fairly strict and limited compensation policy for staff while at the same time lobbying for increased welfare benefits? Can a human service agency have a minimal retirement policy with relatively small benefits (as compared, for example, to other organizations) while at the same time lobbying for increases in social security?

It is important for the policy manager to understand and have a perspective upon the very process in which she or he engages. The provision of skills and the communication of skills does not necessarily provide a knowledge perspective or increase comprehension about the activity in which one is engaged. "Natural" policy managers, just like natural therapists, are frequently able to be helpful, but are not able to articulate what it is that is going on and what it is that they do in a larger, more conceptually coherent perspective. Just as the therapist may stand back and take a look at the counselor-client interaction and from that perspective be able to understand some of the conflicts and strains more clearly, the policy manager needs to find ways to step back from the daily round of conflicts and contentions and in so doing secure a perspective on the structure and patterning of those conflicts.

The policy manager's first task is to ensure that there is a supply of solutions to agency, community, and social problems for processing within the organization. The solutions represent allocations of values in the sense that they advance certain types of value interests and perspectives and retard others. To the extent that the policy manager in the human service organization is implicated in social policy the task is even harder, because transcendent standards involving conflicting ideas about the good life become involved in thinking about ways in which the agency should posture itself within the local community and in decisions made by clinicians. Dolgoff argues in his piece on "Clinicians as Social Policymakers," "where values are not specific, are absent, or are ambiguous, professionals can move the boundaries in various directions in order to get the clients the services needed" (1981:291).

Value Conflicts

Dolgoff seems to assume that values can be clear, present, and not ambiguous. This assumption is also made, in effect, by Selznick, who comments that "where leadership is required . . . the problem is always *to choose key values and to create a social structure that embodies them*" (1957:60; emphasis in the original). This assumption is a conventional one, as Hirschman points out in discussing social actors having a single set of values. Or, as he quotes Sen, being "decked in the glory of their one all-purpose preference ordering" (1982:68).

The problem for the policy manager, however, lies in the fact that values are not likely to be unitary, with set priorities, but are much more likely to be multiple and dual. Values are structured, likely to shift over time, and to be hidden. These five points—*value multiplicity, value duality, value denial, value change,* and *value structure*—become important elements of the policy manager's conceptual apparatus and at the same time that they are tools for understanding become tools for intervention as well.

Value Multiplicity

Rather than assuming that there is a single set of values which we hold and which are ordered, it makes more sense for the policy manager to assume that people, including himself or herself, hold multiple sets of values that conflict with one another. Our minds are probably more like a "value bank" with different value sets available for use (and that press themselves upon us to be used) depending on a range of factors. Different situations may give rise to different values. In fact, as Eric Hoffer (1951) suggested, the person who holds an unmodified value and permits no competition becomes a true believer or zealot from whom we shy away.

Value Duality

Values do not just come in an unorganized mass however. It is my perspective that values come in sets of competing values, something I have called in other connections the dualistic theory of values (Tropman 1978; Tropman and McClure 1979). Edelman, in talking about attitudes toward the poor, expresses this duality well.

One pattern defines the poor as responsible for their own plight and in need of control to compensate for their inadequacies, greed, lack of self-discipline, immorality, pathology, or criminal tendencies. . . . An alternative recurring reaction to poverty defines the poor as victims of exploitative economic, social and political institutions: people deprived by circumstances (not by their personal defects) and likely to become immoral and dangerous unless they are allowed to fulfill their potentialities. (1977:6)

He points out that "everybody has both of them . . ." and argues that "both patterns of belief are present in our culture and our minds, ready to serve our egos when we need them" (p. 6). He concludes:

We find then a pair of opposing political myths for each of the cognitive patterns that define our attitude toward social problems, the authorities who deal with them and the people who suffer from them. Ambivalence is reflected in concomitant myths, each of them internally consistent, though they are inconsistent with each other.'' (p. 8)

Slater (1970) talks about three types of value conflicts: one between the desire for community on the one hand and the desire for competition on the other; one between the desire for engagement with others and the desire for uninvolvement (privacy); and that between the desire for dependence and independence. Boulding (1967) talks about the tensions between a ''grants orientation and an exchange orientation as competing bases of social policy.'' Hirschman (1982) sees competition between public orientations and private ones as a central element in value conflict. It is at least useful to think of values and beliefs as coming in juxtaposed sets and that the emphasis on one creates a corresponding tension with the other, in ourselves, in the agency, in the community, and in the society. What might a set of such conflicts look like? The attached figure gives seven sets developed from an analysis of social policy and the conflicts inherent in it. It is not a complete list nor is it a comprehensive one, but it is satsifactory from the policy management point of view as a beginning presentation of conflicts likely to arise for the policy manager in any of the roles that he or she plays (see table 12.1) Later in the chapter we will have an opportunity to explore how these conflicts may manifest themselves to the manager in thinking about agency policy, community policy, and societal policy.

Table 12.1

individual	family
self-reliance	interdependency
secular	religious
equity	adequacy
struggle	entitlement
private	public
work	leisure

Value Denial

We are not always aware of the value patterns and systems in which we believe. The very complexity of the ''forest of values'' that we possess adds to our lack of clarity about which values operate in what contexts. Human service professionals are no exception to this rule. In a classroom experiment I did some years ago, I found that social work students who were perfectly willing to have a high graduated income tax to provide adequate incomes for the poor were completely unwilling to participate in a grade tax system in which those with higher grades would sacrifice points to a common pool from which points would be allocated to those who had failed. The students were perfectly willing to believe that the economic system was unfair and that awards were capricious, but completely unwilling to apply the same logic to the grading system. While people did not deserve low incomes, students definitely deserved low grades. In the former case there was no attribution of fault, whereas in the latter case low grades were attributed to lack of study and effort (Tropman 1979).

Value Change

If we do in fact have multiple sets of values that tend to come in juxtaposed sets, we must also be aware that our commitment to any particular configuration is not permanent. Hirschman points out that there has been a long-term shift from public to private, a view supported by the analysis of policy postures of the American public through public opinion testing from the early fifties to the late seventies (Johnson et al. 1980). Why might this change have occurred? Hirschman suggests that disappointment in the achievement of a particular value may lead one to an emphasis on an alternative competing value. Kenneth Boulding points out that "value images, like those in the field of choice, are also reinforced by the fulfillment of expectations and may be reorganized by disappointment" (1960:425). He later comments that both foks images and scientific images are changed essentially by the same process, that is, by disappointments of expectations based upon previous conceptions (p. 432). If disappointment "pushes" people to select alternative approaches, the tension between emphasis on one value and corresponding inattention to the other creates a pull in a manner perhaps akin to sibling rivalry. Unattended values may begin to generate competitive pressure. Too much emphasis, for example, on public activity may stimulate the press for private activity, whether or not public activity is disappointing. Too much emphasis on individualism may press someone to think of placing a counterbalancing weight on the family for a while. These shifts and changes can occur within groups, within individuals, within agencies, as well as within communities and societies. A typical dichotomy in the human service organization that Dolgoff (1981) mentions is one between service to the individual versus social action of a societally-based sort. Sometimes agencies go through profound transitions as in the Community Service Society of New York (Goldberg 1980).

Value Structure

The fact that values change and shift within a multiple and dual framework should not be construed, however, to indicate that values flip and flop all over the place without any consistency. Quite the contrary. Commitments can be quite enduring and changes may reflect modest adjustments in the balance rather than complete about-faces. One way to think about this balance is to invoke the concept of dominance and subdominance. For some people one set of values is dominant, though that dominance may be adjusted in time. For others, other sets of values are more dominant. Edelman mentions too that while "everybody learns both of these perspectives one or the other, depending on the social situation, is dominant" (p. 6). In the list of values in table 12.1 it is my contention that those on the left—values of individualism, self-reliance, secularism, equity, struggle, privatism, and work—are dominant within American society. Those involving family, interdependency, religion, adequacy, entitlement, public orientation, and leisure are subdominant. One of the struggles faced by the policy manager lies in the fact that those values espoused by the human service field are more likely to be subdominant and, hence, advocating and developing them is likely also to generate value competition and conflict with the more dominant values.

A Set of Policy Relevant Values

Let us return to the set of policy relevant values displayed in table 12.1. These values occur with a great deal of frequency in policy debates within the human service field and represent a cadre of considerations the policy manager will certainly have to deal with in policy developed for the agency and for the community, or societal policy where the focus is the state or the nation. Let us consider each in turn.

Individual vs. Family American society is individualistic in orientation and celebrates that individualism, for example, in a Superman or a Lone

Ranger. The individual feels that her or his needs should be preeminent, followed by needs of those closely related. On the other hand, a contrary perspective suggests that the family's needs are preeminent and that sacrifices should be made in order to advance family welfare, even though those sacrifices require the setting aside of personal goals and desires. In the human service field family responsibility has been stressed by social workers and others trained in the field. Family intervention often involves treatment of the whole family. On the other hand, the notion that the individual should be free to pursue the course she or he thinks best is very strong.

Self-Reliance vs. Interdependency. Individualism is often associated with the concept of self-reliance. As Slater points out we are a do-it-yourself society. He begins his book with a vignette about a man who tries to do everything by himself and "for which reason and because of his ingenuity they (locals) called him the American" (1970:xii). We also realize, however, that it is not possible to go it alone. Much of our fortune depends upon the society at large, economic and social conditions beyond our control, and even upon the goodwill and support of those close to us. Yet it is somehow difficult for us to recognize and build upon this interdependency.

Secular vs. Religious Orientation. There is a conflict between a secular, more scientific and rationalistic orientation and a religious or mystical and transcendental orientation. From the human service point of view, that conflict is manifest in differences of view historically over what organizations can best provide and administer social services. Should they be public or private with no religious orientation, or should they be, as they have historically been, sectarian agencies with a religious thrust and outlook? Sectarian and secular agencies have sometimes differed as well over the perceived cause of problems in the human condition. Religious agencies have tended, at least historically, to see flaws in character as important and in need of rectification before anything else will be effective. Secular agencies tended to see psychological or social elements as important causes.

Equity vs. Adequacy. We believe that people should be treated not only equitably but adequately. Equitable, or fair, treatment refers to outcomes relevant to the degree of input contributed. This principle has both a positive and a negative application. The old adage, an eye for an eye, a tooth for a tooth, was really a statement of "punishment equity," focused upon returning to one who committed a crime a difficulty proportional to the difficulty created. More severe punishments are thought of as equitable when the crime is more severe. Similarly, benefits are thought to be equitable when they are related to contributions. The student who works hard and does a good job should get a good grade. But we also believe that there should be a minimum and a maximum base with respect to the application of equity principles. Debates over capital punishment are of this sort. While the equity principle would say that one must give up one's life for taking a life, the adequacy principle would say that there is a ceiling and that life imprisonment or some other serious penalty is enough. On the other hand and at the other end, when one thinks of adequate welfare benefits one likes to think that there is some minimum below which one should not go. We think of the minimum wage, for example, or a minimum welfare grant. Sometimes what people can earn (the attributed return on the worth or equity of their investment in the job market) is too low to be adequate. This is explicitly recognized in social security. What a person can receive on the basis of his "equity" contribution may be too low to be adequate, and supplemental security income was created to make up the difference.

Struggle vs. Entitlement. The question of whether one has to struggle for a benefit or whether one is entitled to it as a person and citizen is a central one in the area of human service policy. For example, the means test is really a sort of struggle criterion in which you have to demonstrate need before you can receive a benefit. And that need must be demonstrated on an individual basis and must be revalidated periodically. Other programs are more entitlement based. One is "entitled" to use them whether one "needs" them or not. Consider the senior citizen' discount many stores offer to men and women over sixty-five. That is an entitlement program. There is no question of need. Voting and other citizen rights are considered basic entitlements; one does not have to "earn" them. It is considered appropriate, to give another example, that adolescent children move from the entitlement status they enjoyed—entitled to their parents' support, to food, clothing, and shelter—to a more struggle-oriented environment in which they begin to enter the workplace and provide for their own needs.

Private vs. Public. There has been a historical conflict between the public and private realms within the human service field particularly, but also within the society as a whole. Part of the question is how much should the public weal undertake the provision of social programs and how much should the private realm undertake this responsibility? Communities struggle over the issues involved in public and private schools and argue about which is better. As a nation we struggle over the structure of health insurance and the provision of medical care and argue about public auspices vs. private ones.

At the personal level, there is also differentiation between our public and private selves, between, as Hirschman (1982) points out, public and private orientations to commitments of our energies.

Work vs. Leisure. Our society is work-oriented and people tend to feel that benefits derived through work are legitimate. Leisure—sometimes called recreation—is useful not as an end in itself, but as providing rest and refreshment so that work can begin again. Work programs, which result in positive products and accomplishment, are among the welfare perennials, with programs like work incentive and other workfare programs. They are repeatedly offered as bases through which dependency can be reduced and, if independence cannot be at the same time gained, at least there will be a useful work product. We also recognize, as Machlowitz (1981) did in her study of "workaholics," that some people carry this to an extreme. The workaholic is one who finds no time for leisure. While the argument may be that the main virture of leisure is in recreating one's energies for work, that argument may contain heavy components of rationalization as well. People may like leisure and may like to find time to do some things that they cannot do under the demands of work.

Policy values are:
- Multiple
- Conflictual

(See Exercise 12.1)

Balancing Conflicting Values

Given the importance and heavy commitments involved in the values mentioned, it is not likely that the policy manager can achieve a "once-and-for-all" solution to the problem of value conflict. And, indeed, that is part of the point. One of the key jobs of the policy manager is to continue to work on the problem of values balance, both among the multiple values and between conflicting values. These problems need recurrent resolution and, while this does not make their processing any easier, it does provide a perspective for the policy manager who might otherwise come to believe that the problem has been "solved." Any solution is for a period of time only, and indeed the very crafting of a solution for a particular time sets into motion forces that (among other pressures as well, to be sure) begin to make that solution outdated. In a sense, this is the problem of solution obsolescence. One hears a great deal about the obsolescence rates of various types of training and very little about the likelihood that the solutions we come up with are themselves made obsolete as well. Partly, the problem of solution obsolescence is endogenous; that is, the very fact of achieving a particular solution sets in motion forces—for Hirschman, the force of disappointment—that make that solution unacceptable. However, there are also exogenous factors at work at the same time. A given solution to a particular problem is fine under a certain set of social, political, and economic conditions. If any one of those change or the balance among them changes then the particular solution may be less and less satisfactory.

Given the understanding that no permanent solution can ever be achieved, but rather that solution must be conceived of as a process, there are a few techniques that the policy manager might wish to keep in mind as ways to deal with the onmipresent problem of value conflict. Among them are targeting, blending, averaging, sectoring, sequencing, adjudicating formalization, and power. Let us consider each.

Targeting. In the targeting technique the policy manager targets a portion of the value for one particular group and another portion for another particular group. Where children are concerned, for example, one is more likely to find policies of interdependence in which links to the family are strengthened because the child is not likely to be able to handle an individual and self-reliant role. On the other hand, for adults the policies of self-reliance might be enhanced. For the senior citizen, the conflicts between individualism and familial orientation, self-reliance and interdependence may be the most sharply edged and the values may compete on a fairly equal plane. On the one hand we hope that the older adult can be self-reliant and yet pursue individual goals. On the other hand, there is an increasing need to recognize interdependency and temper individualism. The point here, of course, is that the policy manager identifies different groups as appropriate targets of different value emphases and the final policy reflects that difference.

Blending. Blending implies that aspects of each value are contained within a policy aimed at a particular group. Consider, for example, the professor grading students. The professor may argue that an equitable policy obtains and that people are going to be graded according to the quality of their work. However, the professor may also permit an adequacy criterion to enter, by which a person who does very badly may be able to raise his grade somewhat by doing extra work. Another example is the minimum wage.

While in general we believe that people should be paid what they are worth, it is also argued that there is a basic "minimum" that all (or most) workers are entitled to. If they (or the job) are worth less than that certain minimum, they should not be hired at all (or the job should not be done). One of the problems in blending, by the way, is the so called "notch effect," which occurs when someone moves from an adequacy standard to an equity standard and temporarily loses benefits in the transition. For example, welfare benefits are computed on the basis of family size. Salaries are not. At the bottom range, salaries are likely to be lower than a welfare grant based on the size of a family. Hence, as the large family begins to move from adequacy entitlement to equity struggle, it may slip back. This problem of transition has never been satisfactorily handled by policymakers and will continue to be of concern.

Averaging. In averaging the policy manager seeks to "split the difference" between competing policies. Hence, if it is desired to do something public and private, some public and some private activity might be involved. Suppose that the agency felt that an adequate number of counseling sessions was ten, but an equitable number was between five and twenty, based on ability to pay; the solution might be to create a client average that combined ability to pay and the minimum number required.

Sectoring. Sectoring is similar to targeting except that the bases of value division, rather than being different groups, are different places, different problems. Prices may change at different times and in different locations. At the personal level, for example, we may behave differently at work and at home. We may behave differently during the regular year than when on vacation. In a sense we are sectoring our activities and the agency might do the same thing. For example, it might indicate that a minimum fee for service is $30 an hour for the first ten sessions, but $20 an hour for those after that. Hence, if someone needs more hours, he or she secures a break in price. Different groups may have different values; for example, one might need to emphasize self-reliance values for one client group, while recognizing interdependence values for another client group.

Sequencing. Sequencing refers to the process of alternating values over time and, hence, each new phase provides a corrective for the phase just past. The periods can be short or long. For example, programs can be run in institutions on a day and night basis as in a day hospital and a night hospital; programs that cannot be ran during the school day can be run at night.

Adjudicating. The policy manager can seek to play the role of mediator among various value contentions or particular sets of values that seem to be opposed. This is more an interpersonal than an intellectual approach, because the techniques mentioned can come into play singly or severally. The adjudicating technique brings the contending parties together and seeks to secure their suggestions and agreement.

Formalization in Policy. The ratification phase of policy is one in which the decision among competing values is made concrete by formal action. It may be clear now why decision review and refurbishment are needed. The very act of making a decision creates tensions likely to demand a fresh look and generates disappointments that press for alternative approaches. If the policy manager recognizes this, she or he can be prepared to take the necessary corrective action. A rebalancing of values in the system generates a different constellation of needs that must be met by a different decision structure.

Power. It should not be thought that reasoning and adjudicating strategies are the only ways in which issues are resolved. The application of political and financial force is an alternative way. Policy managers involved in this strategy tend to become more like community organizers. They will mobilize people or money to use the weight of numbers and prestige or of money to secure a particular outcome. It should be stressed that even these activities exist within a value context. In the past twenty years, between 1960 and 1980, we have seen a period which began with a marked rise in the support for public undertaking of social programs and activities and we have seen that view eclipsed and replaced by one with a traditional orientation involving private and voluntary structures as preeminent in meeting needs. Political activity is likely to be more successful if it is aimed at "value-sympathetic" ears. Proposals that the federal government undertake more programs were more positively received in the early sixties than in the late seventies. Nonetheless, the development of political influence and financial support do provide important mechanisms for the resolution of conflicts. Because these resolutions are often good for some participants and bad for others the policy manager will seek higher quality solutions.

Techniques for balancing values include:
- Targeting
- Blending
- Averaging

- Sectoring
- Sequencing
- Adjudicating
- Formalization in policy
- Power
  (*See Exercise 12.2*)

Value Conflicts in the Human Service Organization

Perhaps more than other organizations, human service organizations are value sensitive. As Shapira says:

> The emphasis on values and moral issues has had a two-fold impact on the production on welfare services and their delivery. On one hand, it embued the system with a singular sense of social purpose and commitment. Thus, it commanded the loyalties and devotion of its members much beyond its attraction as a field of employment. On the other hand, it allowed the system to escape salutory effects of reassessment by confrontation of inputs with outputs. Values served not only as a base for defining goals and objectives of the system, but very often (and particularly where social work was the leading profession), as sole criterion for assessment of the means of accomplishing such goals. Insufficient attention has been paid to the development and elaboration of a correspondence between objectives and means. The form of specific service methods and techniques were often chosen on the basis of their consistency with the cherished values rather than because of their demonstrated efficacy. (1971:58)

The central problem here is that values have too often served as a refuge for the social welfare profession in which we have been able to take comfort in assertion rather than accomplishment. The problem has been compounded by the assumption that there was a single set of values, "good" values held by us and more negative and hostile values held by "them."

We have tended to divide values into good and bad, with human service professionals taking sanctuary with the good values, thus creating a distancing, what one might call values as boundary. We were not able to seek a common cause with others who might have been helpful to us, because we believed that they did not have the same values we did, and that we did not have the same values as they. The dualistic approach to values recognizes that most of us have sets of conflicting values and that both are positive. There is nothing inherently more positive about equity than adequacy, nothing inherently more positive about the family than the individual, and so on. Yet the us/them dichotomy has been one of the difficulties with which the human service system has had to contend and one which presents problems for the policy manager.

Another values problem for the human service profession is an extension of the point just made. We are uncomfortable when we find that we have some of the values of those with whom we disagree. Sometimes, as in the grade/tax problem, we deny it. Sometimes we simply feel ambivalent about it. The development of private practice in social work is an example of this ambivalence. On the one hand, many people are involved in this enterprise. The NASW clinical directory lists more than 85,000 individuals available for private practice. On the other hand, schools of social work make little provision for preparing students for such a career. While the profession seems to feel comfortable with "private" agencies, individual entreprenurial effort to solve social problems is thought by many to be inappropriate. And, no doubt, even those who work in private agencies agree.

The policy manager in the human service organization will have to continue to struggle with these problems. If she or he is working on new policy for the agency targeted at staff or clients or is thinking about making recommendations for a community or state-wide policy or even a national policy, these issues come up as troubling and presenting problems. Values refuge problems, values boundary problems, and values denial problems represent aspects of the dilemma to which the policy manager must seek some accommodation.

Conclusion

The role of the policy manager, existing as it does in the realm of ideas and the relationship of ideas to the solution of agency, community, and national problems, is centrally affected by the values system—her or his own set of values and those dominant within the agency, the community, and the society. The historical approach to thinking about values, which divided them into good and bad and which developed a unitary ranking, is in my view, an inaccurate and even harmful portrayal of the values system. In order to function effectively the policy manager needs to have some sense of the matrix of values in which the problems and people with which she or he is concerned exists and have some idea of the constant tensions that manifest themselves in that system. A dualistic, rather than a monistic, approach to the values system is a more useful point of departure. A perception that values tend to come in juxtaposed sets and that raising issues of one automatically raises issues of the other will help the policy manager to achieve a more balanced and more accurate perspective on the series of conflicts that are perennial problems in the human service policy network.

13

SOCIAL POLICY: OLD CONCERNS, NEW PERSPECTIVES

This volume focuses on the policy manager and the policy management process. In it, the focus has been on development of the idea of policy management, with a discussion of some of the problems and difficulties, followed by a discussion of some of the skills the policy manager needs in order to accomplish policy management tasks. The emphasis upon doing policy, however, needs to be supplemented with an understanding of policy as well, and the last two chapters seek to enhance the policy manager's conceptual framework. In the previous chapter, some of the enduring value dilemmas within the policy management process itself were outlined and the continual difficulties and problems that these dilemmas present to the policy management process was the focus of discussion. This chapter will suggest some of the other considerations that affect policy and, in doing so, will broaden the discussion of policy a bit beyond that which has so far been the central focus and return to some of the material in chapter 1. Thus, a discussion of the realms of policy becomes important. One realm of policy of great interest to the policy manager, and relevant to the vague standards to which the human services policy manager is often held to account, is social policy. A more focused and more comprehensible understanding of what social policy is (and it is more than just one thing) is important for the policy manager and thus I will seek to bring out differences in understanding and meanings of the concept of social policy. These two topics—the realms of policy and the kinds of social policy—lead us to consider policy assumptions. In particular two types of assumptions are useful to analyze: assumptions about the causal level of a particular problem and assumptions about the target level of a particular problem.

Policy Realms

The policy manager in a human service organization is working principally to improve the operation of the organization itself through the provision of fresh ideas and innovative solutions, which, with fiscal and personnel capabilities, result in realistic and reasonable new approaches to the solution of dilemmas that confront the agency. However, it is also important for the policy manager to realize that there are more comprehensive policy activities outside the organization for which she or he may have responsibility and in which he or she may have some interest and that there are intra-organizational policies at the level of the work group and even the individual that need to be considered as well. Policy, as a set of rules governing anticipated future action and ratified by legitimate authority, can operate at the level of the individual, the family or group, the organization (the primary target here), the community, and society. The policy manager may well be involved in any or all of these policy targets. Hence, a few examples of each might help to clarify the types of policy involved.

Personal Policy

Personal policy represents those sets of decisions made by the individual and ratified usually by him or her. Decisions, for example, about whether to smoke or not to smoke; whether to consume alcoholic beverages or not, and if so, in what quantity; decisions about personal career trajectories and orientations—all represent the kind of personal goal setting that might be thought of as personal or individual policy. Frequently, experiences that are called personal growth experiences involve a reassessment of the personal policy of the individual, the collection of fresh information, and the reformulation of personal policy objectives.

Personal policy is usually not written, but there are examples that may prove illustrative. The famous New Year's resolution is a case of reformulated personal policy. And with increasing frequency, individuals set themselves specific and written goals or make self-contracts, with the desired results written out and put on the refrigerator as a sort of ratification-by-embarrassment procedure. It should be clear by now that the policy manager in the human service agency may, if she or he has a clinical role as well, be involved with clients in a process that might be called policy review. To the extent that one is involved with oneself or with other individuals in the review of the established set of "rules of the game" that guide our individual behavior in daily life, then, for analytic purposes at least, one can be thought of as involved in the assessment and revision of personal policy. The rewriting and public statement of these is simply a method as useful for the individual as it is for the organization.

Perhaps the best example of personal policy ratified by others within the legal system is the will. The will, of course, specifies what happens to one's property after death, but it is one document of personal policy that has legal force. There are other aspects of personal policy that fall within the great range of contracts executed by individuals, such as putting one's child up for adoption, seeking to adopt a child, borrowing money, or joining the army. So there are numerous examples of other kinds of written policy, and the human service policy manager may become involved at various points with clients in matters of personal policy. Working with older clients may bring up the question of wills and the disposition of materials, of living wills or documents executed by an individual which state one's preference (at the time of "execution" anyway) for the conditions under which he or she would like to be kept alive by extraordinary means. Some individuals do not wish to have extraordinary means applied and seek to absolve others of responsibility for treatment. Child welfare workers may be involved in personal policies with respect to contracting between parents and children about certain behaviors, rule-setting, and so on. Viewing these kinds of interactions for self, or as a counselor for other individuals, as policy matters creates the possibility of a new set of techniques—policy management techniques which can be adapted for work with individuals.

Family and Group Policies

There are a range of family and group policies, including the family policy just mentioned. In the case of the child welfare worker, she or he was establishing a set of guidelines for parents and adolescent children on such issues as time to come home or number of times the car may be used. The will, of course, can also be a family document, with interlocking gifts to members of the family, trusts, and so on. But there are more subtle family policies. For example, consider the policy established by the younger couple about whether or not to have children, when to have children, and how many children to have. These are aspects of family policy, and the discussion of them may be difficult and affect-laden. Other kinds of family policy may be the result of mutual agreement, for example, the specifically tailored marriage contract, which is becoming somewhat more popular today. The marriage contract is a document of no legal standing, which sets forth the assumptions and expectations on the part of one party for the other party. It may involve the bride-to-be securing agreement from the husband-to-be on matters of child care, dishwashing, and a range of other talks of great importance to the marital union.

A number of items of family policy are more accurately described using the policy/practice distinction mentioned earlier. Frequently, the human service worker can be of assistance in engaging in a policy analysis of topics such as these with the family. We are all aware, in working with families, that many may never have discussed items of high interest to each member. Nor have they written out their expectations or specified in any way what one hopes the partner would or might do. A husband, for example, may have married a woman on the assumption that she would not work. That assumption may have been valid for a period, but later she might decide to work. He might then feel there had been an illegitimate policy change, but she may feel that the change is a legitimate aspect of personal growth. Family policy analysis and management (I am *not* referring here to social policy about families, sometimes called "family policy") involve those aspects of discussions or those entire discussions that focus upon understanding, clarifying, establishing, revising, adjudicating, and mediating that set of rules that guide family interaction.

The same type of case could be made for groups, though the bonds typically are not as strong. Groups often have sets of rules and, to the extent that they are formal groups and have decision-making properties, they may be guided by sets of rules we would call decision policies. Roberts' *Rules of Order* is one group of decision rules, but there are a number of others which are important as well. Rules of consensus decision making, for example, may be established. Often the sets of rules for groups are codified in bylaws or other group documents. The human service worker, working with decision-making groups, may well seek to establish sets of rules, as I suggested in the chapter on effective meetings. Those rules are structural or process rules, which govern when things may be brought up or the time an appropriate agenda item is to be submitted, rather than rules that focus upon what decision should be made. As procedures, they helped expedite the flow of matters and only indirectly govern their substance. Informal groups may have unwritten rules; Argyris talks about this in some detail (1982:10).[1]

Focus on group rules and their development is an area where the policy manager may have some activity. It is most clear in the decision-making group, but sometimes more intimate groups, like families, set up rules—rules about who does the washing, who does the cooking on what nights, how much sex the couple will have. These are all procedural rules which help the family unit to function better. Family/child interactions are also assisted by rules of a similar sort—how to give an allowance or how late one can stay out. These are all important aspects of the kinds of things that may be developed to facilitate the procedural activities of the family.

Small group policies, then, tend to be procedural and the policy manager may focus upon them in the greatest degree. They can exist within the decision-making group or the family itself and they can cover a range of activities and areas. They are not all procedural, however. As the examples illustrate, sometimes families set up rules of a substantive nature, such as "in our family, we wear seatbelts." That simply (it is hoped) saves discussing and debating the merits of the issue each time somebody gets into the car. Or, in a small group, they may decide "our group does do this or does not do something else (take political stands, serve alcohol at meetings, etc.),"

---

1. There was a cartoon in the *New Yorker* some years ago that captured this idea perfectly. A group of men were sitting around a table, obviously in a meeting. The chair said, "So then we're all agreed," and each man was saying "aye, aye, aye," but in little captions above them their real thoughts were given: "I don't believe it," "he wouldn't dare," "we'll be the laughing stock . . ."

there again focusing on substantive aspects. The policy manager can find a rich field of attention when group rules become her or his focus of interest.

Organzational Policy

Organizational policy has already been covered in great detail and does not require a great deal of attention now. Basically, it is of two parts: that level of organizational policy which deals with the mission and role of the organization, and those policies and procedures which the organization follows or undertakes. Mission and role policy may, as I indicated in the first chapter, be focused either at the provision of enriched ideas for the mission and role itself or may involve substantive elements relating to fiscal policy, personnel policy, capital investment policy, and so on. These policies assist the organization in carrying out those aspects of its job and, at the same time, assist in more effective and more efficient carrying out of mission and role.

In the case of family, group, and individuals, policy is quite a rare concept. People do not think of themselves as being run by policy and thus the very idea is a bit unusual. It is less rare in the organizational area. It is commonly accepted that organizations are run by policy and thus it is more the idea of looking at it specifically, of managing it, developing it, refurbishing it, that is new. But it is also important to point out that simply because people recognize that, it does not mean that they have a good sense of what policy is, where important policies are, or are sufficiently aware of the distinction between policy and practice to make that understanding anything more than a curious observation on the life of the organization. We name things in order to understand them, locate them, and influence them. The level of organizational policy seems to be an area in which names have been given, but understanding and influence are only now beginning to be developed with any kind of energy and attention.

Community Policy

People in the human service organization tend to become involved, as do others of course, in development of policy for their local community, for their region, for their state. It is really the purpose of the numerous interorganizational committees that many of us sit on to accomplish this task. The whole interorganizational network, in fact, could be thought of as a piece of policy machinery set up to create policies that improve the quality of life in the community and that assure more effective and efficient operation of particular classes and groups of organizations, among other goals.

One aspect of the community, of course, is the network of similar organizations all performing similar tasks. Child welfare organizations runaway homes, or legal services, are all cases in point. Frequently, these organizations will seek to get-together to set and influence policy. Policy-setting goals within a group of similar organizations involve decisions (or may involve decisions) about common and shared services, as well as unique services. The group may decide, for example, that all organizations in one area should offer such and such a service and that beyond it each organization would have a particular kind of specialty. Hence, it decides where duplication of service should and should not occur. I do not want to imply here that this type of decision is totally within the group's own hands. Outside funders, agency-interested persons, state and federal rules may set minimal standards or focus efforts in other ways. But the agencies themselves may get together and try to improve service to the community through what might be called policy sharing and coordination. This policy might be called network policy, because it represents a range of agreements and covenants among those within a network of people doing similar things.

Another type of group that organizations tend to get together with are human service agencies doing different things, where there needs to be some level of coordination and agreement at the client transfer boundary. Hence, mental hospital officials may get together with community-based care officials so that there is agreement on how discharge is to take place, what conditions must be met for discharge, what kinds of follow-up procedures the mental hospital will do or needs to have done, what level of readiness is needed for the community-based persons, and so on. Throughout the human service area, these kinds of adjustments are made.

The policy manager may, therefore, have some degree of extramural focus within the network of similar organizations or within the arena of agencies with links which his organization very closely. Whatever policy emerges from these activities as bilateral (between a set of agencies) or multilateral (among a group of agencies) affects those involved, but does not necessarily influence or create policy within the community. These are two other activities that community policy might focus upon.

Influencing policy involves policy managers from human service organizations as lobbyists and interested persons seeking to shape or structure decisions of other larger policy-making collectivities. Typical targets of policy influence here are local city councils, local boards of education, local United Ways, and other grant-giving organizations; these same types of targets may be replicated at the regional and state level. Some regions have school and other special purpose districts, mental health catchment areas, whose policies may require the attention of the policy manager on behalf of his agency. Similarly, important foci at the state level are the state legislature, the governor's office, and the judiciary. Sometimes the purposes of such policy attention are matters of narrow interest with respect to the agency itself, such as standards for care. In the child welfare field, for example, many state welfare departments set standards that the child welfare agencies would like to influence. The establishment or change of extant service packages is another case in point.

All of the extramural policy attention does not necessarily go to influencing policies that affect the agency so directly. Policy managers may become involved, and frequently do, in the broader area of social policy within the state. Agencies which do not necessarily give any grants might be interested in a more adequate granting posture by the state legislature. Human service organizations may work in a variety of ways to seek a more forward looking, more humane, less restrictive set of state policies in areas such as unemployment compensation, fringe benefits, workmans' compensation, to say nothing of ecologically focused issues.

This kind of role is perhaps better understood than the organizationally focused role for the policy manager. Most workers within human service organizations have, at one time or another, been asked to represent the agency in various kinds of policy discussions involving other agencies or the state itself. Most frequently, these relate to rules and regulations that affect the agency directly and link up with other agencies which may be cooperative or competitive. The participation of the agency in groups and collectivities whose goal is to improve the quality of life in the state itself is not that uncommon.

Societal Policy

The last area in which policy managers may become involved is that of societal policy. Agencies which are national to begin with focus on national policy as a matter of course, but the vast array of human service organizations are local or regional in nature. With a few exceptions, such as the

Veterans' Administration and the Social Security Administration, service-giving activities are not typical of national agencies. Rather, they tend to set standards, establish need, and promote policy. Hence, agencies at the national level may have, as their human service mission, the promotion of a more adequate, more well-balanced human service policy, which may involve the establishment of national standards, the extension of benefits to uncovered individuals, and so on. Other organizations at the state and local level, however, may serve in much the same way, involving community and state activities at the national level. Most human service organizations lack the resources to assign policy managers to this kind of task. Yet, interest in the field itself has led some individuals to pay part of the cost themselves. At the national level, whether the participant is a member of a national agency or a delegate or representative from a local agency, the focus tends to be upon social policy. This requires us to think a bit about what social policy is.

Thinking About Social Policy

Most people in the human services think of themselves as somehow involved in social policy (Berg 1980; Carroll 1978; Gummer 1975; Dolgoff 1981; Jansson and Taylor 1978; Pusic 1981; Shapira 1971). And, indeed, it is in improving social policy that the policy and planning person has a key role, whether that assignment is full-time or a part of a larger assignment or an occasional foray into the field at the request of the executive. And the emphasis is usually on the more practical, more concrete things that one can do to help policy. We are often relatively silent on what the content of policy should be and how it might be better understood.

Social policy is typically thought of as that which is done by government, and many of the works on social policy emphasize that point. But there are other distinctions which can be made about policy that are of equal importance. "Auspices," of course, refers to the authority under which policy is made, and here the distinctions between public and private, social and other policy ("non-social," "asocial"), come into sharp play. Much that private sectors do is social policy too.

"Target" refers to the level of the unit that is to be changed. "Causal assumptions" denote the level at which the cause is thought to exist (Tropman 1976:212). "Level" here refers to social level. We can think, therefore, of a problem caused at the level of the individual and targeted for treatment there. Some mental illness is an example. On the other hand, one perspective suggests that mental illness is caused by large-scale environmental factors and that change in the social system is needed to effect a "cure." Some with a community mental health orientation speak from such a perspective (Brenner 1973).

Social policy differs according to method too (Tropman and Erlich 1979:279 ff). Basically, there are three methods, in the largest sense, which can be used to achieve policy goals. One can hope to secure compliance through agreement (a values methodology), when the policy target wants to cooperate. Or one can assume that the policy target will be relatively neutral, being neither for nor against it, and thus can be led to cooperate through the provision of economic inducements (money, goods, perquisites). Last, a condition may exist in which the individual does not want the policy at all, and various levels of force must be used to secure compliance (Etzioni 1961).

These distinctions are useful ones to keep in mind when thinking about policy generally, but they are not especially crucial to *social* policy—that area of policy with which people in the human services are most likely to be concerned and which the policy manager seeks to manage. To understand the realms in which social policy operates, to understand what social policy is, some additional distinctions must be drawn; the first is the nature of the concept "social" itself.

The Idea of Social in Social Policy

The very meaning of the word social is a confounding and confusing aspect of the idea of "social policy."[2] The *Encyclopedia of Social Work* lists more than fifty entries under social, and clarity is hard to come by. There seem to be, however, three meanings that emerge consistently, each with implications for social policy.

Social as Collective

One meaning of the word social, and the one perhaps most often associated with the idea of "social policy," is as a collective effort, here opposed

2. Words have this curious quality of ambivalence. Take, for example, the word "poor," which means 1) of limited means, 2) sad, and 3) of inferior quality. Or consider the word "discrimination," which means 1) to make distinctions, and 2) to exclude on the basis of prejudice. Another is the word "engage," which means 1) to pledge to marry and 2) to hire.

not to isolation but to an individual effort. Social insurance is that which uses the strength of the collectivity to provide assistance to individuals when needed.

Social as Interactive

A second meaning of social is interactive, and here social is used as a word opposed to isolated. One might consider oneself a social person, referring to the interactive propensities of the individual in question. Social work refers, at least partly, to the process of minded interaction as intended here; social diagnosis refers, in part at least, to the need for an interactive process to be used for the diagnostic efforts between client and worker.

Social as Stratification (Rank)

This use of the word social is one of "stratification." It implies a level, an echelon. At one point in the echelon, the phrase "socially prominent" implies prestige. At another level, phrases like "socially deprived" and "social problem" refer almost exclusively to people at the bottom of the social ladder. And, indeed, when one thinks about one of the common uses of the phrase "social work," one concept implied is that the target of action is those individuals in the lower classes, those at the bottom of the "social ladder." And somehow social policy has been seen, in part, as policy for those who are somehow disadvantaged. This particular stratification meaning of social is perhaps one reason why many social services are changing their names to human services, and people working in the field are referring to themselves as human service workers instead of social service workers or social workers. It seems better somehow to be identified with the whole spectrum of society rather than with those at the "bottom."

Implications for Social Policy

The collective approach seeks to use the strength of the collective to achieve social goals. Groups and committees, the power of "organization," are examples of this approach. Community organization, as a part of social work that seeks to mobilize people, is the beginning of such a method. Central here is using the strength of groups, whether the target is the individual in the group or the group itself.

The interactive use of the concept of social has led to social policy that seeks to modify the structure of social relationships (see, for example Durkheim 1897, 1951). A good example may be found in the work of M. Harvey Brenner (1973), who assessed mental hospital admissions over a long period and found them to be heavily and inversely related to the vigor of the economy. When the economy was flourishing, admissions went down; when it was not, admissions, especially of men, went up. His findings placed in fresh perspective attempts to look at the predisposing causes of mental distress. Durkheim could have made a similar argument about suicide. Social policies, like those of the President's Committee on Juvenile Delinquency, which sought to enhance "community competence" as a way of strengthening the community's ability to handle delinquency, are another example (Lind and Tropman 1969).

Another version of the interactive approach is the use of relationships as such to effect change. The need to provide social work services, for example, to a particular client group, as opposed to simply providing a benefit to the group, implies that the group needs the softening effects of a relationship in order to change.

The third use of the word social implies certain targets of social policy, especially those in the lower classes. The target may be the individual or the group as such. Historically, the settlement house was an example of an agency that aimed a broad sweep of interventions at a special target. Many social agencies today still seek to aim their services here, although they have been criticized for "leaving the poor" (Cloward and Epstein 1973).

Social Policies and Levels of Intervention

These uses of the word "social" are applied from the level of the person or the "micro-social" level to the level of the society or the "macro" level. In the middle is the "meso" level. These levels correspond to the nature of the relationships involved—primary, secondary, and tertiary. A list of approaches occur at the intersection of a particular usage of the word "social" and one of these levels of society is depicted in table 13.1.

Collective

On the collective plane, the strengths of the group itself are exploited for assistance, rather than interaction as such. At the micro level, public goods,

Table 13.1
Dimensions and Targets of Social Policy

Dimensions of Social Policy	Targets of Social Policy			Scope/Participative Involvement
	Micro	Meso	Macro	
Collective	1 Protective laws 2 Schools 3 Parks 4 Tax breaks	1 Organizational improvement 2 Fringe benefits 3 Community mental health	1 Ecological improvement	Broad/Low
Interactive	1 Social case-work 2 Counseling 3 Social Security benefits	1 Social group work 2 Boy/Girl Scouts	1 Social movements 2 National organizations 3 Social Security system	Medium/High
Stratifica-tion/Rank	1 Public welfare benefits	1 Increase community competence 2 Settlement house	1 Public welfare system	Medium/Low
Values Involved	Dominant	Mix	Subdominant	

which use the group to aid the individual with tax breaks, schools, and parks, would be an example. At the intermediate or "meso" level, the provision of fringe benefits, in which the strengths and characteristics of the organizational group are used, can serve to provide additional security for all. Community mental health programs can also serve as an example in which the target of the program is not the health of one individual—that would be community treatment—but rather the mental health of the community as a whole, as manifested in such indices as lower rates of mental illness for the community and lower suicide rates. An example at the macro level is a program of ecological improvement, where the goal is to improve the whole system.

Interactive

I suggest that an interactive approach at the micro level is something like "social casework" or counseling. At the middle or meso level, it is something like social group work in which treatment of an individual occurs within a group and community setting. Organizing a social group of mentally retarded adults to meet for social purposes is an example. At the national level, social movements, mass meetings, and society-wide organizations would be examples, although the mass aspect may move closer to the "collective" dimension.

Rank

In the stratification plane in which social means doing something for some group of disadvantaged, usually those at the bottom of the "social ladder," the three approaches exist as well. At the micro level, proved and direct cash assistance as in public welfare, is an illustration. Within the meso level, "community" approaches which focus upon the organization of the disadvantaged are typical and include such approaches as community development in the field of social work and settlement work. Finally, at the macro level, "social policy," to the extent that it is targeted at the disadvantaged, is illustrative. Most often this policy is called "welfare policy," welfare having become a code word for those whom society believes do not contribute.

Scope, Participative Involvement, and Value Base

There are three other dimensions important to figure 13.1—scope, participative involvement, and value base. Differing dimensions imply different levels of involvement and participation in the policy itself. "Scope" refers to the degree of the breadth and impact a policy has; "participative involvement" denotes the level to which those involved in the policy participated in its formulation, and "value base" indicates whether a dominant or subdominant set of values is used as a primary justification.

Collective Policy. In collective policy, the scope is broad and the participative involvement low, in part, because the larger the number of people, the more difficult it is to secure the involvement and participation desired. Still there are interest groups which present a vigorous picture of interest, but they relate more to issues and single or focal interests rather than across the board. For example, everyone (almost) pays both Social Security and other taxes. Yet the sense of involvement with respect to Social Security seems much greater, more personal, and tangible than involvement with the results of the payment of other federal taxes. There is a bargain in Social Security that moves it into the interactive policy area. Government officials attempt to heighten the sense of involvement in some areas by posting signs indicating results. Anyone who has ever driven on a road that is being repaired and seen the sign that reads "Your Highway Dollars at Work" can understand the connection.

Interactive Policy. Interactive policy is based upon medium scope and high participative involvement, although the nature of the participation may differ somewhat depending upon the level. It can range from participation in a clinical interview, to participation in the contribution to Social Security, to participation in community cohesion that strengthens community life. Thus, while involvement may not be as extensive as in collective policy, it is usually more intensive.

Interactive policy depends for its success upon high involvement. If one will not pay his insurance premiums, if someone is not involved in therapy, or in the success of his or her children, then it is not likely that the policy will be successful. At a more general level, policy which aims to improve the community spirit, or sense of membership in an organization, cannot be successful if it fails to build this sense of involvement. Yet without some initial involvement, the program is almost certainly doomed to failure. Involvement breeds involvement.

Stratification Policy. The stratification level of the word social, implying as it does the plight of those at the bottom of the stratification ladder, suggests medium scope and low participation involvement.

Yet problems of scope and participation have been central in policy aimed at those in dire circumstance. It is one of the classic cases of a values dilemma. On the one hand, we want to be helpful. On the other hand, we do not want to be too helpful. I make this point with no implied irony with respect to the phrase "too helpful"; as the phrase is sometimes used it suggests that people do not want to be helpful at all. This assessment is not accurate, as the policy manager knows and as the chapter on value conflicts suggests. The citizenry does want to be helpful, but not helpful to too many or for too long. Hence, scope is a problem. We have devised means for "regulating the poor," as Piven and Cloward (1971) have so aptly put it, such that not too many apply. My own research on welfare coverage (the proportion of AFDC recipients divided by the proportion of poor by state) suggests that, while there have been important increases in recent years, the levels are still low (Tropman and Gordon 1978). Patterns of means testing and differentiating, actually and psychologically, between the worthy and the unworthy poor, are ways in which the scope of social policy aimed at those near the bottom of the stratification ladder is medium (to low in some cases).

The matter of participative involvement is also a problem and must be ranked as low. Difficulties in involving the disadvantaged in policy concerning them have been notorious (Moynihan 1969). And the problem extends beyond those on lower economic rungs to those who suffer discrimination in all areas—blacks, women, the handicapped, clients generally, students, children, older adults; the list could go on to include other people of color and people of certain ethnic backgrounds. A host of social efforts needs to be made to include recipients of social policy, at least in this sense, because without their involvement policies will continue to miss the mark. Policy managers need to work hard to foster the goals of involvement and participation, not only because of historic commitments and values, but for the pragmatic reason that without involvement policy arrows will miss their mark.

Part of the issue revolves around what the primary value base which supports a policy is. In the case of micro policy targets, dominant values that support the individualistic ethic are present and helpful. Those policies aimed at the macro level—large-scale system intervention and change—have less support. Our recognition of cause and effect is half-hearted at best; even when the social cause seems quite recognizable as in the differential distribution of various diseases or discrimination against blacks and women in salary levels, we seek to find individual explanations for the phenomena (which, as someone commented, is what makes life insurance companies rich and fortune tellers poor!!). We grudgingly accept what the Japanese, for example, take for granted—that collective life is important and influential and needs to be supported.

Conclusion

The idea of policy as developed in this volume is an expanded one. There is certainly a major focus on organizational goals, and the general set of directions that organizations use to guide their activities. But here we note policy concerns extending beyond that single realm into decisions that individuals, families, and communities make. Wherever decisions are made, there is accompanying policy. The policy manager needs to be aware of these other arenas in which policy activity can occur.

Some policy managers will work at the societal level, making policy (or seeking to influence policy) within the federal government or within state governmental systems. For policy managers here, problems of social policy come to the forefront. Questions about what is social policy, and what are the appropriate targets of such policy effort, are often considered. As those discussions go on, a more detailed explication of the issue can help to sharpen the concepts, focus the decisions, and hopefully lead to higher quality policy action.

But it is not only those directly involved in "social" policy who might find an "assumptions audit" helpful. Those at the other levels are also involved, in their own way, in social policy. Human service organizations especially think of themselves as socially responsible and socially concerned, and these perspectives influence their organizational decision making. And while the concern over social policy issues is sometimes less direct for those at the organizational level than those at the societal, it is no less present. Although policy management is a general concern and skill, there are special concerns and constraints involved for those working in the social policy arena, or working on policy matters for social agencies.

CONCLUSION

By now, readers are likely to feel that the whole area of policy management is just "too much"—too many things to do, too many activities to undertake too often. To make matters worse, the topics discussed here are among the more affect-laden (agency goals and purposes, alternative approaches to solving problems in which there may be many hidden costs) and routine (committees, meetings, reports). Yet, as these techniques get put into practice, daily routine will have new meaning and purpose, new perspectives will vivify the more common tasks.

However, the suggestions made here are not all that needs to be done. This conclusion suggests a few new and additional directions the policy manager needs to consider.

Provide Self-Conscious Practice

Most policy practitioners, executives, and other managers have no regular system for discussing and assessing their professional activities. Sometimes when a bad mistake has been made, or prior to or at the time of promotion, an assessment occurs. Sometimes the lack of advancement acts as a stimulus to discussion about the manager's activities. Most frequently she or he "plugs" along until some external force acts to derail.

Policy management's injunction to generate better ideas applies to the self as well as the agency. Sometimes activities are discussed with a mentor, sometimes with a spouse. Both are useful but involved and complex in various ways. The policy manager needs to develop a consultation relationship with someone in the community, but not in the agency, with whom periodic conversations about professional practice can occur and personal assessments and questions can be raised. The analogue is with the consultation provided by one therapist to another about difficult cases. A regular time for self-assessment and a specific individual with whom one talks about one's activities will be of assistance in improving professional practice.

Assess Other Successful Managers

In the course of our daily activities, we meet individuals whom others regard as very successful and accomplished. Often we do not seek more systematically to find out what they do and why. These individuals are a source of knowledge and direction. They can be helpful in suggesting approaches and techniques different from those suggested here, approaches that may work in particular contexts or with particular problems. Others need to be used, in part, as instructors and models. This process is a thoughtful one, in that we need to thoughtfully assess what others are doing and why, and think about how we can use their methods ourselves. And nothing should prevent us from talking directly to them on occasion and asking why they did something a particular way and what alternatives they had rejected.

Involve Superiors, Subordinates, and Colleagues in Policy Thinking

American society emphasizes the technology of "do-it-yourself." It is the land of the one-man band, of "I did it my way." In spite of the mythology to the contrary, much policy activity occurs and, in my judgment, most policy decisions are made in groups. Part of the emphasis here has been on improving the decision-making group as such. But emphasis needs to be placed as well upon developing a policy focused on one's colleagues and subordinates. This may seem obvious but is often ignored, so that the executive really does not have "policy management" capability developing in the organization.

Often the policy manager, because of the nature of the policy manager role, is somewhat alone in the organization. An attempt should be made to broaden the base of support through involving others in policy management—the boss and people above in the organization, colleagues on the same organizational level, and those a step or two below. There are three reasons for such involvement. One, of course, was just noted—since policy decisions tend to be group decisions, such involvement and education tend to "upgrade" the policy system. Second, it makes the "receptor" system—people who receive and comment on the policy manager's recommendations—more knowledgeable and aware. Third, it makes life in the policy management role less difficult and stressful, because there are people with whom one can talk over issues and problems.

If one is in a small agency, there will be only a few people involved. If one is the executive, it means involving the board of directors (which, as suggested in the chapter on policy governance, would be the focus of attention anyway). If one is in a large, megabureaucratic organization, the possibility of involving people is great, but one should begin with a smaller group.

What does "involvement and education" mean here? It can involve several approaches, all designed to increase knowledge about the policy management process and to increase competence in it. The knowledge component can be initiated through sending around materials and articles, and initiating discussion, perhaps during lunch, about the material. It can involve looking at past decisions within the agency (decision autopsy) and seeing how they could have been improved.[1] And, of course, one can seek to involve the group in the strategic planning process for the organization.

Begin Strategic Planning Process

It is important that all organizations in the human service field have a strategic planning group or committee. Such groups are already relatively standard in the corporate world. If we are to be more "proactive" and less

---

1. In this case, it is better perhaps to start with some of the successful decisions that the agency made and seek to understand the good things and how they might be repeated.

"reactive" to the developing world and its complexities, it is important to have a system for thinking about the future and assessing developing alternatives. Such a group can perform many policy management functions and can serve as the vehicle through which the involvement, just recommended, can occur. Such a group seeks to chart the likely course of large (relatively) environmental changes which will affect the agency and deal with them in advance. "Deal" here does not mean one can change the trend, but it does mean that one might adjust the agency's posture in line with expectations.

A Look Ahead

The points outlined here are a few of the things human service agencies should consider if a policy management focus is to be engendered in their organization. The crucial point, however, is to accept the idea of ideas as a resource. Once some importance is attached to the supply of ideas, then the development of procedures to increase it, refine it, and process it within the agency is a logical next step. Policy is simply the end product of an idea generation process. High quality policy depends, first, on the supply of good ideas. Then those ideas require processing, shaping, and targeting. The combination of idea generation and idea shaping is policy management.

I mentioned some reasons in the introduction and in the latter half of chapter 1 for the special problems human service organizations have in the whole process of management itself and policy management in particular. These problems, however, can be handled; while they make the job more difficult, they do not make it impossible. Important here, though, is to differentiate the "idea" from the "idea-logical." Human service agencies tend to have theories of human nature, supported by clinical and practical experience, which can be called "idea-logical" theories. Since the evidence often offered in support of these theories is quite selective, discussions of new ideas and approaches frequently become quite heated and acrimonious. Herein lies, perhaps, the greatest danger. Human services need to take a broad and open perspective toward techniques of intervention, organizational structures, means of self-support, and the like. Precisely because the world is changing, and changing quickly, new approaches are needed. Intellectual and conceptual obsolescence is occuring more quickly than before and more problems arise because of commitments to particular styles and approaches. The policy management process is one which, if not rejected, can bring new ideas and approaches into the organization, can assist staff, boards, advisory groups, and others to become aware of new ideas and to learn from them, and finally, to adopt some of them as appropriate. Thus, policy management not only can improve the current flow of decisions but can, in some instances, prevent a course of action that may lead to organizational demise.

New Horizons

What, then, are some of the emerging horizons of social policy and how might policy management be related to them? One element, of course, is the idea of policy management itself. Thinking about managing, guiding, and shepherding ideas within the human service organization can, in and of itself, improve the quality of policy that the agency uses as guidance both directly and indirectly. It can improve the quality of social policy as well. While it is true that "policy analysis" has been around for a while, it has been contemplative rather than active, reactive rather than proactive, analytically oriented rather than action oriented, in part because ideas themselves were not thought of as targets for intervention. This discussion opens the door, and more elaborate, more useful discussions will surely follow.

A second new horizon lies in recognizing that there are special sets of roles, skills, and machinery which can be used to make policy better. Improving, refining, testing, and writing about them is an important new development. It is almost like finding that one can cook meat rather than eat it raw and leads in time to different ways of preparing it. Policy recipes will soon come.

A third new horizon is the focus upon the policy committee—whether it is an administrative team, a board of directors, or an interorganizational group—as a major policy instrumentality. Perhaps the success of the Japanese experience has forced us to look at this aspect of culture more carefully, with less disdain, and with a more thoughtful eye, in terms of what may be supported and cultivated. It is almost as if one had a horse and regarded it with disdain and contempt until a neighbor pointed out that it could be domesticated. Then interest was piqued.

A fourth new horizon points to the competing set of values that bedevil social policy. Rather than rallying against the conflict; accepting and working with it, developing techniques to balance and accommodate it will yield greater success in forming policy and especially (I think) social policy than has hitherto been the case.

Fifth, the idea that policy as a set of ratified rules exists at the level of the person, group, family organization, community, and state redefines, refocuses, and broadens the targets of our work. Policy is personal as well as public. It is nowhere written that policy must be that which government does, important as what government does is. The rules we run our life by, the rules of our families, the rules of our organizations, all provide a site of analysis and intervention. We have not thought about them as "policy" before, and hence the tools of policy analysis and management have not been brought to play. In the future, however, policy analysis and management techniques are likely to be used more often.

A sixth new horizon is understanding different kinds and aims of social policy. Human service organizations are always interested in social policy—as individuals we seek to further it and we support it—yet there are important differences in understanding exactly what "it" is. The discussion here is a beginning, but only that. More detailed, more elaborate, more empirical approaches will yield greater benefits.

Policy management is a new area and the policy manager a new role. As is so often the case, though, "there is nothing new under the sun." Readers will recognize that they and others they know do some, or many, of the kinds of things discussed here and have the interests and commitments implied. Indeed, the literature suggests roles, like the idea champion, the entrepreneurial manager, and others, which come close to the policy manager. If this book can, for a few, provide the shock of recognition, so that the reader says "So that's what I am!" then it will have fulfilled its first mission. If it can interest others who like the approach, to begin systematically to use techniques of policy management, then it will have fulfilled its second mission. If it can interest human service trainers, professors, and professionals in approaching more systematically the training for and the doing of policy, then it will have fulfilled its third mission.

APPENDIX
PRACTICAL AIDS

This book has been about ideas and how they can be looked at and influenced as targets of management in the human services. The very idea that ideas are subject to management is likely to bring protests. "Such thought will destroy the creative processes of thought itself." Some, perhaps many, will say "Nonsense." I say too much direction will certainly have that effect. But inattention and neglect will have the same effect, although the cause would be different.

American society is a "do-it-yourself," "play-it-by-ear," crisis-oriented society, rather than one that places emphasis upon planning ahead and thinking through alternatives. We must modify our orientation and seek to become more thoughtful about thought itself. Policy, after all, is simply a ratified idea. Careful attention to the conditions and procedures which can enhance the production of many candidate ideas is needed. It can enter them in understandable fashion into the policy debate. And it can, through knowledge of the policy process, develop amalgams of the policy candidates that are, perhaps, stronger than the original candidates themselves and will result in policy of great vigor and higher quality.

Assisting policy managers in the achievement of these goals is a central purpose of this volume. Thinking about thought, about the ideas which turn, shortly, into policy is crucial in the coming decades. Some of the exercises that follow help in that regard. But in the final analysis, whether these ideas or some others are used, a thoughtful approach to policy ideas will yield great gains.

Exercise 2.1: Wicked Problems

Policy management typically deals with wicked problems. Consider your organization and try to identify three to five wicked problems. Write them down. Now consider how a policy management approach involving the systematic generation of ideas, their transformation into proposals, and their subsequent nourishment and shepherding might be of assistance.

Exercise 2.2: Decision Assumptions, Decision Processes, Social Conditions that Affect Decisions

Decision assumptions are different from decision processes and decision processes are in turn different from those social conditions that affect decisions. Consider your organization and answer the following questions:

Decision Assumptions. What are the key decision assumptions of your organization? See if you can list three.

Decision Processes. Try to write down the typical decisions processes in your organization. How would you characterize those processes? Are they democratic? Autocratic? Sometimes one, sometimes the other?

Social Conditions. What key social and structural conditions affect decisions in your organization?

Exercise 2.3: Decision-Making Assessment

Janis and Mann reviewed a large amount of material in order to assess the quality of decision making. They conclude "we've extracted seven major criteria that can be used to determine whether decision-making procedures are of high quality. Although systematic data are not yet available, it seems plausible to assume that decisions satisfying these seven 'ideal' procedural criteria have a better chance than others of obtaining the decision maker's objective and being adhered to in the long run. . . . Our first assumption is that failure to meet any of these seven criteria when a person is making a fundamental decision, one with major consequences for obtaining or failing to obtain important values, constitutes a defect in the decision-making process. The more defects, the more likely the decision maker will undergo unanticipated setbacks and experience post-decisional regret'' (1977:11).

1. Thoroughly canvasses a wide range of alternative courses of action _____

2. Surveys the full range of objectives to be fulfilled by the values implicated by the choice _____

3. Carefully weighs whatever he knows about the costs and risks of negative consequences as well as the positive consequences that can flow from each alternative _____

4. Intensively searches for new information relevant to further evaluation of the alternative _____

5. Correctly assimilates and takes account of any new information or expert judgment to which he is exposed, even when the information or judgment does not support the course of action he initially prefers _____

6. Reexamines the positive and negative consequences of all known alternatives, including those originally regarded as unacceptable before making a final choice _____

7. Makes detailed provisions for implementing or executing the chosen course of action with special attention to contigency plans that might be required if various known risks were to materialize. _____

Consider these seven criteria. Assess your own agency with respect to them, giving yourself an A where the criteria is always used; B where it is sometimes used; C where it is infrequently used; and D where it is never used. Considering A as 4; B as 3; C as 2, calculate your agency's decision quality grade point average.

(Reprinted by permission of the publisher from *Decision Making: A Psychological Analysis of Conflict, Choice, and Commitment,* by Irving L. Janis and Leon Mann. Copyright © 1977 by the Free Press, Division of Macmillan Publishing Co., Inc.)

Exercise 2.4: Problems of the Human Service Organization

Problems of misdirection by budget, subdominant values, turbulent environment, suspicion of quantitative data, lack of information, clinical focus, little stress on external conditions, and little attention to tactical follow-through are problems that confront many human service agencies in particular. In the following list, see which ones, in your opinion, affect your agency the most. Rate each one 0 for little effect to 9 for a large effect. Take those you have labeled 7, 8, or 9 and look at them in more detail, trying to understand why these particular ones affect your agency especially. Consider also those you have marked 0, 1, or 2 and make the same type of assessment.

1. Misdirection by budget _____
2. Subdominant values _____
3. Turbulent environment _____
4. Suspicion of quantitative data _____
5. Lack of information _____
6. Clinical focus _____
7. Little stress conditions of the external environment _____
8. Little attention to tactical follow-through _____

Exercise 5.1: Scientific Correctness of Policy

Think of some current policy in your agency, for example, vacation policy, travel policy, promotion policy, or one similar. Write it out, briefly, in a sentence or two:

Then think about the following questions:
What assumptions about the problem or situation does the policy make?

What do you know about the latest writing, scientific and popular, on this subject? Do you think the policy reflects these new contributions? If not, why not?

Does the policy successfully harmonize conflicts current within the field about the problem or situation it addresses?

Exercise 5.2: What Simon Says Good Policy Should Be

Let us think of two social welfare policies to provide money: one gives money according to the person's need, but the need must be checked and another provides money according to need, but a declaration is accepted.

In which of these policies is compliance easy? Why?

Is noncompliance any more difficult in either? Why or why not? How could noncompliance be made more difficult?

Can you think, in going over the policies of your agency, of policies that make compliance easy? Or some that make noncompliance difficult?

Exercise 5.3: Good Policy Involves Political Sensitivity

Think of a recent policy change that affected your agency. It can involve clients, staff, or any other group. Then consider the following questions:

Knowing. Were the political positions of groups involved considered? Were the feelings and sensitivities of these groups taken into consideration?

Clearing. Were early policy ideas and directives shared with relevant groups?

Checking. Were early drafts of the policy shared with those involved?

Involving. Were those affected by the process involved in the process?

Modeling. Did the process through which this policy change came about (items 1–4 above) serve as a model for other changes (or did people say, "NEVER AGAIN!!!")?

Many of these questions you will not, I suspect, be able to answer or answer well. Think for a moment about what that inability indicates. Perhaps you do not know as much about the process of policymaking as you had thought? Perhaps you know more. If you think you know less, what does this suggest about the things you might do?

Exercise 5.4: Thinking About Cost Parameters

Try to call to mind some recent discussion you had with a colleague at your agency about the financial aspect of a program. Think of something that someone wanted to add to the agency—a new office location, a new service, or something similar. Write it down in a sentence or so here:

Now think about the Relative Budget Constraint. Was the argument based upon the constraint (the amount of money in the system)? In what ways?

Leaving aside the RBC, was the cost or price of the item acceptable? Was it too high? Too low?

Leaving price aside, is it worth it for the agency to undertake the program or service? If you answer "no," think about the price at which it would become "worth it." If the answer is "yes," think of the price at which it would become "not worth it."

Exercise 5.5: Policy Is Linked to Values

One of the value conflicts deeply rooted in the human service profession is the conflict over dependency. On the one hand, we want to provide help. On the other hand, we want to foster independence and self care. Think of other value conflicts in the human service profession. What conflicts are they? List them briefly.

Can you think of policies derived from these conflicting values? How have the conflicts been resolved. Has it been a process of (a) accommodation; (b) alternation (first one, then the other)? Write down what you think.

Suppose you overhear an argument among some men and women. One of the men says that people should get off welfare and get to work. Another says he agrees, but that it's OK for women and children to get help. But not, he adds, students. A third person enters the discussion saying they are both wrong—it is need, not anything else, that should be the only criterion.

What are the values involved in this discussion? Can you spot several? Make a list of them.

It is widely said that the 1980 period will be a conservative one. If this should be so, how can human service providers adjust their programs to attach to ascending values?

Consider the case of a pregnant woman thinking about an abortion and seeking help at a Catholic agency. What are likely conflicts between client and worker on a values basis?

Exercise 5.6: Policy Must Contain Sufficient Guides to Action

Call to mind a recent policy decision in your agency. For this exercise, it would be helpful to have a written copy of the policy statement in front of you. It can usually be found in the board of directors' minutes.

Specificity. Consider the policy statement. Do you think it is sufficiently specific? Does it specify target groups, range of application, how decisions will be made? If not, what additions or subtractions would make it more specific?

Implications. Consider the implications of the policy. Have any unforeseen implications developed yet? Can you think of any which might develop?

Applicability. Does the policy state when, to whom, and for how long it is to apply? Are there trigger conditions (preconditions) or limitations (e.g., only $400 for travel money)?

Ease of Administration. Is the policy (or has it been) easy to administer?

Administrative Discretion. What is the relationship between directed and discretionary elements within this policy?

Exercise 5.7: Good Policy Is Reviewed and Refurbished

Call to mind a recent area of disagreement among the staff in your agency. It might concern smoking at staff meetings, length of interviews with clients, appropriate client workload, or whatever. Jot it down for easy reference.

Policy vs. Practice. Can you distinguish between policy and practice here? Was there an actual policy which had, by custom, come to be violated (no smoking policies fall into this category)? Had there been no policy but only diverse practices people thought of as policy?

Applying Practices within the Agency. Was the disagreement the result of nonuniform application of policy? Was it a result of multiple understandings of practice? Was there a systematic use of an extant policy to serve as emergent need for which no policy had been as yet developed?

Monitoring. Considering this troublesome policy area, had any procedures been developed for monitoring either the agency activities under the policy (for example, after six months, how is the smoking policy going?) or to assess the variety of practices for dealing with a particular item of difficulty.

Fine Tuning. When a new policy was passed, or issued by the executive, was some "fine tuning" (small corrective adjustments) made after a period of time?

Seventh-Year Refurbishment. If the policy or policy area you have in mind is old enough, consider whether it was reviewed and updated within the seventh year.

Exercise 6.1: Oiling the Policy Machinery

Think of a particular unresolved problem in your agency today. Write it down in a sentence or so.

Then, consider the Persons, Roles, Tasks, and Processes which need to be involved in order to establish and implement policy to correct that problem. List them by category.

Exercise 6.2a: Psyching Out the Policy Context: Values, Money, Power

Pretend that you are going to apply to your local United Way for a small grant in policy management training. Consider the policy context of such a proposal.

Values
1. What are the current United Way value orientations in your community?
2. What are the kinds of things, as far as you know, that the United Way considers VALUE-able in your town?
3. If you don't know the answers to these questions, how can you find them out?

Money
1. What is the funding situation of the United Way in your community? Does it have small grant possibilities? If not, are there agencies that do?
2. What kinds of budget requests are likely to be most successful? Are there certain items that are not considered fundable?
3. What else do you need to know about the financial system?

Power
1. What are the key policy committees that will need to approve your request? (Include your own agency and funding agency committees here.)
2. Who are the key individuals who can be helpful or harmful to your request?

Exercise 6.2b: The Generalized Policy Context

Knowledge of the policy context is relevant for a particular project, as in Exercise 6.2a. In that case, we seek to begin with a project and then to look at the context. However, the reverse of that progress is possible. It consists of knowing what values are "current," what the most recent "policy theory" is, where money is, how much is available for funding, and who controls access to these moneys. Thinking about your community for a moment, try to answer the following questions:

Values
1. What ideas and perspectives on human service and its delivery are now popular in your community? State? Nation?
2. Are there any initiatives you could propose from the perspective of your agency that would fit here?

Money
1. What kinds of programs seem to be funded in your community? State? Nation?
2. Are there any programs in your agency that could be shaped to meet these types of interests and orientations?

Power
1. Who are the powerful individuals with respect to values and financing within your community? What organizations are powerful with respect to values and financing?
2. What attempts have been made to contact these individuals and organizations and develop a relationship upon which further more specific proposals can be based?

Exercise 6.3: The Policy Community

Consider the following issue: In a small American community there is some interest expressed to your Family and Children's Service in sponsoring a program in foreign adoptions. Your boss asks you to "pull together interested persons and organizations for an exploratory meeting." Whom would you suggest and why? Such a list is almost sure to be a "first pass" at listing the policy community. Thinking of your community, list twenty persons or organizations whom you would seek to pull together and the reason for your choice.

Exercise 6.4: The Policy Elite

Inspect the list you developed in Exercise 6.3. Which of the persons or organizations could almost certainly *block* action? Which of those persons or organizations could probably *put something across?* List them in two columns headed Block and Put Across.

Those persons on both lists are the policy elite; those on one list only are the subelite.

Exercise 6.5: Writing the Policy Agenda

Consider the issues needing policy attention in your agency. See if you can identify several of them and make a list.

Now look at the list carefully. Do you agree with the order you initially used for listing? Make a fresh list arranging the items in order of importance. Then make a third list arranging the items in order of ease of handling.

Are the lists similar? If not, have you followed a common tendency and put off the most important items?

Exercise 7.1: Playing the Policy Manager Role

Most policy managers are not specifically appointed to the position. They rather tend to be informally acknowledged and are the people we know who are good at identifying the crucial problems for discussion, who can pull together materials for discussion, who can alert and encourage us to plan ahead, and who can be sensitive to interpersonal issues as well as task issues. Few of us have all these qualifications. But we can learn them. This exercise asks you to try some experiments in your own agency or work place. Use the staff meeting as a point of focus.

Crystalizing. At the next staff meeting, wait until several points of view on a problem have been expressed, then see if you can offer a view that captures the essence of the problem. A glance at the agenda before the meeting, a little thinking, a few pre-meeting notes, and some within-meeting notes on what was said will be helpful.

You will have succeeded if people comment that you made a very good point.

Compiling. At the next staff meeting, wait until there is some issue under discussion which needs, but does not have, facts available. Offer to compile the relevant facts and bring them to the next meeting.

You will have succeeded if your offer is accepted.

Taking a Proactive Stance. Think about the issues facing the agency which are *not* currently being dealt with. Pick one you think needs discussion. Chat with the boss and ask if it can be brought up for discussion at the next staff meeting. (Do not suggest a solution here!) Offer to prepare a short introduction to the issue and explain why you think it is pressing.

You will have succeeded if you can make the presentation. It is not necessary here that people agree with you.

Playing Task Roles. At the next staff meeting, see if you can assist the group in sticking to its task. Also, see if you can make a comment supporting one who has made a good contribution.

You will have succeeded if the group gets back on the track or the person you supported expresses appreciation.

Exercise 7.2: The Busy Executive

Bill is the model of a busy executive. He is in early, at eight or a little before, attending to problems of his agency, Children's Helpers. There are the phone logs to check, the daily time schedules to skim, and the daily petty cash disbursements to look at. He feels that this is an excellent way to begin the day because it gives him a grip on the details that make the agency run. By the time he finishes these chores, there is usually some staff member who has a complaint, and he listens to that, Throughout this period, the phone rings with this crisis and that crisis, and the pattern repeats itself throughout the day, until he can, at long last, leave the office. He is vaguely troubled because he never gets to the long-range planning committee's report and he does not really know how to deal with some differences in therapeutic approach coming up in the agency.

> Consider this small vignette and outline what you think Bill's problem might be. Do you think he is attending to policy issues? Why or why not? How might he organize himself to spend more time on the issues he thinks important?

Exercise 8.1: The Policy Committee

Think of a committee you have served on recently. Review in your mind the last couple of meetings and recall some of the issues before the meeting. Then:

1. Consider whether or not a decision was made. If a decision was made, go to point 2 below. If not, ask yourself why not. What were the factors that prevented a decision from being made at that point? Were they interpersonal ones? technical ones? flaws in the committee process? Consider, having diagnosed the problem, ways in which you might help the group move to a decision next time.

2. If a decision was made, ask yourself whether it was a "good" decision, one of high quality. Criteria for grading decisions are not, as yet, very explicit. Still, think of what could have been a "better" decision than the one that was made, and what could have been a "worse"

decision. (Ignore here narrow self-interest as a criterion—whether you got your way or not). List them below.

The decision made was:

A better decision than the one made would be:

A worse decision than the one made would be:

By looking at the basis (or bases) you used to make this classification, you can begin to develop some criteria for a good decision.

Exercise 8.2: The Web of Committees

Consider an issue in your agency that has not yet been settled. Make a note of the committees that will need to have some input, in approval terms, review terms, or informational terms.

Fill in the blanks in the diagram. The squares are for committees which give approval; the circles are for committees which review and comment; the triangles are for committees to which information is appropriately given. Place numbers 1, 2, 3 . . . in terms of the (rough) order in which the committees would be consulted.

Exercise 11.1: Writing Policy Documents

Call to mind the last report you wrote for a group of decision makers—a board, finance committee, staff meeting, or whatever. In thinking now about that report, did you:

1. First and foremost, seek to communicate the central idea under discussion?

2. Put the conclusion first?

3. Work to a point in time? (Some decision point or meeting point, or was the report late?)

4. Get ideas on paper quickly?

5. Rewrite, after checking and clearing?

6. Prepare psychologically for the process of review and revision?

7. Know the several audiences for whom you were writing? Was there a distinction in your mind between interior and exterior language?

As you think about these questions, make a mental note of your strong points and your weaker points. Then seek an occasion to prepare a small report and try some of these hints. (You can also use the KNOWER system described in this chapter.)

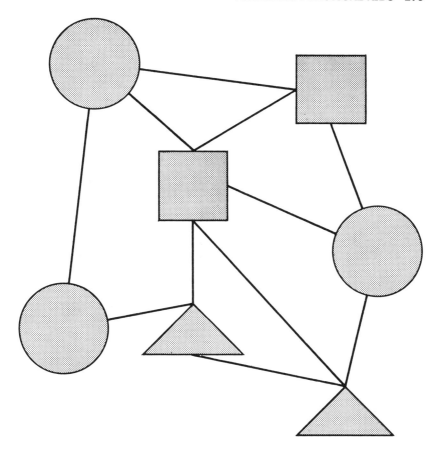

Exercise 11.2: The Knower System for Policy Writing

Make a small 4×6 card outlining the steps of the KNOWER system and keep it at your desk. Make a copy of the outline on pp. 204–205 and keep it as well. When the next opportunity to draft a report comes, give this system, or elements of this system you think will fit, a try.

Exercise 12.1: Value Conflicts

Consider a policy issue in your agency. Write it down.

Consider the value conflicts outlined in this chapter. Do any apply to this policy issue? How many? In what way?

Exercise 12.2

Consider the policy issues in Exercise 12.1. In terms of resolving them (could) were some of the techniques for values balance listed in this chapter (be) used? Why yes or no?

REFERENCES

Altman, Stan. 1979. "Performance Monitoring Systems for Public Managers." *Public Administration Review* (January/February), 39(1):31–35.

Amara, Roy. 1982. "Management in the 1980s: New Environments, New Social Values, and New Technologies Will Breed a New Type of Manager." *Technology Review* (April), 83:76–82.

Argyris, Chris. 1982. *Reasoning, Learning, and Action: Individual and Organizational.* San Francisco: Jossey-Bass.

Austin, David M. and Michael L. Lauderdale. 1976. "Preparing Public Welfare Administrators." *Public Welfare* (Summer), 34(3):13–18.

Barber, B., 1978–79. "Control and Responsibility in the Powerful Professions." *Political Science Quarterly* (Winter), 93:599–615.

Beckman, Norman. 1977. "(A Symposium) Policy Analysis in Government: Alternatives to 'Muddling Through.' " (Introduction.), *Public Administration Review,* 37:221–222.

Bennis, Warren G. 1979. "RX for Corporate Boards." *Technology Review* (December/January).

—— 1978. "The Crisis of Corporate Boards." *Technology Review* (November).

Berg, William E. 1980. "Evolution of Leadership Style in Social Agencies: A Theoretical Analysis." *Social Casework* (January), 61(1):22–28.

Berry, Waldron. 1981. "Beyond Strategic Planning." *Managerial Planning* (March/April), 29(5):12–15.

Bland, D. H. 1979. "Managing Change." *Corrections Today* (July), 41:48+.

Bopp, W. J. and W. P. Rosenthal. 1979. "Participatory Management." *American Journal of Nursing* (April), pp. 670–672.

Boulding, Kenneth E. 1967. "The Boundaries of Social Policy." *Social Work* (January), 12(1):3–11.

—— 1960. "Decision Making in the Modern World." In Lyman Bryson, ed. *An Outline of Man's Knowledge of the Modern World*. New York: McGraw-Hill.

Bozeman, Barry and L. Vaughn Blackenship. 1979. "Scientific Information and Governmental Decision-Making: The Case of the National Science Foundation." *Public Administration Review* (January/February), 39(1):53–57.

Brenner, M. Harvey. 1973. *Mental Illness and The Economy*. Cambridge: Harvard University Press.

Buell, Bradley et al. 1952. *Community Planning for Human Services*. New York: Columbia University Press.

Carroll, Nancy K. 1978. "Beyond Parochialism in Social Welfare Administration." *Journal of Education for Social Work* (Spring), 14(2):31–37.

Catridis, D. 1978. "Market Forces and Distribution Policies." *Ekistics* (Summer), 45:346.

Cloward, Richard and I. Epstein. 1973. "Private Social Welfares' Disengagement from the Poor: The Case of Family Adjustment Agencies." In G. Brager and H. Specht, eds. *Community Organization*. New York: Columbia University Press.

Cohen, Michael and James G. March. 1974. *Leadership and Ambiguity: The American College President*. New York: McGraw-Hill.

Cohen, Michael, James March, and Johan P. Olsen. 1972. "A Garbage Can Model of Organizational Choice." *Administrative Science Quarterly* (March), 17(1):1–25.

Cohen, Susan I. 1980. "Incentives, Iterative Communication, and Organizational Control." *Journal of Economic Theory* (Fall), 22:37–55.

Cohn, David M. 1980. "Strategic Business Planning: A Critical Management Tool for Survival." *Managerial Planning* (January/February), 29:4–10.

Curtis, Donald. 1980. "Management in the Public Sector: It Really Is Harder." *Management Review*, October, pp. 70–74.

Daft, Richard L. and Patricia J. Bradshaw. 1980. "The Process of Horizontal Differentiation: Two Models." *Administrative Science Quarterly*, September, pp. 441–456.

Day, Phyllis J. 1980. "Charismatic Leadership in the Small Organization." *Human Organization* (Spring) 39(1):50–58.

Deutsch, Claudia H. 1981. "Trust: The New Ingredient in Management." *Business Week*, July 6, pp. 104–105.

Dillon, Ray, 1979. "Evaluating Your Social Awareness Expenditures: A Pragmatic Approach." *Managerial Planning* (May/June), 27(6):25–41.

Dolgoff, Ralph L. 1981. "Clinicians as Social Policymakers." *Social Casework* (May), 62(5):284–292.

Donnelly, Robert M. 1981. "Strategic Planning for Better Management." *Managerial Planning* (November/December), 3–6 and 41.

Drucker, Peter F. 1980. "Deadly Sins in Public Administration." *Public Administration Review* (March), 40:103–106.

—— 1973. "Managing the Public Service Institution." *Public Interest* (Fall), no. 33, pp. 43–60.

Dunn, William N., ed. 1980–81. "Symposium on Social Values and Public Policy." *Policy Studies Journal*, 9(4):519–636.

Durkheim, Emile. 1897, 1951. *Suicide: A Study in Sociology*. New York: Free Press of Glencoe.

—— 1893, 1967. *The Division of Labor in Society*. Introd. by George Simpson. New York: Free Press of Glencoe.

Dye, T. R. 1978. "Oligarchic Tendencies in National Policy-Making: The Role of the Private Policy-Planning Organizations." *Journal of Politics* (May), 40(2):309–331.

Edleman, Murray. 1977. *Political Language*. New York: Academic Press.

Eldridge, William D. 1981. "The Legitimation of Social Work Planning." *Social Service Review* (June), 55(2):327–335.

Elmore, R. F. 1979–80. "Backward Mapping: Implementation Research and Policy Decisions." *Policy Science Quarterly* (Winter), 94:601–616.

Etzioni, Amatai. 1961. *A Comparative Analysis of Complex Organizations*. New York: Free Press of Glencoe.

Fairholm, Gilbert W. 1979. "A Reality Basis for Management Information System Decisions." *Public Administration Review* (March/April), 39(2):176–179.

Felsenthal, Dan S. 1980. "Applying the Redundancy Concept to Administrative Organizations." *Public Administration Review* (May/June), 40(3):247–252.

Fiedler, F. E. et al. 1979. "Organizational Stress and the Use and Misuse of Managerial Intelligence and Experience." *Journal of Applied Psychology* (December), 64:635–47.

Filho, Paulo De Vasconcellos. 1982. "Strategic Planning: A New Approach." *Managerial Planning* (March/April), 30(5):12–20.

Finsterbusch, K. and M. R. Hamilton. 1978. "Rationalization of Social Science Research in Policy Studies." *International Journal of Comparative Sociology* (March/June), 19:88–106.

Flynn, Rob. 1979. "Urban Managers in Local Government Planning." *Sociology Review*, New Series (November), 27(4):743–753.

Ford, Charles H. 1980. "Management by Decisions, Not by Objectives." *Business Horizons* (February), 23(1):7–18.

—— 1979. "MBO: An Idea Whose Time Has Gone?" *Business Horizons* (December), 22:48–55.

Forester, J. 1980. "Critical Theory and Planning Practice." *American Planning Association Journal* (July), 46:275–286.

Frankfather, Dwight L. 1981. "Welfare Entrepreneurialism and the Politics of Innovation." *Social Service Review* (March), 55(1):140–146.

Frohman, Alan L. and Steven P. Ober. 1980. "How to Analyze and Deal with the Basic Issues." *Management Review* (April), pp. 46–50.

Gelman, Sheldon R. 1981. "Who Should Administer Social Services?" *Social Work* (July), 26(4):327–332.

Gil, David. "A General Framework for Policy Analysis." In John E. Tropman et al., eds., *Strategic Perspectives on Social Policy*. Elmsford, N.Y.: Pergamon Press.

Gillespie, David F. and Dennis S. Mileti. 1979. "Action and Contingency Postulates in Organization-Environment Relations." *Human Relations* (March), 32(3):261–271.

Glaser, E. M. and T. E. Backer. 1980. "Durability of Innovations: How Goal Attainment Scaling Programs Fare Over Time." *Community Mental Health Journal* (Summer), 16:130–143.

Goldberg, Gertrude S. 1980. "New Directions for the Community Service Society of New York: A Study of Organizational Change." *Social Service Review* (June), 54(2):184–219.

Gottesman, Leonard E., Barbara Isizaki, and Stacey Mona McBride. 1979. "Service Management: Concepts and Models." *Gerontologist* (August), 19:378–388.

Gray, Bonnie J. and Robert K. Landrum. 1979. "Are You Ready for Tomorrow's Management Style?" *Business (Atlanta)* (November/December), 29:32–38.

Greanias, George C. and Duane Windsor, eds. 1982. *The Changing Boardroom.* Houston: Gulf Publishing Company.

Gummer, Burton. 1979. "A Framework for Curriculum Planning in Social Welfare Administration: Implications for Curriculum Development." *Administration in Social Work* (Winter), 3(4):385–394.

—— 1975. "Social Planning and Social Administration: Implications for Curriculum Development." *Journal of Education for Social Work* (Winter), 11(1):66–73.

Haft, Robert, 1981. "Business Decisions by the New Board: Behavioral Science and Corporate Law." *Michigan Law Review* (November), 80:1–67.

Haga, W. J. 1980. "Managerial Professionalism and the Use of Organization Resources." *American Journal of Economics and Sociology* (October), 35:337–348.

Harari, Ehud. 1974. "Japanese Politics of Advice in Comparative Perspective." *Public Policy* (Fall), 22(4):537–577.

Harman, Wilfried. 1964. "Administration." In J. Gould and William Kolb, eds. *Dictionary of the Social Sciences.* New York: Free Press of Glencoe.

Harrison, W. 1964. "Policy." In J. Gould and William Kolb, eds., *A Dictionary of the Social Services.* New York: Free Press.

Hasenfeld, Y. and John E. Tropman, 1979. "Interorganizational Relations." In F. M. Cox et al., eds. *Strategies of Community Organization.* 3d ed. Itasca, Ill.: Peacock.

Herbert, W. R. 1979. "Effective Time Management." *Public Management* (January), 61:9–10.

Hibbard, Michael. 1981. "The Crisis in Social Policy Planning." *Social Service Review* (September), 55(3):557–567.

Hillsman, Roger. 1964. *To Move a Nation.* New York: Doubleday.

Hirschman, Albert O. 1982. *Shifting Involvements: Private Interests and Public Involvement.* Princeton: Princeton University Press.

Hoffer, Eric. 1951. *The True Believer: Thoughts on the Nature of Mass Movements.* New York: Harper.

Huseman, Richard C. et al. 1980. "Planning for Organizational Change: The Role of Communication." *Managerial Planning* (May/June), 28(6):32–36.

"In Search of Rational Organization (Symposium)." 1979. *International Social Science Journal,* 31(4):561–707.

"Inter-Organizational Relationships: Substantive Policy Areas." 1980. *Town Plan Review,* 51:300–321.

"Issues of the 80s: The Managerial Environment." 1981. *Los Angeles Business and Economy* (Winter), 6:4–15.

Janis, Irving and Leon Mann. 1977. *Decision Making.* New York: Free Press.

Jansson, Bruce S. and Samuel H. Taylor. 1978. "Search Activity in Social Agencies: Institutional Factors That Influence Policy Analysis." *Social Service Review* (June), 52(2):189–201.

Johnson, H. R. 1980. *American Values and the Elderly.* Ann Arbor: The Institute of Gerontology of the Univesity of Michigan.

Jones, James A. 1972. "The Researcher as Policy Scientist." In Irving Spergal, ed. *Community Organization: Studies in Constraint.* Beverly Hills: Sage.

Kahn, Alfred J. 1969. *Theory and Practice of Social Planning,* New York: Russell Sage Foundation.

Kelman, Sander et al. 1981. "Planning the Planners." *Social Policy* (January/February), 11(4):46–51.

Kernbert, O. F. 1979. "Regression in Organizational Leadership." *Psychiatry* (Fall), 42:24–39.

Kerrigan, John E. and David W. Hinton. 1980. "Knowledge and Skills Needed for Tomorrow's Public Administrators." *Public Administration Review* (September/October), 40(5):469–473.

Kerrigan, Mark L. 1979. "Decision Making in the Management of Energy Regulation." *Public Administration Review* (November/December), 39(6):553–555.

Kidder, Tracy, 1981. *The Soul of a New Machine.* New York: Avon.

Kirton, Michael. 1980. "Adapters and Innovators in Organizations." *Human Relations* (April), 32(8):213–224.

Klein, Harold E. and William H. Newman. 1980. "How to Integrate New Environmental Forces into Strategic Planning." *Managerial Review* (July), pp. 40–48.

Levine, Arthur L. 1979. "The Role of the Technoscience Administrator in Managing National Science Policy." *Public Administration Review* (March/April), 39(2):122–128.

Lind, Roger and John E. Tropman. 1969. *Delinquency Planning and Community Competence.* Final report submitted to the Office of Juvenile Delinquency and Youth Development. Ann Arbor: University of Michigan.

Lindblom, C. E. 1959. "The Science of Muddling Through." *Public Administration Review* (Spring).

Lorant, John H. 1980. "On Managerial Professionalism." *American Journal of Economics and Sociology* (October), 39(4):418–421.

Lukton, Rosemary Creed. 1978. "Social Policies, Social Services, and the Law." *Social Casework* (October), 59(8):523–529.

Lynn, Laurence F., ed. 1979. "National Research Council Assembly of Behavioral and Social Science Study Project on Social Research and Development." *Studies in the Management of Social R & D: Selected Policy Areas.* Vol. 3. Washington, D.C.: National Academy of Science.

Machlowitz, Marilyn. 1981. *Workaholics.* New York: Mentor.

Madison, D. L. et al. 1980. "Organizational Politics: An Exploration of Managers' Perceptions." *Human Relations* (February), 33(2):79–100.

Magill, Robert S. 1975. "An Introductory Policy Planning Course for Graduate Students." *Journal of Education for Social Work* (Winter), 11(1):99–104.

Maines, D. R. 1978. "Reply with Rejoinder." *Sociological Quarterly* (Summer), 19:491–498.

March, J. and H. Simon. *Organizations.* New York: Wiley, 1958.

Marker, Gail. "Guidelines for Analysis of a Social Welfare Program." In John E. Tropman et al., eds. *Strategic Perspectives on Social Policy.* Elmsford, N.Y.: Pergamon Press, 1979.

Martin, John. 1979. "Business Planning: The Gap Between Theory and Practice." *Long-Range Planning* (December), 12:2–10.

Mayntz, R. 1979. "Public Bureaucracies and Policy Implementation." *International Social Science Journal,* 31(4):633–645.

Mazzolini, Renato. 1981. "How Strategic Decisions Are Made." *Long-Range Planning,* 14(3):85–96.

McTighe, John J. 1979. "Management Strategies to Deal with Shrinking Resources." *Public Administration Review* (January), 39(2):86–90.

Michael, Stephen R. 1980. "Feedforward versus Feedback Controls in Planning." *Managerial Planning* (November/December), 29(3):34–38.

Mileti, Dennis et al. 1979. "Structure and Decision Making in Corporate Organizations." *Sociology and Social Research* (July), 63(4):723–744.

Montjoy, Robert S. and Laurence J. O'Toole, Jr. 1979. "Toward a Theory of Policy Implementation: An Organizational Perspective." *Public Administration Review* (September/October), 39(5):465–476.

Moore, Mark H. 1982. "Policy Managers Need Policy Analysis." *Journal of Policy Analysis and Management* (Spring), 1(3):413–418.

Morris, Seymour, Jr. 1980. "Managing Corporate External Affairs." *Managerial Review* (March), pp. 48–53.

Moynihan, Daniel Patrick. 1969. *Maximum Feasible Misunderstanding: Community Action in the War on Poverty.* New York: Free Press.

Mueller, C. R., Jr. and S. Mueller. 1980. "How to Find out Everything You Wanted to Know about Your Organization But Were Afraid to Ask." *Corrections Today* (March), 42:8–10+.

Myrick, J. R. 1979. "Rejoinder." *Public Administration Review* (May/June), 39(3):300–301.

National Information Bureau. 1979. "The Volunteer Board Member in Philanthropy." New York: National Information Bureau.

Naylor, Thomas H. 1981. "How to Integrate Strategic Planning into your Management Process." *Long-Range Planning,* 14(5):56–61.

Naylor, Thomas H. et al. 1979. "Design of a Strategic Planning Process." *Managerial Planning* (January/February), 28:3–7.

New FSAA Publications Aimed Toward Managers in Human Service Agencies. 1979. *Social Casework* (March), 60(3):179.

Nye, F. Ivan and Gerald W. McDonald, eds. 1979. "Family Policy: Should This United States Have an Explicit Family Policy?" Special Issue. *Journal of Marriage and the Family* (August), 41(3):447–664.

Parsons, Talcott. 1960. *Structure and Process in Modern Societies.* Glencoe, Ill.: Free Press.

Penson, J. K. 1977. "Innovation and Crisis in Organizational Analysis." *Sociological Quarterly* (Winter), 18:3–16.

Peter, Thomas J. 1980. "Putting Excellence into Management." *Business Week,* July 21, pp. 196–197+.

Peters, B. G. 1979. "Bureaucracy, Politics and Public Policy." *Comparative Politics* (April), 11:338–358.

Piven, Frances F. and Richard Cloward. 1971. *Regulating the Poor.* New York: Pantheon Books.

Purham, John C. 1979. "Non-Profit Boards Under Fire." *Dunn's Review* (October).

Pusic, Eugene. 1981. "Social Planning, Social Policy, and Political Change." *Social Service Review* (September), 55(3):411–418.

Ramus, A. G. 1978. "Misplacement of Concepts and Administrative Theory." *Public Administration Review* (November/December), 38(6):550–557.

Reeser, Clayton. 1981. "Tactical Planning." *Managerial Review* (November/December), pp. 10–13.

Rein, Martin and Lisa Peattie. 1981. "Knowledge for Policy." *Social Service Review* (December), 55(4):525–543.

Rice, George H. 1980. "But How Do Managers Make Decisions?" *Management Decision,* 18(4):194–202.

Rittel, W. J. Horst and Melvin M. Webber. 1973. "Dilemmas in a General Theory of Planning." *Policy Sciences* (July), 4(2):155–169.

Sachs, Wladimir M. and Marybeth L. Meditz. 1979. "A Concept of Active Adaptation." *Human Relations* (December), 32(12):1081–93.

Scioli, Frank, Jr. 1979. "Problems and Prospects for Policy Evaluation." *Public Administration Review* (January/February), 39(1):41–45.

Scotch, C. Bernard and Virginia B. Haskett. 1978. "Preparing Social Workers for an Age of Accountability: Understanding Cost Analysis." *Journal of Education for Social Work* (Fall), 14(3):107–113.

Scurfield, Raymond M. 1981. "Clinician to Administrator: Difficult Role Transition?" *Social Work* (November), 26(6):495–501.

—— 1980. "Educational Preparation for Social Work Administrators: A Survey." *Journal of Education for Social Work* (Winter), 16(1):49–56.

Selznick, Phillip. 1957. *Leadership in Administration*. New York: Harper and Row.

Seward, Jack. 1972. *The Japanese,* New York: Morrow.

Shapira, Monica. 1971. "Reflections on the Preparation of Social Workers for Executive Positions." *Journal of Education for Social Work,* 7(1):55–68.

Shatshat, H. M. and Bong-Gon P. Shin. 1981. "Organizational Communication—A Key to Successful Strategic Planning." *Managerial Planning.* (September/October), 30(2):37–40.

Shils, Edward. 1975. *Center and Periphery*. Chicago: University of Chicago Press.

Simon, Herbert, Donald Smithburg, and Victor Thompson. 1950. *Public Administration*. New York: Knopf.

Slater, Phillip. 1970. *The Pursuit of Loneliness*. Boston: Beacon.

Solomon, Lewis D. 1978. "Restructuring the Corporate Board of Directors: Fond Hope—Faint Promise?" *Michigan Law Review* (March), 76(4):581–610.

Sosin, Michael. 1979. "Social Welfare and Organizational Society." *Social Service Review* (September), 53(3):392–405.

Sprafkin, Benjamin R. 1978. "Long-Range Planning for Family Service Agencies." *Social Casework* (December), 59(10):614–620.

Steinberger, P. J. 1980. "Typologies of Public Policy: Meaning Construction and the Policy Process (with Discussion)." *Social Science Quarterly* (Summer), 61:185–207.

Steiner, Gilbert Y. 1979. "Reply with Rejoinder." *Journal of Politics,* 41(1):315–319.

Terrell, P. 1979. "Private Alternatives to Public Human Services Administration." *Social Service Review* (March), 53(1):56–74.

Thomson, William. 1979. "Eliciting Production Possibilities from a Well-Informed Manager." *Journal of Economic Theory* (June), 20:360–380.

Trecker, Harleigh B. 1980. "Boards Can Be Better: The Production Board Meeting." Hartford: Community Council of Hartford, Conn.

Tropman, John E. 1972. "A Comparative Analysis of Community Organization Agencies." In I. Spergal, ed., *Community Organization: Studies in Constraint*. Beverly Hills, Calif.: Sage.

—— 1979. "The Grade Tax." *Policy Analysis* (Summer), 5(3):393–395.

—— 1979. "The Loci of Social Change." In John E. Tropman et al., eds., *Strategic Perspectives on Social Policies*. Elmsford, N.Y.: Pergamon Press.

—— 1982. *Organizational Governance*. Plainfield, Vt.: Freymann Rocklin.

Tropman, John E. and John L. Erlich. 1979. "Introduction to Planning." In F. M. Cox et al., eds., *Strategies of Community Organization,* 3d ed. Itasca, Ill.: Peacock.

Tropman, John E. and Alan Gordon. 1978. "The Welfare Threat." (December), 57(2):697–712.

Tropman, John E. et al., eds. 1981. *New Strategic Perspectives on Social Policy*. Elmsford, N.Y.: Pergamon Press.

Unni, V. K. 1981. "The Role of Strategic Planning in Small Businesses." *Long-Range Planning* (April), 14(2):54–58.

Van de Ven, Andrew H. 1980. "Problem Solving, Planning and Innovation." *Human Relations* (October/November), 33 (10):711–740; 11:757–779.

Van de Ven, A. H., Gordon Walker, and Jennie Liston. 1979. "Coordination Patterns within an Interorganizational Network." *Human Relations* (January), 32(1):19–36.

Van Leunen, Mary-Claire. 1978. *A Handbook for Scholars.* New York: Knopf.

Vogel, Ezra. 1979. *Japan as Number One: Lessons for America.* Cambridge: Harvard University Press.

"Wanted: A Manager to Fit Each Strategy: Meshing Strategic Planning with Executives' Skills." 1980. *Business Week,* February 25, pp. 166+.

Weber, C. Edward. 1979. "Boards' Role in Planning." *Managerial Planning* (May/June), 27(6):21–24.

Weber, Joseph and Nellie Hartogs. 1974. *Boards of Directors: A Study of Current Practices in Board Management and Board Operations in Voluntary Hospital, Health, and Welfare Organizations.* New York: Oceana.

Weiss, Janet A. 1979. "Access to Influence: Some Effects of Policy Sector on the Use of Social Science." *American Behavioral Scientist* (January), 22(1):437–458.

Westhues, Anne. 1980. "Stages in Social Planning." *Social Service Review* (September), 54(3):331–343.

White, Sam E. et al. 1980. "The Effects of Group Decision-Making Process and Problem Situation Complexity on Implementation Attempts." *Administrative Science Quarterly* (September) pp. 428, 437–440.

Whittington, C. and Paul Bellaby. 1979. "The Reasons for Hierarchy in Social Service Departments: A Critique of Elliott Jaques and His Associates." *Sociology Review.* New Series (August), 27(3):513–539.

Williams, T. A. 1979. "In Search Conference in Active Adaptive Planning." *Journal of Applied Behavioral Sciences,* 15(4):470–483.

Wortman, Max S., Jr. 1981. "Strategic Management Issues in Governmental and Non-Profit Organizations." *Survey Business (University of Tennessee)* (Spring), 16:22–27.

Yelaja, Shankar A. 1975. "Social Policy Practice." *Journal of Education for Social Work* (Fall), 11(3):101–106.

Zander, Alvin. 1982. *Making Groups Effective.* San Francisco: Jossey-Bass.

Zelman, William N. 1977. "Liability for Social Agency Boards." *Social Work* (July), 22(4):270–274.

Zimmerman, Shirley. 1979. "Policy, Social Policy, and Family Policy: Concepts, Concerns, and Analytic Tools," *Journal of Marriage and the Family* (August), 41:487–495.

Zoffer, H. J. 1981. "Restructuring Management Education." *Management Review* (April), 70:37–41.

INDEX